THE SEARCH
FOR
THE REAL SELF

*Unmasking the Personality Disorders
of Our Age*

James F. Masterson, M.D.

THE FREE PRESS

NEW YORK

THE FREE PRESS
A Division of Simon & Schuster Inc.
1230 Avenue of the Americas
New York, NY 10020

First Free Press Paperback edition 1990

Manufactured in the United States of America

16 18 20 19 17

Library of Congress Cataloging-in-Publication Data

Masterson, James F.
The search for the real self.

Bibliography: p.
Includes index.
1. Personality disorders—Treatment.
2. Psychotherapy.   I. Title
RC554.M276   1988   616.89   88-11237
ISBN 0-02-920292-2

Contents

Preface

THE search for meaning is the search for expression of one's real self. This book describes how one's real self begins to develop in early childhood, what its capacities are, and how one identifies it and articulates it through testing and experiment in the environment to bring one's real self into harmony with the outer world through work and love relationships.

The Search for the Real Self is also about those with an impaired real self who are unable to accomplish the task of finding a fit with their environment, and are compelled to resort to self-destructive behavior patterns—evidence of a false self—that protect them from feeling "bad" at the cost of a meaningful and fulfilling life. The false self, unable to experiment, induces a lack of self-esteem as the person has to settle for rigid, destructive behavior that avoids life's challenges but leads to feelings of failure, lost hopes and unfulfilled dreams, and despair.

These behavior patterns—officially called "personality disorders"—are not only increasingly prevalent among people seeking professional help today, but also reflect major psychological themes in American culture at large: fear of abandonment, emphasis on the self to the exclusion of others, difficulties in intimacy and creativity and with assertion of the real self.

People with personality disorders were previously considered untreatable. However, no longer must they endure their condition, for new therapeutic vistas have been opened by clinical research that has dramatically improved the effectiveness of psychotherapy to help some overcome the problem completely and others improve significantly. The book unmasks these prevalent disorders of our age by showing how and why they develop, what they look like, and how psychotherapy helps them to change.

The psychological struggles that dominate and constrict the lives of some people, and to a lesser degree confront us all, have their origins in the developmental hurdles that must be surmounted to achieve a healthy real self. When these hurdles are successfully overcome, we develop the capacities necessary for healthy growth and adaptation to life's challenges and opportunities. Only when firmly grounded in a strong real self can we live and share our lives with others in ways that are healthy, straightforward expressions of our deepest needs and desires, and in so doing find fulfillment and meaning.

Winston Churchill's description of Soviet foreign policy as a mystery wrapped in a riddle inside an enigma dramatically highlights the clinical dilemma of working with people whose real self was severely impaired and whose lives had become dominated by a false self. Before we understood personality disorders as we do today, they had been coming to psychotherapy for decades, describing symptoms, sharing with therapists and counselors their inhibited, painful, and unfulfilling lives. Confused and uncertain, they presented life stories that were perplexing and paradoxical, inconsistent and contradictory.

If our patients were confused, so were we. Even when we tracked a single patient, the story that unfolded seemed riddled with confusing, contradictory symptoms. To cover our confusion, we diagnosed these patients as "borderline" because they were sicker than the neurotic but not sick enough to be classified psychotic. They were on the border, somewhere in between. Although this wastebasket term seemed appropriately descriptive, it really said more about our ignorance on the subject than about what was wrong with the patient.

Since so little about borderline and narcissistic disorders was understood, treatment failures were common. Amidst all the inconsistencies surrounding these patients, the only consistent finding was that they failed to get better. Clinical reports attested to this failure. There were no systematic studies.

At times, we could see patients begin to improve and activate themselves in some areas, but on other occasions neither we nor they could make any headway. A therapist would see gross symptoms subside quickly, putting the patient more in touch with reality for one moment, only to watch the patient engage in some bizarre acting out or addictive behavior in the next moment. The very inconsistency of symptoms usually alerted the clinician to diagnose the patient as a borderline or narcissistic personality disorder. But this diagnostic approach based on symptoms was misleading in that it focused on the most puzzling, paradoxical, and superficial aspects of the disorder. Reading the literature on borderline patients told us more about the complexity of the problem to therapists than about the patient with a borderline personality disorder.

Each specialist's view of the problem was conditioned by his own background and training. Psychiatrists with their emphasis on the clinical descriptive approach used a plethora of labels, suggesting that the problem might be some form of schizophrenia: incipient schizophrenia, latent schizophrenia, ambulatory schizophrenia, pseudo-neurotic schizophrenia, and chronic undifferentiated schizophrenia. Other therapists favored labels such as chronic severe personality disorder, chronic severe character disorder, and narcissistic character disorder. On the other hand, analysts trained in classical instinct theory, which emphasized oedipal conflict, viewed the problem as a neurosis originating at the oedipal stage around age four or five and they treated it accordingly. The treatment technique—interpretation of the unconscious—did not meet the patients' therapeutic needs and therefore treatment did not work. These difficulties reinforced the conclusion which the profession was slowly coming to, namely, that borderlines were untreatable. In point of fact, these patients were falling into the no-man's-land between the descriptive psychiatric approach and the classical analytic approach. Since there was no successful treatment for them, therapists were inclined to recommend supportive therapy only.

This negative attitude about the difficulties of successfully treating borderline and narcissistic patients survives to this day in many areas where therapists have not become aware of the newer discoveries. It, too, often continues to be the prevailing attitude in lay circles and the media, which is one of the important reasons I wrote this book. Not all, but many patients, given the proper therapeutic support, can and will overcome their developmental problems and their real selves will emerge.

In the early years of my career, I began a follow-up research project on hospitalized adolescents, little realizing that it would put me on the trail that would eventually lead to an understanding of the origins and development of the borderline and narcissistic problems and an effective treatment process for dealing with them. In those early days when I became intrigued by the borderline dilemma, I found myself serendipitously in the midst of two complementary research experiments: Mahler's work on the early development of the normal self through mother-child observation studies and my own adolescent patients describing and demonstrating dramatically the failures of that same normal process.[1] Pulling the two together opened a major door to understanding the mystery.

The final breakthrough emerged from object relations theory, a theory of early pre-oedipal development of the self and its associated structures. I reported my findings in a paper that integrated these three lines of work, along with the contributions of other researchers in the field, into a concept that the borderline personality disorder was due to a developmental arrest of the real self in the pre-oedipal phase. This paper was presented at a 1975 symposium honoring Margaret Mahler. I felt confident that I had finally unraveled the mystery—at least for myself—and that a whole new way of looking at borderline psychopathology had opened up. The perceptual stereotypes that had characterized the misunderstanding of borderline patients for so many years had been overcome.

The new approach involved two shifts in my thinking. First, there was a shift from the descriptive to the psychodynamic. No longer was I content to work with borderlines merely in terms of their current symptoms. I wanted to know and deal with them on the psychodynamic level, where the problem began and how it persisted over time. Second, there was a shift in focus, from the oedipal to the pre-oedipal stage as the critical developmental phase where the roots of the problem lay. These shifts in understanding led to dramatic changes in the psychotherapy, which led to much better results. In addition, understanding the consequences of the impaired real self provided new insights into how the healthy, real self develops and how to facilitate that development.

My hope is that this book will help both lay readers and professionals in the field understand the intricate backgrounds of people suffering from a borderline or narcissistic disorder. By understanding the origins of these disorders and the treatment that has proven successful in so many cases, readers may glean valuable insights for dealing with family members, friends, colleagues, and patients in whom the real self has never fully emerged. For individuals with a severely impaired real self, psychotherapy can now provide a life preserver to rescue the deprived and abandoned in their struggle and a beacon to guide them to overcome their trauma, reconstruct their psyches, and rejoin the mainstream of life. I hope the chapters that follow, and the lives of the patients presented in them, shedding light on the struggles and vulnerabilities of the developing self, will lead us all to better understanding of our own selves, our vulnerabilities, and our relationships with others.

Acknowledgments

I am grateful to Brunner/Mazel for allowing me to adapt material from my earlier books for use in this volume. I would like to thank Tom Cowan for his expert help in the preparation of this book, as well as senior editor Laura Wolff, editorial supervisor Edith Lewis, and copy editor Kennie Lyman at The Free Press.

I have often thought that the best way to define a man's character would be to seek out the particular mental or moral attitude in which, when it came upon him, he felt himself most deeply and intensely active and alive. At such moments there is a voice inside which speaks and says: "This is the real me!"

William James in a letter to his wife, 1878

I

THE FALSE SELF
The Internal Saboteur

"I'M afraid I'm about to make a mess out of a romance," confided Jennifer, 35, a tall, blonde, blue-eyed actress. She wasn't referring to the domineering character she played on an afternoon soap opera, whose talent was making messes out of other women's romances. She meant her own.

The popular, strong-willed character Jennifer played on television had become her professional trademark, and recently she played a similar character in summer stock to rave reviews, demonstrating to herself that she could handle the stage as well as the camera. But neither the reviews nor her fan mail really made her feel very good about herself or her talent as an actress. Without a strong director and a well-crafted script, she had little natural insight into acting, and she knew it. She was not a method actress, drawing on experiences from her own life, for there was little firm direction or self-understanding about what was going on in her life, which she frequently felt was "rather worthless." After visits to her parents who disapproved of her career as an actress, she even doubted whether she should stay in acting, and more than once she seriously considered giving in to their wishes and embarking on some other line of work.

Jennifer had been in psychotherapy with me for a little over a year, and her on-again, off-again, relationship with Rodger, a 37-year-old dentist, seemed again to be headed for the brink. I had

1

asked her often what she saw in him, and her reply was always along the same lines. "He's solid, stable, in a good profession. I like being with a man I can rely on. He's got a successful career and it gives my life some balance."

What Jennifer was still unable to perceive was that the relationship was neither solid nor stable, but unreliable, and did not balance her life. Furthermore, in spite of her protestations, she seemed to need this very unreliability, as this was only the latest in a series of shaky, short-term relationships she had been involved in.

I asked her what the current problem was, although, from earlier episodes, I anticipated what her answer would be. "It's getting close to Easter, and Rodger's getting cold feet about his promise to get married in the spring. In fact, it's not just his feet that are cold. His feelings for me seem to be cooling down too."

I reminded her that even though he often told her that he loved her, his feelings for her were always cool and that this was one of the reasons they had split up so often in the past, only to get back together again, until another incident brought it home to Jennifer that Rodger was a basically unfeeling, dispassionate person, who found it hard to show any deep affection. She agreed but said that he hugged and kissed a lot, which pleased her and apparently offered her some amount of satisfaction, since, unlike her sexy television character, Jennifer was not all that interested in sex. She responded more to gentle, affectionate foreplay, and Rodger had no complaints about this and seemed to enjoy their physical relationship.

"Look, I'm getting old and have never been married. Thirty-five is halfway there, isn't it? Soon there won't be anyone for me. I know I love him, but he just won't commit himself and we've known each other almost a year now. What's wrong? Am I too demanding for wanting commitment? Is it me or him? Or both of us?"

In the past we had talked about her fears of rejection that underlay an inordinate need for reassurance and affection. This was partially aggravated by a career in which rejection played such a major part. Jennifer had learned to rely upon her relationships to see her through the hard times when she did not have steady work. She hated to be alone and had no other consistent interests or activities, although she could easily develop temporary interests under the inspiration of a new friend or acquaintance. She realized that she needed to fill up every moment of her life and would complain that when not busy she felt empty and directionless.

She wondered if the nature of acting required the actor to have an empty core at the center of his or her identity, a point many of her actor friends took pride in because they believed it allowed them to portray a wider range of characters. She feared that this trait would keep her from ever finding her real self, which in her heart she knew was a far cry from the hardboiled women she could portray so convincingly on the stage and television.

Jennifer's need for reassurance began long before she landed her first acting role. Rodger was only the latest in a long line of men who seemed unsuited for her. The pattern was always similar: she would get involved, put demands on a man to show more affection or make a commitment, he would back off, Jennifer's fear of losing him would grow, and the relationship would fall apart. Now she was about to replay once again this same scene that she had been repeating since she was a young girl in high school.

"I saw Rodger over the weekend, and we made love. He was very nice to me. But then I felt sick all over, even nauseated. I got so tense I had to leave and go back to my apartment. I knew I couldn't be with him for a couple days. Then I felt guilty and lonely and went back to him, and we talked about the wedding, but he said he wasn't sure the time was right. Again I felt miserable and returned to my apartment alone. I can't bear to be apart from the only person who loves me, even though I know he's not the right person."

Pam, 19, dropped out of college in her freshman year because she suffered severe panic attacks. In high school she had been an outstanding student, but lack of self-esteem prevented her from really taking credit for her accomplishments or capitalizing on them to prepare for a career in science. In college she didn't apply herself and led a rather isolated life, cut off from others, even students she considered her friends. She found reasons not to go to athletic events or campus parties, usually relying on the excuse that she had to study; but once alone in her dorm room, she would seldom crack a book. Her interest in science waned, and she turned down invitations to join science clubs and the campus ecology projects for which the college had an outstanding reputation in the community and which were among the reasons she had chosen it in the first place.

On some days she felt so depressed she found herself unable to leave her room. She would stay in bed and daydream, occasionally about a better life, but most often simply to relive the cannibalistic fantasies that had fascinated her from childhood when they took the form of fairy tales, such as Hansel and Gretel or Little Red Riding Hood, in which children are eaten by evil adults or animals. At times she would imagine that she was the child; at other times she was the devouring monster.

"I didn't care. I felt helpless, alone. Nobody loved me. So I would just stay in bed all day and lose myself in my fantasies."

Daydreaming in itself is not a self-destructive activity. Fantasy is often the mainspring of creativity. Many famous works of art, scientific discoveries, and business ventures first began in the whimsical musings of their creators. The significance of daydreaming depends on its content and, more importantly, on why we engage in it. As a form of experimentation and rehearsal, free from the constraints of reality, we can give free play to our emotions and ideas, testing them, wondering about them, and then make plans to implement them. Healthy fantasies are spontaneous and flexible, able to roam and move around playfully—all essential prerequisites for creativity.

Pam's fantasies, however, were pathologic for two reasons: they were about cannibalism, and they served no other purpose than to engulf her in a fantasy world as an escape from her depression and panic. Often on vacations or weekends home, she would stay in her room and refuse to see old friends who called her. She got into arguments with her parents over her lack of interest in school or dating and over what they called "throwing your life away." She usually ended such arguments by telling them that she had a lot of things to think over and would retreat into her room where she would indulge in her daydreaming and fantasy life. Rather than enriching her life, or giving her ideas about how to reshape old patterns that weren't working for her or to create new patterns, her daydreaming kept her immobile, trapped in her feelings that she was helpless and unlovable.

Martha's situation was a variation on Pam's. She too thought herself unlovable and dropped out of college in her junior year because of depression. "I just couldn't get myself to go to class anymore so I would sit around the dorm, watch game shows on television, and eat. Now that I've put on so much weight, I don't like myself and don't want to be on campus where you have to compete so hard to get dates. I might as well stay out till next semester and try to diet. Maybe being away from it all will get my mind off things, and I won't pig out so much." But getting away from what she thought was the problem didn't work. At home she continued to overeat and put on thirty pounds.

In addition to her problem with obesity, Martha had had roommate problems at school that stemmed from her inability to assert herself and command her share of the room. "When I tell my roommate what I think about things, or what I want to do, she always has these little ways of letting me know she doesn't approve. Then I get scared to death because I've offended her. It totally wipes me out. I give up trying to say what I want."

And giving up, for Martha, meant retreating into herself, lying around passively, watching television and eating.

Eating disorders are poignant examples of self-destructive behavior, whether they take the form of anorexia, a severe food deficiency resulting in considerable loss of weight, or overeating resulting in obesity. Bulimia, an eating disorder in which the patient regurgitates food, does not result in weight loss or gain. Bulimics tend to pass for normal and often have good jobs and function well in them. But all severely deviant eating patterns are pathological and symptomatic of more serious but less obvious problems that must be dealt with if the person hopes to begin or resume a normal eating pattern.

When Jennifer, Pam, and Martha each came to see me initially, none of them could articulate her problem specifically. Jennifer knew she had "trouble finding the right man," and Pam felt that no one loved her, and Martha was depressed because of having failed to stay in college and because she had gained so much weight. In addition to these problems, each described herself as confused, uncertain about why she often felt depressed, and worried that her life was stuck in a rut that wasn't going anywhere; but none of these women had a clear idea why her life was so unfulfilling.

The problems of these three women are not uncommon. Psychiatrists are increasingly meeting people with complaints that do not fall neatly into the traditional categories of psychiatric problems, such as an obsession or a phobia, that have been typical of patients since Freud's day. Instead, they complain about their lives in vague and general terms, stating that they get little satisfaction from their work, they are bored or frustrated in their relationships, they can't seem to pull their lives together and find enjoyment in work or love. Eventually, the vague discontent acquires a sharper focus and the patient unravels a long history of difficulties in loving and working. Subsequent sessions deal more specifically with distinct problems in maintaining relationships or deriving satisfaction from work.

For June, a 34-year-old clerical worker whose difficulties were more severe than those just described, making it through the day required enormous effort.

"I have to force myself to function every day to go to work. I feel dead but have to keep going. It's a daily temptation not to slit my wrists or jump out of windows or in front of speeding cars."

June's job entailed filing workmen's compensation claims and she could slip easily into the routine, once she arrived and began work, but the effort required just to leave the house in the morning and return home in the evening sapped her of any energy that could be used creatively in other activities. She lived a lonely life, isolated from others, at home with her mother and a younger sister who had two small children. She had had no boyfriends or social life since high school.

"Nothing has seemed real for the last eighteen years," she explained. When talking about herself, June often used "she" and "her" or "that thing." "Outside of plodding through work everyday, all the thing wants to do is sit at home in her chair and do nothing," she once confessed. Her life was routine, rigid and uneventful, week following upon week, month after month, and the years were piling up without hope for the future.

For 12 years June went to a parochial school where she worked hard and was well liked by the nuns and other children. In high school she became involved in music, sang in the local choir, and even played small roles in the community theater's local productions. Her father thought she should pursue a career in television or radio since she had a good speaking voice and had stage presence. For a time she seriously considered it, but when her parents divorced in her senior year, her father moved to the West Coast, and without his encouragement, she soon lost interest in the idea. Although she became "very quiet," she seemed to have as much going for her as other girls her age, and family and friends expected her to embark on a satisfying adult life after graduation. But graduation was not a commencement. "It was the beginning of the end," she admitted. "I didn't know what I would do." Eighteen years later, and after five years of therapy, June still didn't know what to do or where life was taking her.

The stories of these four women reveal some of the common problems of people who unknowingly sabotage their real happiness in love and work, as well as in recreation and hobbies. In love, they allow the fervor of romantic fantasies to camouflage severe flaws in the relationship or they project their own problems onto their partners. Individuals, like Jennifer, who have difficulty with an intimate relationship, sabotage it by clinging or distancing behavior which often causes their partners to leave them.

People like Pam retreat into a fantasy world to avoid feelings of low self-esteem, but avoidance behavior simply reinforces their feelings of worthlessness. Martha's low self-esteem led her to overeat, put on weight, feel guilty about that, and in turn, experience intensified feelings of worthlessness, which she tried to assuage by eating. She was trapped in a self-destructive cycle that merely encouraged her overindulgence in food.

June was the type of person who remains in a job far below her talent and interests and drifts through the years, never taking the steps to discover and get a more challenging job that would stimulate her interests and capacities and make her feel good about herself. A person in June's situation could very well live out her entire life caught in an inflexible routine that provided little satisfaction or enjoyment.

Many people are caught in a knot of self-destructive behavior and are unable to see it or appreciate how they themselves have tied it. Each believes the problems lie somewhere "out there," surrounding them but beyond them, rooted in external circumstances. They also believe that the solutions to their problems are "out there" too—the right man, the perfect woman, a more appreciative boss, a more interesting job, the right diet.

Not knowing what to do with one's life, not being able to make up one's mind or decide on a career can become a lethal form of self-sabotage. The habit of postponing decisions or indecisiveness to avoid taking action can deprive a life of any lasting satisfaction and happiness. The human mind can provide an endless reservoir of self-justification, of "good" reasons to conceal the "real" reason for just about anything. "The time isn't ripe," "I'm not ready for that yet," "I need more information," "I need more experience before taking such a big step," "I'm still too young," "I'm now too old." The list of rationalizations goes on and on.

Consider the situation of Harold. After divorcing his wife, a childhood sweetheart, Harold decided to sell out his interests in one of the family companies for which he worked. Although only in his late 20s, he now was in the enviable position that many people only dream about: he was independently wealthy, freed from the necessity of earning a living for the rest of his life if he so chose. Nevertheless, Harold was not the type who could simply live off his investments. He knew he needed something to do, some meaningful activity, especially one that would provide human contact. But deciding on a career posed enormous problems for him.

When he began working in the family company he had not really considered what it would mean for him personally. As the eldest son in a family with strong traditions and intense loyalties, he was expected to join one of the firms and he complied. Selling his interest in the company and striking out on his own had been a momentous turning point in his life, causing most members of the family to raise their eyebrows and a few even to disown him, which raised important issues of identity and personal values for him. Now he couldn't decide what he wanted to do.

In therapy, he often seemed like the little boy gaping at all the candy selections in the grocery store, afraid to make a choice and spend his nickel on something he wouldn't like. He had trouble concentrating. He was ambivalent about all his interests, afraid that whatever choice he made would put him into psychic jeopardy. He was convinced that he would fail utterly in any line of work that he chose on his own and that he would make a fool of himself. He wanted to avoid humiliation no matter what the cost, especially since some members of his family were openly predicting that he was headed for ruin, so he sank into a state of passivity.

He ended up unable to do anything. When he came to see me, his self-esteem was at its lowest ebb.

Vocational testing showed him where his abilities lay, but testing cannot provide motivation or tell a person what he or she *wants* to do. Finally, desperate to do something and increasingly depressed over his inability to make a decision, Harold took some classes in the community college, hoping they would help him find a direction. He enrolled in night courses in accounting, law, and painting. He also became a backer of a little theater group, took up jogging, and realized considerable success from business investments other than the theater—an achievement that made money for him but didn't fit his self-image or satisfy his need to be recognized for his work. The college courses helped him pass the time but did little to show him a future career. He couldn't decide whether he wanted to pursue any of these fields professionally or merely as a hobby.

Of course, choosing a career is a serious endeavor and should be done with care, foresight, and self-knowledge. But Harold's problem is typical of people who procrastinate and thereby sabotage their lives by involving themselves in activities that distract them from making hard decisions and commitments. No amount of vocational testing will tell a person what kind of work or activity will bring her unique gratification and fulfillment. At best, tests only indicate one's aptitudes, something many of us already know. Experimenting with classes to test one's level of interest, enjoyment, or skill is a reasonable approach, if it leads to commitment, rather than serving as postponement. A productive and satisfying life requires commitment to something one can do well or that offers pleasure. The fortunate person finds both in his commitments.

Most people who come to therapy with problems relating to career decisions fall into one of three categories. The first type are those who don't know what they want to do with their lives. They have usually done a lot of thinking, daydreaming, maybe even some serious studying of the options, but nothing appeals to them or everything seems to have a vague general appeal. The second type are those who do well in their jobs and are considered successful (even by their own standards), but they don't get any enjoyment or satisfaction out of their work. They might be working at jobs below their levels of competence, or the nature of the tasks may not interest or challenge them. A third category contains the people who know what line of work they want to pursue and have every reason to believe that they would be both successful and happy in it but are unable to find the motivation to make the move.

Here is how a young executive explained a dilemma somewhat similar to Harold's. "I'm not doing what I want because my ideas of what I want are filtered through the perception of what others want: how I work; how I think; how I dress; even my hobbies and how I relate to women. Then I blame what's wrong on my lifestyle. I blame *what* I am doing rather than my motivation, or *why* I am doing it. I'm good at perceiving what pleases other people, and I give them what they want. But I think I pay a terrible price for it. I make changes in my lifestyle, but nothing works. I'm a chameleon; I adapt to suit the environment, to please others rather than myself. All my life I've felt trapped, suffocating inside my skin, yearning to be free."

One balmy summer day after an appointment with a client, Beverly, fifty-six, an interior designer, stepped out onto Fifth Avenue in Manhattan and was suddenly swept by an intense feeling of freedom. Here's how she described it:

"I just left my client and discovered I had some free time. I was walking down the street and suddenly I was engulfed in a feeling of absolute freedom. I could taste it. I knew I was capable of doing whatever *I* wanted. When I looked at other people, I really saw them without being concerned about how they were looking at me. I was expressing myself with people, talking to them in the stores as I shopped; the feeling and expression flowed spontaneously. I didn't have to plan what I would say or how I would act. I was just being myself and thought that I had uncovered the secret of life: being in touch with your own feelings and expressing them openly with others, not worrying so much about how others felt about you."

lack of self-conscious

For Beverly, moments like this were extremely rare. In fact, after she told me of this particular afternoon, I asked her when she last felt like that, and she couldn't remember for sure. She thought it might have been several years ago. True to form, however, the feeling of exhilaration and freedom didn't last.

"Then just as suddenly as it came, it disappeared. I panicked and started thinking about the million things I had to do at the studio, of errands I needed to run after work. I began to feel nauseous and started sweating. I headed for my apartment, running most of the way. When I got in, I felt that I had been pursued. By what? Freedom, I guess. To calm down I began eating and couldn't stop. I found I had cut off all feeling. I was disgusted. I turn into a robot or a computer whenever I feel like my real self."

Beverly can't handle too much freedom. In spite of the fact that we live in a culture that idealizes and worships freedom and self-expression, an alarming number of us are secretly terrified of it. Many people feel uncomfortable without someone or some routine controlling them; they grow anxious at having to manage their lives on their own.

Once when Beverly was riding the train back to Manhattan from a job upstate, she pulled out a notebook and wrote a poem, something she hadn't done since she was in college. The poem pleased her, and she was proud of it. For a moment she contemplated how nice it would be to have the leisure time every day to sit down and write, but as soon as she realized that this would mean having time on her hands and being on her own, she panicked, tore up the poem, and walked down to the end of the car to throw it in the trash receptacle.

Throughout her life, Beverly has tried various hobbies and avocations—ballet lessons, oil painting, and horseback riding—and each of them (she admits today) gave her a great sense of freedom and pleasure. She also dropped each activity shortly after taking it up.

Whenever Beverly experiences the rush of freedom, she sabotages it out of fear and panic. Instead of indulging in the moment and enjoying it, she cuts off feeling good by cutting off all feeling whatsoever. Then as if punishing herself for having tasted the forbidden fruit, she engages in self-destructive behavior such as overeating.

Ricky, a teenager whom I treated in the hospital back in the early seventies, wrote an essay just before he was discharged. In it he described a young man hitchhiking down a highway with a joint of marijuana in his hip pocket. A highway patrolman pulls over to question him about his destination, suspects something fishy, searches him, and finds the marijuana. The patrolman picks him up and hauls him off to jail. When Ricky was released, his essay came true. Within a month, he was arrested for possession of marijuana while walking down an interstate highway. In a short time, he was back in the hospital.

Ricky is like an ex-con who wants his chains back, a "repeat offender." He is a rather extreme example of how our idealization of freedom and independence masks the many problems they can bring. We give them lip service, but in actual practice not all of us can handle them very easily. Some of us need the large corporation, the union, the group, even the hospital or prison, where we can remain relatively anonymous and have our destinies programmed for us. People like Ricky are more comfortable and function better when they have someone else—a boss, a leader, a jailer—to rely upon for direction. They would rather be dependent in a hostile environment and combat it every day than manage their own lives. In this way they avoid having to confront their own anxieties and discomfort about activating and asserting their real selves.

The people we have just met are unable to cope effectively with life without resorting to self-destructive behavior that may protect them from "bad" feelings but also prevents them from living their lives. They have little sense of self-worth, admit to feeling inauthentic most of the time, and derive very little enjoyment from their work or relationships.

Let us now focus on individuals who seem to be the opposite: they seem to have more than adequate feelings of self-worth. Consider two men who seem to have the fulfilling lifestyles these other individuals only dream about. Daniel and Stewart are both talented, charming, self-confident men, successfully pursuing careers that tap their talents and interests and provide a wide range of professional and social opportunities. They seem to be in control of their lives and receive the necessary recognition for their achievements and praise from their colleagues.

And yet neither Stewart nor Daniel is happy, and the curious paradox is that both are unhappy in the same way as the other people in this chapter. In spite of the facade of success, self-confidence, and self-esteem, both men admit that they feel false, that their lives are driven by a need that never seems fulfilled, that they, too, are caught in a web of self-destructive behavior, and believe that deep inside they are worthless. Each wishes, just like the others we have seen, that on a deeper level, he could be more in touch with his true feelings and that the person he would like to be, the person he would call his real self, could emerge.

Stewart, 35, admitted that he wasn't "feeling too good these days," which was his way of telling me that he was drinking heavily again. As in the past he would get drunk several nights a week. Not "feeling good" is disastrous for Stewart, whose childhood fantasy was that he could walk on water.

As an adult, he puts it this way: "I'm usually pretty confident about myself. I feel in charge of my life, my work, myself. I'm always enthused and charged up. But I have to be the best. Like with tennis. I know it's not just that I enjoy the game; I enjoy the *praise* for winning a match more than the actually winning. I need people to admire me and say I'm really good at something. The best.

"Over the weekend I entered this tennis tournament at the country club and really blew it. Worst I've played in months. I knew I wasn't going to do very well because I don't practice much, especially this time of year when I have to work late. The other contestants were mostly tennis bums who are out there every day till they drop. I shouldn't have expected to do too well. Maybe I'll practice more and get in shape for the next one."

Stewart doesn't always put two and two together and come up with four. If he knew ahead of time that he wasn't up for the tournament and he expected to do poorly, he should not have had to drown his disappointment in gin and tonic. But Stewart's life is filled with disappointments springing from his need to be the best. He drives a Cadillac but has his heart set on a Mercedes. He is on the board of directors of a prestigious arts foundation but is finding the projects and shows it has been sponsoring lately to be banal and substandard according to his tastes. He has a comfortable position in a prominent Wall Street brokerage firm, but he admits that the job isn't providing much satisfaction, considering the long hours he puts in evenings and weekends. Stewart admits he's a workaholic, but as he puts it, "workaholism should pay off." What he really means is if he keeps busy enough he won't have to confront what he calls his "worthless self."

Stewart is separated from his wife of 12 years and, on nights he doesn't work too late, usually drops by bars to meet women.

> The other night I was at this bar and I was in my "perfect self," I was "on." Nothing could stop me from making it with a girl I had seen there a few times before. I knew the night would turn out the way I planned. I was overstimulated, high, almost manic. And sure, I scored. But then I wasn't satisfied. Maybe she wasn't sexy enough. Or smart enough. I don't know. She wanted us to get together again, but I got frightened. I can't seem to stay interested in a woman for any length of time. It's like tennis. I really like the game but just can't get motivated to stick with it and get really good. And if I'm not good—the best—I don't enjoy it, and I give up. Whether it's tennis or a relationship, what seems to matter most to me is that it makes me feel on top rather than that it endures.
>
> After just a few nights together with a woman, I feel phony. Sometimes I think I'm basically shy, and when I'm in my "perfect self" I'm cut off from my real feelings. At work, I feel trapped, like I have to constantly be the best, put everything I can into my work just to win the praise of my supervisors and colleagues. If I want to feel okay, I have to be the best businessman, athlete, lover, bridge player—you name it. I just can't seem to enjoy doing these things in themselves. It's like there always has to be a trophy waiting with my name on it. Otherwise, it's not worth it.

At the moment, when things don't seem to be worth it and the admiration he expects others to shower upon him doesn't materialize, Stewart numbs his disappointment with gin and tonics.

"I charm people, but I don't let myself get involved," explained Daniel, 53, a lawyer, who was proud of this fact when he first began seeing me. He thought it made him more successful in his career. Now he isn't so sure.

"At work I can usually get applause from my colleagues and clients, even assistants and secretarial staff. I'm known for being a lot of fun to have around. And I'm good. I've always been an achiever, and other people really have to take second place to that. Out of sight, out of mind, I've always said."

Daniel realized that he was attracted to the legal profession because it allowed him to function like a fact-gathering machine. He even used the word "machine" to describe his ability to work smoothly and continuously. "I like being in control of things. If I have the facts, I can serve my clients better, and ultimately myself. I can get more done. Feelings get in the way." In school, he would throw himself into his work in order to avoid feelings, to preserve a safe distance between himself and others. "Feelings were unimportant," he told me. As he became more successful in his career, he became even more of a machine.

I pointed out to Daniel that he had built his life around busyness and that he was a committed workaholic. He was addicted to "not feeling." He was "terribly restless and panicky" when he had nothing to do. On weekends he suffered from the "weekend neurosis" if he didn't schedule tasks and chores into his life that would bolster his self-image and keep him from realizing his true feelings about his work, his partying, life, himself. As he put it, "The idea of a task that doesn't make me feel great is impossible." At one point he was thinking of giving up golf, which he enjoyed, because the friends with whom he played began teasing him about his spate of bad luck. He couldn't take their joking and drew the conclusion that they didn't appreciate him.

Daniel had been married for 25 years to an attractive woman whose main purpose in life, as he saw it, was to support all his activities and enhance the image he held of himself. She was an appendage to his life, and when she failed to admire and adore him he would fly into rages, sometimes not speaking to her or even acknowledging her presence for two weeks at a time. He had treated his three children much the same way while they were growing up; and after they left home, they practically severed all ties with him, visiting only a few times a year, even though they live within easy travel distance. Today Daniel thinks his children are ungrateful for all he did for them.

After his wife finally left him, he began dating other women to fill the gap in his life and feed him the praise that he needed in his off hours. He couldn't stand to be alone or doing nothing. He needed an audience 24 hours a day. In fact, it is difficult to distinguish a workaholic's "off hours," for he never slows down or knocks off. With women, too, Daniel felt angry, impoverished, and depressed if they didn't give him the recognition that he felt he craved and deserved.

"I pretend I'm interested in them," he confided about his method of getting to know new women. "But what's more important is that they be interested in the things I like to talk about and that we have a compatible sexual arrangement. If I can't have sex when I need it, I'm just no good. I begin to lose interest in conversation and making love, if I don't feel that I'm on top of things."

The problem that Daniel faces—a variation on the one confronting Stewart—is that he obviously can't be "on top of things" and "feeling good" all the time. At some point the frustrations of reality would impinge on this feeling, and both men would have to face up to not being the best at everything. Both would have to come to grips with the profound feelings of inadequacy about their real selves that lay beneath their driven and frustrating lives.

This smorgasbord of symptoms, complaints, life problems, and self-destructive behavior has not been haphazardly thrown together. While the cases above may seem to be unrelated, a veritable litany of diverse personalities, each with his or her unique brand of failures, lost hopes, and unfulfilled lives, they are all variations on a single theme. Each is an example of a person living a life dominated by a false self. The young executive who feels trapped and suffocating inside his skin, who changes to suit others like a chameleon changes its colors, articulates well what the others would all admit is wrong with their lives were they to perceive it as clearly as he does: They feel they are phony. The lives they lead are not directed by, or reflective of, their real selves. On a deeper level, often too deep to be perceived or admitted, each of them feels like a hypocrite, a robot programmed by a false self to sabotage any satisfaction that could be derived from working or loving.

Loving and working are the ways we express ourselves. As Freud pointed out, building the abilities "to love and to work" are the primary goals of healthy development and of psychotherapy. For love and work are the building blocks of a gratifying adult life. They give meaning to life, but not if one's primary goal is to avoid feeling bad and all love and work activities must be channelled toward that goal. What we have seen in each of the individuals above is a person dominated by a false self, a person who loves or works in an impaired way, convinced that self-destructive behavior is necessary to prevent feeling bad, even though such an attitude can only lead to dead ends in the search for the real self, which alone can give meaning to life.

How do we find "meaning" in life? This question has alternately excited and terrified human beings throughout the ages and will inevitably continue to do so as each generation arrives, only to experiment and test for itself the time-honored advice that has preceded it. And yet, testing and experimenting are not wasted efforts. Ultimately, no human being can find genuine meaning in her life merely by accepting the meaning handed down from those who have gone before. Personal meaning must be created, not accepted, and the process of creating it requires testing and experimentation. A false self will neither test nor experiment; it is a defense against experimenting.

Each of us must find ways to articulate and bring our inner real selves into harmony with the outer world. Most of us do so through love and work, by discovering partners, projects, or pastimes that will satisfy our needs. None of the individuals above has been able to do that.

In the case of June, the clerical worker who lives at home with her mother and her younger sister, her search for meaning ended when she graduated from high school. Daniel, the workaholic, appears to have hit upon a suitable lifestyle that he finds rewarding; namely, being the best at everything and throwing himself into an unending round of work and more work. But he is locked into this style which is not an adaptive one; it fails him in situations where he can't be best, or on top, or constantly busy, and when he has to relate to women who won't reflect back to him his grandiose image of himself. Beverly, the interior designer who is deathly afraid of freedom, is clearly blocked by not being able to enjoy those moments when she can get out of her usual way of dealing with life and explore other possibilities. She panics and runs home to the safety of food and her apartment. Jennifer, the actress, can deal with men only by demanding a level of reassurance from them that even the most accommodating would not be able to deliver. Without it, she falls apart, feels unloved, and breaks off the relationship.

In each of these cases we have met a person whose capacities to meet the challenges of an ever-changing world are impaired to a considerable degree. You may know people like them or individuals who exhibit these traits on a lesser scale. On the surface some of them exhibit a facade of mastery, an ability to deal with a narrow slice of life, but they do so in pathologic ways. They accept the message from a false self that self-destructive behavior is their only way to deal with the conflict between their feelings and the demands of reality. They believe the false self's message that they shouldn't cut—or even hope for—a larger slice of the pie.

In all these men and women a false self has substituted a defensive fantasy for genuine self-assertion, a fantasy that promises protection in love and work. In personal relationships, the false self promises to defend against the intimacy that could lead to engulfment or the pains of abandonment by substituting fantasy relationships with unavailable partners for real relationships. On the job, the false self assures the person that he can avoid the conflicts and anxiety that would come from honest self-assertion with authority figures and peers, competition, and discipline by not working up to his full capacity or ability.

Allowing the false self to control one's life results in a severe lack of self-esteem. And rightly so, for the real self is too impaired, too weak and ineffectual, to merit esteem. When a person senses that he is merely reacting to life like a robot, rather than responding like a human being, he often glimpses what so many people refer to as the "essential phoniness" or utter hollowness of life. They blame "life" rather than their own problems and withdraw into a shell where they can avoid the real problems, remain passive in the face of challenges, and deny the real mess they have made of their lives.

Being dominated by a false self means settling for a rigid manner of dealing with problems and challenges. Why would one prefer self-destructive behavior that is not able to accommodate or adjust to a variety of environmental roles? Why would someone prefer to be dominated—and sabotaged—by a false self when it means never realizing heartfelt goals and dreams that could truly make life worthwhile? What is the false self's lure that can sidetrack us from exploring the vast possibilities of life and discovering which ones fit our unique personalities and give us a sense of meaning and belonging? In short, what is the false self's power base?

Listen to how Ann, 30, explains why her false self has such a hold on her. "I'm not worthy of anything because I don't have a real self. I am a vampire living off other people. So needy. I know I delude myself, afraid of looking inside to find my real self. If I let my real self out, I'll be all alone, without anyone to fall back on. I am preoccupied with surfaces—how I look, other people, what they think. It's so hard to deal with my real self. To finally see my real self is to be like a prisoner released after twenty years: Everything seems too alien; I'm afraid of it because I don't have a grip on myself. It's too frustrating. I need to be able to crawl inside someone else's skin. It terrifies me to think of saying, 'This is me; this is my skin.' So I cop out on myself by being some other person, living with some other person's fantasy. It becomes my fantasy. I know it's not my real self. It's fake. But I'm fake. If I let my real self come out, I'll be all alone, and I can't handle that."

For Ann, a persistent and overwhelming fear of letting her real self out controls her life. To avoid the fear and the depression that would result if that real self did emerge, a false self arises to restructure life and make it "safe." But it is a perverse rescue operation, pulled off by an internal saboteur. What Ann and all the people in this chapter have done is to make a contract with the false self. Although each writes it in his or her own way, the bottom line is the same for all of them: "I'll give up searching for my real self and all that would make me truly happy in exchange for never feeling the fear of being alone with my real self or the pain of abandonment."

Although most people have occasional doubts about their identities, their self-worth, and their true happiness, and wonder if they are making the most of their lives, they are not dominated by a false self. In healthy people, a real self emerges that can realistically assess these moments of questioning and self-doubt, and cope with difficulties and disappointments, without resorting to self-destructive behavior to avoid feeling depressed or worthless. Once we understand what the real self is and how it develops, we can identify the experiences that may thwart its development and allow a false self to take control.

2

THE DEVELOPMENT
OF THE REAL SELF

CONCEPTS of the self have been around a long time. Poets and philosophers have discussed the self and written about it since ancient times wherever reflective men and women have paused to consider their true nature and purpose in life. Psychologists and psychoanalysts have been analyzing the self for at least a hundred years since Freud began practicing; and over the last century the popularization of psychodynamic theories, especially Freud's and Jung's, has allowed discussion of the basic psychological components of the self to filter into popular literature. In the past 25 years we have watched the concept of the self become an almost national obsession. From the "do your own thing" advice of the 1960s through the Me Generation of the 1970s, what Christopher Lasch has called the "culture of narcissism" has pervaded all areas of popular thought. Self-expression, alternative lifestyles, the artistic explosion that came with the new video technologies, and "new age" transformational therapies of the 1980s remind us constantly of the advice Polonius gave Laertes, "to thine own self be true."

One would think that after so much hype about the self, we would not need another book on the subject. If any generation in human history should produce experts on the nature and purpose of the self, it should be our own. But poets, philosophers, and even many psychotherapists do not look at the self from a clinical point of view. Although their works may be inspiring, uplifting, and motivating, they have not worked analytically with the self in terms of its origins, development, and capacities. Depending on their theoretical persuasion, analysts have tended to either minimize or overemphasize the self at the cost of investigating the psychological complexity of its development in early childhood and its functioning in the personality.

Freud, as the father of psychoanalysis, led early pioneers in the field down a path that would encourage work with the self in only its barest outline. Freud was primarily concerned with the instinctual drives—sex and aggression—and more or less took the self for granted. In the course of his study of the effects of oedipal conflict and castration anxiety on normal development and on the development of neuroses, Freud outlined pre-oedipal development and therefore sketchily described the pre-oedipal development of the self; but his probing explorations of the oedipal stage took most of his energies, and further and deeper study of the earlier development of the self was left to others.

Early psychoanalysts followed Freud's lead with the result that much was said and written about the self indirectly but there was no sharply focused study or understanding of how it is structured and how it functions.

Another factor that led generations of psychoanalysts farther afield from the self was the unfortunate fact, pointed out recently by Bruno Bettelheim, that when Freud did speak of the self, which he called the "soul," the word was lost in translation. In his famous "three provinces of the . . . soul," the more humanized terms *I*, *it*, and *above-I* were translated as ego, id, and superego. What Freud called the "structure of the soul" became "mental apparatus," and the phrase "organization of the soul" was translated as "mental organization," all of which fostered the impression that Freud was concerned with the mechanics of the human mind, not the mysteries of the human soul.[1] It is ironic that the term was lost over the decades, because it was Freud's belief that one must think in terms of the soul or self to understand his system of psychoanalysis.

In talking about the "self," Freud used the word *ich*, in two senses: the self as the whole person and the self as simply the ego or agency of the mind. These two concepts have persisted down to the present, inspiring two distinct schools of psychoanalytic thought about the self. The difference between the two concepts is strikingly depicted in the classic split between Freud and Carl

Jung in 1912. Both men were interested in how and why a person develops psychosis, but they targeted different problems in the early years of life. For Freud, the psychotic reached the oedipal stage and then, discovering that the oedipal conflict—the sexual attraction to the mother and the ensuing rivalry with the father— was too threatening, regressed to the earlier pre-oedipal stage where the conflict could be avoided. Jung, on the other hand, felt that the psychotic's self never reached the oedipal level, that development was arrested at a pre-oedipal stage where the self's major concern is the attempt to emerge from its identity with the mother. Jung was probably closer to the truth than Freud at that time.

Jung emphasized the self as a primordial image or archetype that expresses a person's need for unity, wholeness, and the highest human aspirations. This focus on wholeness characterized what would become the holistic school of psychoanalytic thought and initiated a shift, for the Jungians, away from the intrapsychic base, away from the importance of the ego, id, and superego and their conflictual roles. At times verging on the popular notion of the "whole person," the concept of the whole self minimized the contribution of early development to the contents of the unconscious. It split the unconscious into a personal and a collective unconscious, placing the primary importance on the collective, which operates somewhat independently of the individual person's unique intrapsychic structure. In so doing, the Jungians downplayed the depth of the individual's unconscious for the unconscious structures that all people share in common.

Freudians, on the other hand, concentrated on the *ich* as ego, an agency of the mind. Their concept of the self tended to become like an abstract institution or agency that operated on a set of mechanical principles almost divorced from the person's individuality.[2]

In recent times, a movement among Freudian ego psychologists, such as Hartmann and Jacobson, has introduced the idea of the self into Freudian theory, restoring this vital notion and placing it within the context of the classical theory of id, ego, and superego. However, their emphasis is still not focused on the more personal, creative aspects of the self.[3]

What is called for is an approach that unites the Freudian school's emphasis on the complex effects of early development on

intrapsychic structures (ego, id, superego) with the recognition of
the personal subjectivity and creativity of the more holistic theories. A more complete theory of the self, what I call the real self,
must take into account creativity and the subjective experiential
aspects of the individual, which the Freudians minimized (or considered secondary dividends of successful therapy, not part of its
essence) as well as the intrapsychic depth that the Jungians tend
to overlook. I don't believe we need to shy away from the importance of the ego in order to emphasize the whole person, nor do
we need to minimize the intrapsychic structures and the conflict
between them in order to recognize that the liberation of creativity
can be a major result of therapy. Creativity is more than a byprod-
uct of therapy; it can be a direct result. An intrapsychic emphasis
can reach into the depths of the unconscious while still retaining
a place for unique experiential developments of the self. The concept of the real self includes both the intrapsychic *and* the unique,
individual aspects of the whole person.

The real self, from the perspective of object relations theory, is
made up of *the sum of the intrapsychic images of the self and of significant others, as well as the feelings associated with those images, along
with the capacities for action in the environment guided by those images.*
The images of the real self are derived mostly from reality and to
a lesser extent from fantasy—what one wishes as well as what one
is—and its motives are directed toward mastery of reality tasks as
a way of maintaining psychic equilibrium. The false self, on the
other hand, is derived mostly from infantile fantasies, and its motives are not to deal with reality tasks but to implement defensive
fantasies: for example, avoiding self-activation to promote the fantasy of being taken care of which then becomes a way of "feeling
good." The purpose of the false self is not adaptive but defensive;
it protects against painful feelings. In other words, the false self
does not set out to master reality but to avoid painful feelings, a
goal it achieves at the cost of mastering reality.

The real self can be viewed as mostly conscious, creating images
and representations of the individual and the world, identifying
our unique individual wishes and expressing them in reality, as
well as maintaining the continuity and relatedness of the various
images. The real self consists of all our self-images plus the ability
to relate them to each other and recognize them as forming a sin-

The environ (parent)
allows for the real self
only possible
in good enuf
environment

gle, unique individual. These self-images are the images we have of ourselves at particular times and in specific situations. They include our body images, whether they are conscious or unconscious, realistic or distorted. The real self allows a person to recognize within herself that special "someone" who persists through space and time, who endures as a unique entity regardless of how the various parts of it shift and change.

Confusion can arise in trying to completely and clearly separate the concepts of the real self and the ego. Not only did Freud himself not do it but the definitions differ depending on the theoretical perspective. From the perspective of ego psychology, the real self and its functions are encompassed in the term "ego." From the object relations perspective, the real self does not encompass the ego but functions as a parallel partner, utilizing some ego functions to accomplish its tasks, while the rest of the ego carries out the traditional functions described by ego psychologists.

The ego through its defense mechanisms maintains intrapsychic equilibrium by regulating the internal interaction between the id, superego, and reality. In addition, it also helps the real self with its tasks. For example, reality perception is essential in order to carry out a reality task. The self can be viewed as the representational partner of the ego, although it is more than that because in addition to having representational aspects of ego functions, it also has its own agenda which is to identify and express one's unique wishes. The ego can be viewed as the executive arm of the self, although it is more than that in that it also regulates the balance between id, ego, and superego.

Erik Erikson's analogy of the heart and lungs is helpful in understanding the unconscious, automatic regulating role of the ego. As our hearts and lungs operate automatically, without our being aware of them, to maintain our physical equilibrium, so do the ego defense mechanisms maintain our psychic equilibrium without our having to activate them consciously. We can rely on a reservoir of stored intrapsychic memories and habits that save us from having to think through every act and feeling of every minute each day, which would ultimately block our ability to function meaningfully in the real world. Erikson further explains that each personal identity has what he calls an ego aspect and a self aspect. The self aspect (or self identity) emerges when the ego aspect (or ego identity) successfully integrates and synthesizes the various self-images that are formed in the psychosocial experiences of the individual[4]; in simpler terms, when you manage a relationship or a task using your own unique style the experience is integrated to reinforce your self-image.

The real self keeps the various subordinate images related to one another, allowing us to see how the self-images and behaviors are linked so we can recognize them as our own and as honest expressions of ourselves. It keeps us aware of our essential, separate, unique identity and allows us to adapt creatively to changing situations so that we can continue to express the continuity and uniqueness of our identity and feel "real."

We are very much a kaleidoscope of self-images, like pieces of colored glass, forming and reforming shapes, patterns, and designs, always changing even though the pieces stay the same. The shifting patterns always resemble each other and seem to be variations of one another, suggesting that no matter how much we change, something basic in us holds its own. In addition to the self-images we can see through the kaleidoscope of our lives, there is also another self: the self who holds the tube up to the light and turns the end, allowing the pieces to fall and reassemble and form new patterns. This is the functional aspect of the real self that expresses, organizes, and observes the patterns of our lives.

When Malcolm Cowley wrote his memoirs at age 85, he was not concerned with the question "Who am I?" but "Who *was* I?" What he discovered was not always what he expected, but he hoped that the process of putting his life and memories down on paper would reveal to him "the person who is possibly the real me."[5] In writing an autobiography or a memoir, or whenever we look back seriously over our lives, we are confronted with a kaleidoscopic vision of ourselves, of a single life made up of many roles, situations, people, behaviors, ideas, hopes, disappointments, and successes. As genuine reflections of the real self, were they all equal? In what ways were they, or were they not, "real"? And are they still real in some ongoing fashion that contributes to the unique individuals we are today?

In looking back over your life, or pausing to consider where you are at the moment and from whence you've come, you can recognize the various separate self-images that reflect your intrapsychic real self. Many of these are based on relationships: son, daughter, brother, sister, husband, wife, parent, friend, neighbor, enemy. Many self images derive from our work and recreations: doctor, secretary, lawyer, teacher, salesclerk, poker player, jogger, poet, artist, swimmer. The clubs, organizations, and institutions we belong to, or have in the past, also round out the real self: Republican, Democrat, Catholic, Jew, Elk, Junior Leaguer, Scout. We each wear many hats, play many roles, cross and recross many bridges. We have personal and professional self-images, some known only to ourselves and those closest to us, others displayed publicly for everyone to see.

Under the guidance of the real self, we can identify our individual wishes as they change over the years and discover realistic ways to achieve them in our lives. The real self allows us to take the steps to carve out our individual places in the real world by finding the appropriate job, lifestyle, or mate. Our lives are then characterized by a harmonious interaction between the intrapsychic real self and the external environment, which, in turn, maintains our self-esteem.

The real self can accept and modulate the various, even conflicting, self-images and resolve any apparent, temporary confusions. It can integrate diverse aspects of our lives to form a whole. It becomes the guidance system that motivates much of our behavior and keeps that behavior on the appropriate path. The real self is the person writing his memoirs as well as the various persons he was in the past. The real self knows how to relate them to each other to form a whole life, a whole self. The real self understands that what we are today is the product of the ever-shifting roles, behaviors, and circumstances that made up the many self-images that fitted us over the years. They fitted us then, and when viewed through the wisdom of the real self, they still fit today.

Until about 25 years ago, most of what we knew about psychological development was gleaned from patients in therapy remembering and retelling childhood experiences, and it suffered from the inevitable gaps and distortions to which memories are subject. As Margaret Mahler pointed out, what we knew of normal development was often abstracted from patients' accounts of what went wrong. Far better, as we were to learn through Mahler's own studies, was to piece together a picture of "what goes right" through actual face-to-face studies of normal young infants and their mothers.

Beginning with Mahler and others in the late 1950s, child observation studies of normal healthy two- and three-year-olds with their mothers in real life situations have added greatly to our understanding of the processes involved in the child's successful attempts to separate from the mother physically and psychologically and develop a separate, autonomous real self. Based on observations of children and their mothers over several years, psychoanalysts and psychologists have identified the various stages of development through which a child passes as she develops a real self and learns to express it through her own unique personality, setting up many of the coping patterns that will stay with her for life.

We have learned that the building blocks of the real self consist of biological endowment (although to date, research has not revealed what these building blocks exactly consist of or to what extent they influence the development of the self), the child's experience of proprioceptive and sensory sensations from his own body, as well as pleasure in increasing mastery in coping with the environment. In the early years development takes place through interactions with the mother or principal caretaker. As Mahler put it, "Insofar as the infant's development of the sense of self takes place in the context of the dependency on the mother, the sense of self that results will bear the imprint of her caregiving."[6]

A newborn baby has one primary goal: comfort, i.e., to seek pleasure and avoid pain. Like every human organism, the infant experiences hunger and various types of discomfort arising internally and externally, such as the internal discomfort of a full bladder or the external unpleasantness of a stuffy, overheated nursery. The child can and will take care of the full bladder; the overheated room is beyond his means. A sensitive mother or father, of course, will lower the temperature or open a window.

For many years it was thought that in the first three months the infant was a passive *tabula rasa* acted upon by the parents.[7] In recent years a second wave of baby watchers with newer investigative techniques have focused their studies on these three months and their findings have drastically changed the *tabula rasa* theory. They have found that the baby's perceptual capacities emerge very early: at four weeks the baby develops a special response for the mother and father, and by seven weeks the baby can organize visual observations. Thus the baby becomes a far more active partner very early in its development through an active dialogue with its caretakers. Despite the fact that many contemporary men are more interested and involved in parenting than their counterparts in previous generations, in most families the mother is still the primary caretaker, particularly during the infant's first months of life. Hence the delineation between specific experiences and feelings the infant has involving each parent. This dialogue then becomes crucial for the emergence of the self.

At this point in life, the child still feels "fused" with the mother. There is not yet a sense of "I" and "not-I." The process of birth has physically separated the child from its mother, but as the child perceives himself and his mother intrapsychically, there has been no separation as yet. From the child's point of view, he and mother are still one and everything in the environment is part of his self *and* part of the mother.

After two or three months, however, things begin to change, as the baby begins to discover his skin, and slowly learns that he has boundaries. Although the concepts of "inside" and "outside" are still vague, he begins to grow aware of the fact that some things are outside him, including mother. As this perception grows, he realizes on a very primitive level that some needs are satisfied by the mother alone, that it is she, not the child, who brings about some pleasurable feelings and relieves unpleasurable ones. He begins to discover that she is not part of his own body, as he once perceived her. Nevertheless, because the mother comes and goes within his orbit, she is still perceived as part of himself, although not strictly speaking a bodily part any longer.

She is a mysterious part of him, another half who is different from him, an all-powerful partner or pole of his being who organizes things and provides for his needs whether it be milk, a diaper changing, or a comforting hug. The child gradually becomes aware that the mother is indispensable for his sense of well-being. She is the master organizer of his life, mediating every perception, action, insight, and every bit of knowledge so that he comes to identify with her and her actions; and she will continue to organize for him until he develops his own internal organizer.

During these second and third months the baby will look more directly into its mother's face and focus more closely on her eyes. Eventually in the fourth or fifth month he expresses his special bond with her by the specific smile that leaps to his face only for her. Prior to this stage, infants use a nonspecific, social smile that charms everyone from nurses to grandparents, but though we hate to admit it, the child doesn't really mean anything personal by it. The special smile for mother, however, is different. It means something. When mother enters the room or comes into view, the baby honors her with this special smile of delight, and in so doing honors the unique relationship that he is beginning to understand *4 or 5th month* he has with her and her alone.

At this stage of development the baby is also more alert when awake. The attention is more clearly directed outward toward the environment and is steadier, more constant. The child doesn't drift in and out of alertness as much as she did a few weeks ago. She seems to be less preoccupied with herself. She responds more readily and predictably to the world around her. At six months the child is pulling at mother's hair, nose, glasses, necklace, trying to put food into her mouth. Now we notice that sometimes when mother holds her, the baby will stiffen her body and strain to push away to get a better look at the mother. When she was newborn, her body molded easily and comfortably into the contours of the mother's body and arms, a metaphorical posture that indicated she felt symbiotically fused with her.

Now she wants something more. She watches the mother intently, scanning her face and body, even as she scans the environment around the two of them from her safe and secure vantage point in mother's arms. Soon the young human being's sense of "I" is different from "mother" and the "world." In these days and nights of feedings, crying, and being held and doted on, the child's sense of self begins to emerge, a self that will be distinct from the world around her and will persist throughout life.

The baby first finds this new identity in a physical way by paying more attention to his own fingers, hands, arms, and toes, feeling himself, making sure he is there. He watches his movements in a mirror. By 12–18 months the child recognizes the image in the mirror as himself. He can point to it and say his name or use a personal pronoun, or if he isn't talking yet, he can point to the mirror and then proudly to himself.

7- or 8ᵗʰ month until 1½ years - love affair with the world

In the stage from the seventh or eighth month until the child is about a year and a half old, the real self is activated by the endless forays to explore the marvels of the world; and indeed, everything in the world is truly marvelous. The child has a "love affair with life" as he learns to sit up, scoot, crawl, and walk. He plays with toys, touches and tastes everything that he can get his mouth on. As he sits up by himself, stands by holding onto a chair or piece of furniture, and learns to walk, he gains a new visual perspective of the world.

Fueled by the mother's interest and enthusiasm in the discoveries of this emerging self, the child simultaneously practices the motor skills needed to make those discoveries as well as the psychological skills that will later become the capacities of the real self—self-activation, self-expression, and creativity. At this stage, the quality of mothering is crucial. The mother's ability to pick up the cues and signals from the child's emerging self, her own ease of self-expression and creativity, her imagination—these compose the fertile soil in which the child's real self grows and develops.

Soon the child takes that first step by himself. When he actually walks on his own, the world becomes an even larger arena, as he puts more physical distance between himself and mother. Narcissism is at its peak. The child is able to search for toys, pick things up by himself, feel them, taste them, and bring them to adults. He is omnipotent, almost drunk with power, oblivious to his own limitations, busy and elated by his discoveries and his release from the confining world of the mother. Not even falls and bumps or other frustrations can stop him.

And yet the little adventurer is not as fearless as he might seem. The world might be his oyster, but mother is still home base. The child scampers off, lost in the thrill of the moment, but frequently returns to mother. He might come back simply to touch her leg briefly or grab her skirt. Perhaps he wants to toss the ball or block or rattle into her lap. Over and over, the child returns for emotional refueling, for reassurance that mother is still there.

The age-old game of peekaboo is more than just fun. It becomes a mini-drama of the real self's dilemma. In it, the child ducks behind something and temporarily loses the mother's image, delighting in the fact that he is not really fused with her; and yet almost as if he can not yet tolerate too much separation, he quickly makes the mother's face reappear. The child is practicing crucial tasks that will be important for the rest of life: the ability to be separate and yet negotiate closeness and distance from others, to go away and come back, to tolerate (even impose) isolation and find companionship, to be single yet social, to be for one's self and for others.

Take for example the simple ruse of running off, away from mother, hellbent for nowhere, only to have mother hot on his heels to sweep him up in her arms before he gets too far away. Almost as if the ruse were mutually agreed upon, the child has no intention of escaping for good. He learns that mother will be there to rescue him and protect him from himself as well as the real environmental dangers of which he is still unaware: the busy street at the end of the yard, the top step of the basement stairs, the low table filled with breakable objects.

Like peekaboo, this is a game of loss and recovery, of losing and regaining both mother and freedom. In one sense, it is play; but in another, it is serious practicing for the many situations in life where the individual must balance his need to be dependent on others with his desire for freedom and independence. It is also a vehicle to develop his capacity to deal with separation anxiety.

The child needs emotional "supplies" for the emerging self and will keep returning to mother to receive them, in the form of her acknowledgment and support for the unique displays of self-expression and achievements the child demonstrates through curiosity and play. But as she approaches the end of her second year of life, she develops a growing concern over mother's whereabouts, a concern not as intense or noticeable in the earlier months when she practiced leaving and returning to mother by charging off into the room and happily running back. In fact, the new concern doesn't seem like practice at all. It is serious business. We can see it on the child's face—she looks worried, hurt, fretful, sometimes even panicky.

Even as her ability to walk and master the world increases, the child's need for reassurance that she is not totally on her own also increases. She must balance her growing independence with assurance that mother shares her life and supports her struggling efforts to develop as a separate, autonomous person in her own right apart from the mother. She needs both mother's encouraging presence and space away from her. Her desire to explore the world on her own is tempered by her wish for reunion with mother, and even this wish is tempered by the child's fear of being engulfed by the mother. Life now becomes a kind of dance, alternating between "shadowing" the mother visually, keeping her in view, and darting away from her. Even while playing in another room, alone or with a playmate, the child needs to know where mother is and may, in fact, scamper back to touch base, to get refueled. By means of this interplay of advance and retreat on the part of the child, the original fantasy of being fused symbiotically with the mother disappears.

The increased need for reassurance parallels and reinforces the child's realization that he is indeed separate from mother. In the physical sense, he learns to put increasing amounts of distance between himself and her; and on an intrapsychic level, he experiences himself as an object separate from the object that he is learning to regard as his mother. As intrapsychic separation occurs and the real self emerges, the child develops an image of himself that is entirely separate from his image of mother.

The child now stands at an important crossroads in the development of his real self. He is ambivalent about his need for mother, fearing his new embryonic self will be "engulfed"—taken over by the mother—and disappear. His budding personality is now emerging as he learns to assert himself in his own unique ways when dealing with other children, finding his toys, relating to adults and strangers, making his needs known to those who can alleviate them. Unlike peekaboo, loss and recovery are not swift and immediate. He becomes frustrated, and his frustration tolerance, once high and unassailable, is lower. Things bother him, he can't always get his way, he falls down and it hurts. And in these new encounters with reality lie the origins of the temper tantrums that will characterize the "terrible twos."

Living with a child through this stage is not easy. It can try the best of nerves in the most sympathetic and understanding parents. And yet these are the months in which the child's real self will emerge under the protective care of parents who can accept his ambivalent and indecisive behavior and support his emerging self. He teeters at a major threshold in personality development, torn by conflicting needs and desires. The toddler must learn to cope with the world in his mother's absence, and learning to do so requires him to venture out and be separated.

During these initial years, the father plays a pivotal role in the development of the child's real self. Whereas the child must separate the mother's image from the fused symbiotic unity he initially shared with her, no such task is required with the father. On the contrary, the father-image has always been separate and distinct, coming, as Mahler says, from outer space as it were; the father is a kind of knight in shining armor whom the child becomes aware of just at the time when the child himself embarks on his first important quest to see the world. Right when the child needs him, the father pops in and out of view, representing a vast and exciting world that is totally non-mother-and-child. His appearances and activities, even though the latter may be many of the same as the mother's, "rescue" the child from its sole dependence on the mother-image. Like the world of toys and the other mysterious rooms of the house, the father is someone to practice on. He is different and stands for nonmother experience. Exploring reality through him has a special quality of exuberance.

On the intrapsychic level, the child can use the father to test his emerging self-image as distinct and separate from that of the mother. With the mother, the child can often feel sucked back into the mother's orbit in a frightening and engulfing way. With the father, however, the child can experience his own otherness and individuality without the fear of engulfment. Father, coming from the outside world of reality rather than the fused symbiotic state, does not trigger symbiotic fears. When father is firmly established as both an exhilarating adventure into worldly reality and a safe haven where the child can test his intrapsychic perceptions about that reality, we can be reasonably assured that the toddler will continue to achieve his own individuality and the important psychological separation from mother, and the real self will emerge with confidence.

In the course of the intricate process of separating psychologically from the mother, the child separates "good" images from "bad" images even as he separates his own image from that of the mother. In the process, he ends up splitting his own "bad" self-image from his "good" self-image and the image he holds of the "bad" mother from the image of the "good" mother.[8] During times

Age 3
hold both
good + bad
images of
self

when the child feels good—warm, fed, comfortable, safe—a "good" self-image arises. When he feels bad—hungry, tired, uncomfortable, frightened—he develops a "bad" self-image. These images are held apart by splitting them into two distinct images. The real self, as we have indicated, is a master at holding various self-images together, and one of its first tasks, when the child is around age three, is to fuse and hold together the two parallel images of the self.

The same effort must be undertaken in terms of the two mother-images. Every toddler holds two parallel images of his or her mother: a "good" mother-image made up of the experiences in which the mother provides pleasure, comfort, warmth, affection; and a "bad" mother-image from those experiences in which the mother frustrates the child's impulses, shows displeasure, punishes, or in fact physically harms or inflicts pain on the child. In normal development, the real self fuses these two images of the mother into one. Over time the child must learn to perceive both himself and mother as whole, constant individuals. There are not two selves, two mothers, one good, one bad. Although this fantasy arises as the child differentiates and separates himself from the mother, it does not last. Split objects fuse into wholes, and the child learns that they are constant.

This realization of wholeness and constancy is part of the wider knowledge that life itself is ambiguous, colored in shades of gray, rather than stark whites and blacks. For a young child, the world is truly unpredictable and kaleidoscopic; and it is an enormous feat to acquire the realistic perception that objects hold together, that the mother who scolds is the same mother who hugs, that the self that breaks the lamp is the same self who learns to balance food on a spoon and aim it successfully into the mouth. Life is both rewarding and frustrating. So is mother. So is the self.

Clearly, the images the child holds of the mother, father, himself, and the world in general may be distorted, skewed, and incomplete. Take for example the child's perception of the physical environment. The room with its furniture looks enormous, the preparation of food is mysterious and magical, the place that father disappears to when he leaves in the morning is terra incognita, and as the unexplored lands on Renaissance maps indicate, "here be monsters." The point is not how accurate and complete a child's representation of mother, father, or the world really is; every child's set of psychic representations is subjective and incomplete. What's important at this period is their wholeness. Completing our images of mother and father is a life-long task, always destined to fall short of the mark. But wholeness is another matter. The real self has the ability to learn at this early age of life, but with difficulty, that objects are whole and incorporate both their good and bad aspects. There is one self and one mother.

At the same time as the split is being healed, the child, through identifying with the mother, takes into himself functions the mother had performed for him before his ego was developed enough to perform them for himself. Now he begins to assume control over his own ego functions. He develops better reality perception, frustration tolerance, impulse control, and ego boundaries.

Instead of allowing the images to remain split into their good and bad components, the child learns to repress the negative aspects into the unconscious. Personality development depends on repression because the drives and feelings that are repressed enter the unconscious for sublimation. They become the raw material for creativity, the pool of energy that fuels our desires to become doctors, lawyers, mothers, fathers. If a person can't repress, he or she can't sublimate because there isn't the psychic energy to respond to life in creative and successful ways.

In the best family situations, trial and error—on the part of the parents as well as the child—gradually build up the child's confidence that the world is neither a totally threatening nor a totally pleasurable place, but an ambiguous place, an arena of opposites: safety and danger, success and failure, comfort and pain, power and helplessness, companionship and loneliness. There will be moments of happiness and elation as well as times of frustration and sorrow. Most of all, the child learns that his mother also embodies good and bad qualities. At times she rewards and comforts; at other times, she is distant, aloof, punishing. But the child discovers that his mother loves him with his emerging and separating self no matter what and that she sincerely wants him to explore the world and develop and grow in his own unique way. And as he does so, the real self emerges and develops its capacities to cope successfully with life.

The real self is stabilized intrapsychically between ages three and four, but the journey is far from over. In fact, it has only just begun. Although the intrapsychic system is in place, the years of childhood are spent learning to put that system to work in the external environment—learning how to dress, eat, get along with others; discovering interests and talents and learning how to develop them into satisfying activities.

During the grammar school years, children are exposed to a wide range of interests and activities, some of which they will get intensely involved in as hobbies or pastimes, many of which they will drop only to take up something else. At this stage the possibilities of life are too rich and various to make hard, fast decisions and commitments. The young boy, when asked what he wants to be when he grows up, may answer, "Either a truck driver or an astrophysicist." The unlikelihood that both would appeal to the same individual is explained away when we remember that during these years, referred to as the latency period, the child is testing skills and interests to see what activities reinforce the real self. In answering the question, the young boy is really saying that he still hasn't discovered what niche would make him feel most like himself and allow him to express his own unique characteristics.

In adolescence, the real self tests its ability to handle sex and freedom from parents, finding ways to articulate itself in an expanding world of opportunities and obligations. During these years teenagers venture into the unexplored territory of personal and sexual relationships, seeking answers to questions about their real selves. Infatuations, romances, crushes, and "best friends" may come and go as adolescents seek foils and complements to test and understand their own identities. Outwardly they may appear to be auditioning their friends and acquaintances for their personality traits, values, sexual preferences, and compatibility, but inwardly they are seeking to learn more about themselves.

For most people, all of life is a period of growth and development, experimenting and testing, searching through trial and error for harmonious ways to allow the intrapsychic structure of the real self to express itself in the physical world through relationships and work. All the issues are not resolved by the end of adolescence. While it's true that most people arrive at some definite conclusions regarding their needs and interests in their early twenties—they get their act together, as it were—and settle down in careers and relationships, it is not uncommon for them to rethink the issues again in midlife, perhaps divorcing and remarrying or switching careers.

As children and young adults, we learn to stand on our own two feet both physically and psychologically, and in doing so, we develop patterns of feeling and thinking that serve as an internal guidance system for coping with problems and difficult situations. These patterns incorporate the specific strengths and capacities of the real self, which shape the way we handle relationships and express ourselves in work and other pastimes.

3

THE REAL SELF
IN ACTION

IN contrast to the individuals we met in Chapter 1 whose real selves were severely impaired, a person with a healthy real self can manage not only the routine ups and downs of daily life but also serious crises as they develop. Social, personal, financial, and professional crises, while always upsetting to one's normal pattern of life, are not paralyzing or totally defeating to a person with a healthy real self. In fact, people guided by a healthy real self often grow and mature through crises, coming out of them richer, more understanding, and compassionate human beings.

Let's take a look at a young woman with a healthy sense of her real self to see the types of strengths and abilities the real self provides:

Terry grew up in an Irish-German family in the Midwest. She was a vigorous and active baby who walked early and showed genuine delight in exploring and learning about the world. Both her father and mother encouraged her curiosity and spent a lot of time with her from the time she was little, sharing her interests and stimulating her to develop her skills as a child and do her best in school.

During her childhood Terry showed a marked interest in playing with animals and learning as much about them as she could. Over the years she raised gerbils, rabbits, a cat, and two dogs. Each time she got a new pet, her parents impressed upon her the importance of taking good care of it, and so she learned responsibility. As Terry got older, it became clear that she had a real talent for training and caring for animals, and she loved doing so. Spending time with her animals provided her with long hours of enjoyment and happiness. Her interests, however, went beyond caring for animals. She had many friends, played a number of sports, and always enjoyed reading and music.

Terry was among the first generation of women in her family to go to college; she majored in arts and sciences, torn between her love of literature, science, and animals. She was active in the drama club and was a member of the college newspaper staff. A strong-willed, attractive woman, she was well liked by both men and women. She usually had a boyfriend whom she saw steadily, but her involvement with a special boy never cut her off from other men or groups on campus. Terry was considered outgoing and fun. She never lacked friends with whom she could share her problems, dreams, and aspirations.

In her senior year a crisis developed. She applied to and was accepted by a school of veterinary medicine out of state. When she announced this to her parents, they were quite upset. They had always assumed that Terry's love of science and her volunteer work in local hospitals would lead her to nursing or medical school. In fact, her father, a doctor himself, had his heart set on her going to a well-known medical school in town. Her mother was more open-minded about the career issue but didn't relish her daughter's moving so far from home. Both parents made their feelings known, and Terry was made to feel that she was letting them both down by her decision to enter this graduate program. To compound matters, Craig, her boyfriend of two years, had gotten serious; he talked of marriage off and on and harbored an unspoken assumption that they would move in with each other after graduation. He had been hired by a major company in town and was looking forward to setting up housekeeping with Terry. He took it hard when she broke the news to him. Had she been dominated by a false self, she would not have been able to withstand opposition from those close to her. Her decision would not have been anchored in what she believed was best for herself, and she would have automatically given in to her parents' and Craig's wishes rather than run the risk of losing their approval.

At veterinary school Terry achieved academic success and great personal satisfactions and rewards. Each passing week confirmed that she really wanted to be a veterinarian. She and Craig corresponded at first and called each other weekly, but as the months passed, his affection for her cooled and he became involved with someone else. On her first Thanksgiving visit home, he told her about his new girlfriend and Terry became very upset. However, even though she loved him very deeply, Terry was able to envision a life without Craig. She had had enough experience at meeting and going with men in high school and college to know that she could survive without him.

The weekend was filled with other tense moments and disappointments, as Terry's parents continued to express their disapproval over her career decision, particularly her father who thought she was wasting her talents on animals rather than using them on people. When she returned to school, Terry felt awful. For a week, she seriously doubted her ability to continue, feeling rejected by both her parents and Craig.

She eventually realized, however, that her studies meant a lot to her and her dream of becoming a veterinarian led her back into her normal routine of classes and study. A guilt-provoking letter from her mother, pointing out that going away to school was what caused her to lose Craig, convinced Terry that she should not spend the entire Christmas season at home as she had promised over Thanksgiving. She talked her decision over with a professor with whom she had a friendly relationship. He agreed that it would do her no good emotionally to subject herself to her parents' criticism and put-downs for the entire week. She called her mother and told her that she would only come home for three days and then return to school. Someone with an impaired sense of self would not have been able to handle this situation as smoothly as Terry did. Either she would have gone home for the entire holidays and felt awful because of her mother's criticism or she would not have gone home at all and felt guilty for letting her parents down.

In the spring semester, Terry lost her part-time job at a blood bank where she had made extra money for school expenses. Although she had a scholarship, she relied on the extra money for clothes, meals out, and entertainment. She had found a new boyfriend, but because he was a graduate student himself without a lot of money, they usually did things "dutch-treat." Not having the money she had relied on from her job put a bit of a strain on their relationship, but they made do.

Throughout her years in veterinary college, Terry gradually learned how to rely less and less upon her family and friends back home. She made new friends, found part-time jobs when she could, and developed a new life for herself that was different and more rewarding than she imagined going to medical or nursing school and living at home or living with Craig would have been. When problems arose, she found herself getting over the initial disappointment, usually by talking things over with friends or teachers.

When her thesis advisor left the college in her last year, her own course of studies was put in jeopardy, since no other faculty member had expertise in her line of specialization. She was threatened with having to shift her emphasis to a related field against her wishes. With the support of other students, she protested her case to the appropriate review board and won permission to continue even without a supervisor.

After graduation, Terry returned home and lived with her parents for a few months while beginning her practice at an animal research clinic. Her parents had by this time come to accept her career choice, but the years of living away from them had taught her that she would not be able to stay at home for long and still maintain her sense of independence. Her real self kept the inevitable tensions in perspective, reminding her that the present situation was only temporary and she would soon be on her own again. After a few months she found a suitable apartment and moved out.

Happy in her career and her independent lifestyle, Terry soon began a relationship with Steven, a young man at the animal clinic. Not ready to marry or settle down, she refused his suggestion that they move in together, arguing that since they saw each other each day at work, she needed her time alone away from him. He honored her wishes, and they continued to see each other. Terry's adult and professional life was off to a good start.

Terry's experiences are typical of the normal opportunities and challenges a young person might encounter in making the transition from college to graduate school or career. Important life-changes such as these test us on many levels, calling upon our resources for independent action, decision-making, creativity, self-confidence, and the ability to maintain our self-esteem and integrity in the face of unfamiliar, perhaps even threatening, situations. While the particulars of important life-changes vary from individual to individual, and even from stage to stage in each person's life, they all test how well the real self emerged earlier in life. The success or failure that accompanies our attempts to negotiate the transitions of adult life hinges on how well we negotiated that first important transition, the separation from the mother and the awakening of our own unique real self.

Certainly Terry's problems and crises were not more nor less upsetting than those of most young men and women. What carried her through them was a strong sense of her own self-worth that was based on reality—accurate perceptions of the people in her life and of her own abilities and options—and her fair sense of being entitled to a rewarding life. Her real self served as a reliable guide that steered her life along the lines of her best interests. Because she had developed a healthy real self through childhood and adolescence, she had the capacity to meet the problems and challenges of life, change what needed changing, and accept what could not be changed. And, as the popular maxim puts it, she knew the difference between the two.

In handling many obstacles at a major turning point in her life, Terry drew upon several key capacities of the real self that pulled her through the setbacks and enabled her to keep moving ahead towards the goals she had set for herself.

First, *the capacity to experience a wide range of feelings deeply* with liveliness, joy, vigor, excitement, and spontaneity. From college through veterinary school and into her first professional job, Terry's emotional responses matched current life situations. She was happy when good things happened, disappointed and sad, or angry, when bad things occurred. The real self does not block feelings or deaden the impact of emotions but provides a sense of what is appropriate.

Allowing for differences in personality and temperament, there is an appropriate range of anger and disappointment to feel when a boyfriend or girlfriend breaks off with us, when we lose an advisor at school, when a parent expresses disapproval or makes us feel guilty. Even feeling guilty should be a measured response, varying in intensity and duration according to the stimulus. In Terry's case, her real self knew that choosing a career that was not in line with her father's wishes was not wrong and feeling guilty over it would only undermine her decision and her performance at school.

The healthy real self provides for the experience of emotions both good and bad, pleasant and unpleasant. These are a necessary and fundamental part of life, and the real self does not erect barriers against these feelings or go into hiding. It accepts the wide range of feelings and is not afraid to express them.

Second, *the capacity to expect appropriate entitlements.* From early experiences of mastery, coupled with parental acknowledgment and support of the real self, healthy individuals build up a sense of entitlement to appropriate experiences of mastery and pleasure, as well as the environmental input necessary to achieve these objectives. We come to expect that we can in fact master our lives and achieve what is good for us.

Terry learned early in life that self-activation would bring positive responses from the environment. She had a talent for taking care of animals, and her success in science courses at school led her to realize that she could expect success and enjoyment from a career that combined both. In terms of relationships, her mother's support of her emerging self instilled confidence that her real self could expect positive responses from others. She had had enough success in high school and college to reinforce this belief so that breaking up with Craig was not the end of the world for her. She was hurt, disappointed, and moody for awhile, as was to be expected, but she got over it. She expected to, and in fact did, meet someone else.

Third, *the capacity for self-activation and assertion.* This capacity includes the ability to identify one's own unique individuality, wishes, dreams, and goals and to be assertive in expressing them autonomously. It also includes taking the necessary steps to make these dreams a reality and supporting and defending them when they are under attack. Terry politely defied her parents' wishes by going to veterinary school and, when a change in faculty threatened her major field of study, defended her right to continue it.

Fourth, *acknowledgment of self-esteem.* This capacity allows a person to identify and acknowledge that he has effectively coped with a problem or crisis in a positive and creative way. It is what kept Terry going even when it seemed that her world was falling apart. Many people with a tendency to see only the bad side of things, including what they mistakenly believe is their own lack of talent, are oblivious to their victories. In order to make it through the bad times, they need to be able to remind themselves that they are worthwhile individuals with skills and abilities.

As important as recognition by others is, self-recognition is even more important. We cannot always rely on others to refuel our sense of self-esteem. The real self must do it. Regardless of whether or not the world acknowledges our worth, the real self has the capacity to keep it foremost in our minds and the capacity to assert itself when necessary to renew the belief that we are worthwhile individuals, entitled to setting and reaching our goals.

Fifth, *the ability to soothe painful feelings.* The real self will not allow us to wallow in misery. When things go wrong and we are hurt, the real self devises means to minimize and soothe painful feelings. When Terry's mother accused her in a letter of ruining her relationship with Craig by going off to school, Terry's real self got her involved in her studies and helped her put the matter in perspective so that the guilt quickly abated. The real self also advised her to avoid extended stays with her parents, a wise decision since they would only lead to more painful feelings—in anticipation of the visit, in enduring it, and in the memories left in its wake.

Sixth, *the ability to make and stick to commitments.* The real self allows us to make commitments to relationships and career goals. Despite obstacles and setbacks, a person with a strong sense of the real self will not abandon her goal or decision when it is clear that it is a good one and in her best interests. Terry stuck to her decision to be a vet in spite of financial problems, loss of her advisor, and lack of support from her parents whom she truly loved and who had usually supported her in the past. She had a goal, and she met it.

Seventh, *creativity.* There are many definitions of creativity. The one that I like, based on helping people allow their real selves to emerge, is the ability to replace old, familiar patterns of living and problem-solving with new and equally or more successful ones. For example, any time we change our residence, we are forced into adjusting more or less creatively to new physical conditions. Psychically we also move into new situations that make demands on our creative resources. We must devise ways to cope with loss, as Terry did when Craig broke off his relationship with her. We may have to rethink priorities when we do not have sufficient finances to realize all of them, as Terry did when she no longer had the extra money coming from her part-time job.

Not only is creativity the ability to find solutions for life's problems in the world around us, it is also the ability to rearrange intrapsychic patterns that threaten to block self-expression without which there can be no creativity. We may need to learn how to view things differently to eliminate false impressions and replace them with accurate, realistic ones. We may need to diffuse the negative memories or feelings that we associate with certain activities or situations so we can engage in them from an emotionally neutral or positive stance.

Eighth, *intimacy*, the capacity to express the real self fully and honestly in a close relationship with another person with minimal anxiety about abandonment or engulfment. We saw Terry handle this in two relationships:

Without Craig, she could have felt so abandoned as to become paralyzed in her ability to study and continue her work. When he ended the relationship, she did not block or repress her feelings (the first capacity of the real self); she felt hurt, lonely, and rejected, and rightly so. She had been dumped. But fear of abandonment, fear that it would happen again if she gave her heart to another man, did not keep her from beginning a new relationship.

When she returned home after graduation, Terry realistically assessed Steve's suggestion that they move in together, realizing that it would be too much too soon and would prevent her from realizing other goals. A more insecure woman who could not envision her life without a man would probably have moved in immediately, or if not, would have doubted the wisdom of her decision not to do so. Terry had enough sense of self-esteem to say no to Steve without fearing rejection if she hurt his feelings. And she had a strong enough capacity for intimacy to maintain the relationship while also pursuing her other goals.

Ninth, *the ability to be alone*. The real self allows us to be alone without feeling abandoned. It enables us to manage ourselves and our feelings on our own through periods when there is no special person in our lives and not to confuse this type of aloneness with the psychic loneliness, springing from an impaired real self, that drives us to despair or the pathologic need to fill up our lives with meaningless sexual activity or dead-end relationships just to avoid coming face to face with the impaired real self. We saw in Terry the ability to organize her life around worthwhile pursuits, some of which required leaving family and friends behind in order to achieve a goal. She learned that the ability to find meaning in life comes from within and that although she related well to and enjoyed others, she was not dependent on them to activate her real self.

Tenth, and lastly, *continuity of self.* This is the capacity to recognize and acknowledge that we each have a core that persists through space and time. We are confident that the "I" of one experience is continuous and related to the "I" of all our other experiences. The Terry who did well in college, loved Craig, defied her parents, was short of money, stood up to her graduate school administration, passed exams, worked with animals, lived alone, and applied for jobs and landed a good one was the same Terry. Whether up or down, in a good mood or a bad one, accepting failure or living with success, a person with a real self has an inner core that remains the same even as he grows and develops. At the end of life, it is the same "I" who was born many years ago who passes on.

In this next example, Mary and Denny, we can see how the capacities of the real self emerge and sustain a family as well as a husband and wife as individuals. In their early 40s, they have three teenage children. Both of them take family responsibilities seriously, and over the years the two have been good parents, encouraging their children along the lines of interests that they show whether it be in school, sports, social activities, or hobbies. Mary and Denny have the capacity to share in their children's tumultuous moods and show sympathy and concern while remaining distanced enough to allow the children to grow independently. The parents know they can provide an emotional anchor for their children when they need it. Individually their own affective responses are appropriately handled. When bad things happen, they worry and share their concerns with each other, ready to help the other pull through difficult and disappointing times. Similarly, they share together in the joys of family life and show genuine delight in the children's happiness.

Both partners have a realistic sense of their entitlement to a good life with their children, each other, socially, and professionally. Like most mothers, Mary learned by trial and error how to be a mother, raise children, and supervise household matters. As her proficiency grew, she learned to expect success. On occasion, when plans failed or things did not go as she had hoped, Mary did not let her confidence lag nor did she doubt her abilities. Her real self knew that she had the skills and wherewithal to care for her family.

Denny, too, learned from his experiences as a young and then not-so-young father that he could raise three children, provide for the family financially, and maintain a stable, loving relationship with Mary. At work he was, over the years, promoted from a junior level through department head to senior management position. During this process, he acquired a sense of competence and professionalism that he learned to rely on when things weren't going his way.

When their youngest child began high school, Mary decided to take night courses in real estate at the local community college. Denny supported her in this, but the children objected, since it meant changes in the evening meal schedules and the necessity for them to pitch in and help prepare dinner a few nights a week and clean up afterwards. These new responsibilities often conflicted with their own after-school activities, and they required the family to reorganize and work more closely together. In spite of the children's griping, Mary asserted herself, confident that it was in her best interests to pursue a career and diversify her life at this stage. She defended her decision against the children's complaints and found ways to minimize the painful effects of whatever initial guilt she felt over not continuing in the traditional role of mother that she had played till then.

Because of illness, she missed a number of classes and failed her real estate exam the first time around. In spite of these setbacks Mary remained committed to her goal and persevered, repeating one course, and finally passing the licensing exam. When she be-

gan her career with a neighborhood real estate agency, Mary had
to devise creative ways to handle clients, show houses, and close
deals while still fulfilling her responsibilities at home.

As her real estate career progressed, Mary discovered through
both successes and failures what was required to do the job well.
As a woman with appropriate self-esteem and realistic perceptions
of her own experience, Mary knew that, in her life, success and
failure usually balanced each other, and she did not let lost sales
discourage her conviction that she could make it as a real estate
agent.

While Mary was pursuing her real estate career, Denny went
through difficult times in his own work. Based on a recommendation by an outside consulting firm, he decided to reorganize a major department in his company. He knew it would initiate months
of unrest both in the department and throughout the company.
But Denny was a self-confident man who knew that he had the
talent to direct the changes and handle the hurt feelings and disappointments that would arise. He viewed the project as a challenge
even though it would produce a crisis.

Part of the reshuffling involved firing employees whom Denny
liked personally; although sad he was able to contain the painful
feelings by recognizing the necessity for the change, remaining self-
confident in his decisions, and directing the operation assertively
and fairly according to what he knew was right. Thanks to his
strong sense of self-worth, he weathered the grumbling and office
politicking, which he knew was unavoidable, and remained committed to the reorganization effort.

One recommendation made by the consulting team was that
Denny hire an assistant to whom he would delegate many of his
own duties. This required changes in Denny's own office routine,
many of which he found difficult at first, but he had learned early
in life to approach new situations creatively, as opportunities
rather than stumbling blocks, and he learned to derive satisfaction
from working through them. This was his approach in hiring the
assistant and devising a new flow chart of duties and responsibilities.

As was to be expected, Mary and Denny's relationship was
strained during the months when they were each engaged in their
new enterprises. They were busier than usual, more tired at the

end of the day, and had their minds on other matters. They had less time and emotional energy for each other. Yet neither lapsed into feelings of being unloved, unwanted, or taken for granted. Over the years they had learned how to express their feelings for each other in a variety of ways and remain intimate both sexually and nonsexually. During this time, they stayed close to each other and relied on their love for each other, their mutual respect, and trust to see them through the trying weeks and months.

Terry, Denny, and Mary are three typical individuals with healthy real selves capable of carrying them through crises with clarity, single-mindedness, and confidence. In presenting these cases in summary form, as I have done here, I'm afraid the soul-searching, the moments of self-doubt, and sleepless nights may have gotten lost. Certainly these three people occasionally felt depressed and alone, questioned themselves, wondered if they were embarking on the right track, got angry at others and themselves, and on occasion "lost it." Yet despite their human frailties, they, like most of us, continued to find meaning in their lives and hope for the future.

Were we to trace their development during the first three years of life, we would undoubtedly see a common pattern in the way their parents and other important caretakers raised them. Each one's mother and father had his or her own unique set of personal characteristics, yet in each family we would spot the same supportive presence that the real self needs to emerge strong and healthy. Each of these people received the support, in different ways, from a mother or father who, we can be sure, was far from perfect. There are no perfect mothers. There are no perfect fathers. Fortunately, perfection is not required for the development of a healthy real self. The mother and father who are simply "good enough" are sufficient.[1]

The real self does not insulate us from the negative feelings and frustrations that are part of human life. It is not a cocoon or isolation ward from the world's sufferings. But as the real self emerges in early childhood and develops through later stages into adolescence, an individual grows confident that she really has a unique, capable identity that can withstand being buffeted by failures and disappointments. The real self has the capacities to function successfully in the real world.

The real self has a sense of continuity; it creates a tough core at the center of one's personal identity that remains the same from one experience or crisis to another. A person recognizes that he is *somebody*, who lives, works, and loves in a certain way, and it is taken for granted that the somebody is a worthwhile, competent human being, not immune to the sufferings of life, but capable of withstanding them and growing because of them. This is the truth that, if learned well in the first three years of life, contributes to the development of the real self that remains with us into adulthood, reminding us that no matter how temporarily confused we might be in any particular situation, we are indeed worthy and have a coherent center and wholeness upon which we can rely. Therefore, we can successfully integrate the many different roles we have to play in life, and we can secure recognition from others for both our achievements in specific roles and for the whole person, the real self, that is more than the sum of our individual accomplishments.

4

FEAR OF ABANDONMENT

The Self Under Siege

In order to establish a coherent sense of self, the child in the first three years of life must learn that she is not a fused, symbiotic unit with the mother. As Mahler's and others' studies have clearly indicated, the mother and child (and father) engage in a kind of choreographed give and take, a dance of release and return, risk and retreat, learning and testing. The child runs off, the mother runs after her; the child explores and comes back to her for reassurance; she ventures out, buoyed by the excitement of discovery, and returns for emotional refueling when the adventure becomes too threatening or her own fragile sense of identity and permanence wears thin and feelings of abandonment overwhelm her. In the development of normal, healthy children, the mother acknowledges and supports her child's efforts. In the development of individuals dominated by the false self, these patterns of self-expression and maternal support did not take place. Why?

Three factors account for the failure of some children to separate and express themselves in ways that will develop and strengthen the real self: nature, nurture, and fate.

Just as each human being is born with genetic endowments that

51

will develop and guide physical growth within specific limits, so too each of us begins life with different genetic potentials that will affect our psychological capacities. We won't all become Olympic gymnasts, no matter how many years we practice. Nor will we all be able to take our places beside Shakespeare or Keats as poets. Physical and intellectual limitations are built into us at conception; within certain parameters, training and practice can improve our talents, but we are ultimately constrained by a set of limitations beyond which we simply were not destined to go.

The same is true of the real self's capacities. At conception, children most probably receive at least some of the potentials for the psychological capacities that can be developed over their lives. Part of our genetic inheritance and biologic makeup includes limitations and deficiencies in these psychological abilities. For example, some children and adults are naturally shy, reserved, hesitant; others are outgoing, extroverted, adventurous. Some need strong direction; others take charge by themselves. Some will always need the companionship of other people to a greater degree than will others. In some individuals, the ability to commit themselves to causes or careers or other people is stronger and more dominant than in others. Talent for talent, and skill for skill, we are not all equal, and we did not begin equal.

In my own studies with adolescents who are not able to function successfully on their own, I noticed that a few who seemed to improve with treatment while in the hospital reverted to their pathologic behaviors shortly after leaving. The latest follow-up studies indicated that they have never recovered.[1]

How to explain the fact that they survived childhood without a clinical breakdown, broke down in adolescence, then seemed to repair it in the hospital, but fell apart on discharge? As described in Chapter 2, as the self emerges from the maternal image it internalizes or "takes in" both the image of the mother and the auxiliary functions she had performed for it. These functions (reality perception, impulse control, frustration tolerance, ego boundaries) contribute greatly to the capacity for autonomous self-activation.

The fact that this image and the associated functions had not been internalized in these patients was disguised during childhood because fate was kind and did not expose these children to excess separation stress and because there is an "umbrella of dependency," which allows the child to depend on external parental authority to help him function. In other words, the child is not expected to function autonomously. However, adolescence removes the umbrella and exposes the growing child to tasks of emancipation and the need to function autonomously. At this point, his underlying difficulty with self-activation emerges in a clinical syndrome. The teenagers in my study seemed to improve in the hospital because the presence of external authority figures on whom they could be dependent reproduced the earlier childhood environment. They appeared improved, but the changes could not endure when the support of the therapist and the hospital was removed. The fact that they fell apart on discharge strongly suggested that they did not have the basic capacity to internalize these interactions either in infancy with the mother or later with the therapist, and this lifelong inability to separate and become autonomous was probably due to an innate genetic deficiency. The possibility that it might have been due to severely damaging developmental experiences was unlikely since their early histories were no worse than the early histories of other adolescent patients who did better in the study.

Currently there is little research evidence regarding the exact nature of this type of genetic deficiency, but we have seen that some severely impaired individuals, whose conditions cannot be directly attributed to failures in nurturance or to acts of fate, do not respond to therapy of any kind; we assume that the root of the problem in these cases lies in a genetic or biologic deficiency. For example, studies have shown that the infantile psychotic will not respond to even the best mothering. In these cases, it appears that some innate deficiency, not inadequate mothering, is responsible.[2]

So nature has seen to it that we will not all go through the first three years of life with the same ease or difficulty. Some of us will separate from our mothers and express our own uniqueness more easily; some of us will have a harder struggle to do so. Nature has not endowed each of us with the same psychological seeds for developing a real self, and as adults each person has her own unique range of strengths and weaknesses in the real self's capacities. What is present at birth will grow and develop, just as in a tree, the fruit, flower, leaves, bark, and structure are contained in the smallest of seeds.

How fully, smoothly, or quickly the child's innate psychological potential develops depends in part on the mother's, and to a lesser degree the father's, psychological ability to provide the environment in which the seeds of the real self can grow. The child's self-image emerges from the symbiotic image of the mother. In most families the mother is the primary caretaker and the father plays a secondary role, hence the emphasis on the mother's abilities to foster and nurture psychological growth. In this context, nurture refers not to the physical supports, such as protection, warmth, or food, but to a more specific form of nurturance that allows the unique, individuative qualities of the child's real self to emerge. Parents must be able to identify and to respond with positive emotional support to the unique, individual aspects of the young child's emerging self, which will thrive in an environment that is physically stimulating yet safe, socially challenging yet manageable for the child's stage of development, intellectually exciting yet emotionally secure.

The key is the mother's ability to perceive and to support the child's emerging self, for without that support, he experiences her as withdrawing and disapproving of his efforts. The mother may respond inadequately for a variety of reasons. She might be psychologically disturbed—borderline narcissistic, psychotic, psychopathic, or manic-depressive. She may be unable to respond adequately because she herself has suffered a loss and is depressed or even physically ill or actually absent. Her unavailability produces the climate in which the child's real self will not be able to emerge.

In my study of adolescents who had an impaired sense of self,[3] I found that many though not all of them had mothers who themselves suffered from an impaired real self. The mothers too feared separation, and attempted to prevent it at all costs. In these cases the cost was the normal development of a real self in their children. For one example, a mother who failed to develop a confident sense of self tended to foster the continuance of the symbiotic union with her child, encouraging him to remain dependent in order to maintain her own emotional equilibrium. She seemed to be overwhelmingly threatened by her child's emerging individuality, which sounded as a warning that he was destined to leave her, eventually forever. Not being able to handle what she perceived as abandonment, she was unable to support the child's efforts to separate from her and express his own self through play and exploration of the world. Her defensive maneuvers to avoid her own separation anxieties entailed clinging to the child to prevent separation and discouraging his moves toward individuation by withdrawing her support.

In short, she could not accept her child as he actually was, growing and developing with needs that must be addressed. She perceived the child as a perpetual infant—or worse, an object—to be used as a defense against her own feelings of depression over separation. Consequently, she was unable to respond to the child's unfolding individuality. The child, in turn, learned to disregard, even fear, parts of his potential self that he realized threatened the mother. In time, he suppressed those feelings, wishes, and activities in order to continue receiving approval from her. Both mother and child then denied to themselves that this interaction was destructive to the child's growth.

The mother's unavailability to supply the emotional fuel dampened or thwarted the child's desire to individuate and become his real self, with the result that the child engaged in clinging or distancing behavior. The clinging relationship was mutual, occurring at a time when the mother was not able to release the child because to do so would unleash her own separation anxieties. Therefore, both mother and child had a vested interest in clinging to each other, and the child's psyche became fixated at this point in development. If the mother's clinging was too intense the child became afraid of being taken over or engulfed, and defended against this fear by distancing himself emotionally from her and others but also, because he feared abandonment, giving up further individuation.

The vulnerability of the parents of adolescents with an impaired real self came from their own impaired real self, caused in part by the nurturing style of their own parents. This led them to repeat with their own children the behavior they had experienced with their own parents. Consider Nancy's mother Grace. Grace was a rigid, angry, depressed, moralistic woman, who at times played the role of martyr. Her strengths lay in her basic, conscious commitment to do what was right for herself and her family once that was made clear to her. She was a bright and talented woman, quite capable of finding other interests once her children were grown.

Grace's own mother was described as a depressed, angry, highly inconsistent woman who acted out much of her resentment and frustration against Grace. She was also moralistic and rigid in setting limits for Grace. For example, she constantly accused Grace of smoking, checking her breath every time she returned from school, although there was no real basis for her suspicions. Her inconsistency was clearly demonstrated by her insistence that Grace take dancing lessons although she forbade her to go to teenage dances. Grace complied with her mother's restrictions with some awareness of a growing anger and fear over her mother's behavior.

As a mother herself, Grace had difficulty setting limits on Nancy's behavior from early childhood. She had determined to be quite the opposite of her own mother, to control her anger and behave in a rational manner, which led her to ignore Nancy's behavior until it became intolerable to her. Then she turned from being indifferent to excessively punitive. She would withdraw from Nancy, feeling guilty and frightened, thus effectively reproducing her own mother's behavior. At one point she went to the school and emptied Nancy's purse in front of her peers to see if she had cigarettes. She also obtained the combination to Nancy's locker and rummaged through it looking for cigarettes and drugs.

The fathers of patients who exhibit the false self were equally unavailable to them as an "uncontaminated" member of the family orbit who could support the child's unique self-expressions, her efforts to explore the world that is not-mother, and her attempts to master reality. The specifics vary from family to family, but in general the father of the borderline child does not intrude on the mother-child relationship. His influence is almost always, by default, a reinforcement of the mother-child's exclusive clinging relationship, rather than as a force to oppose it by leading the child away into the broader world.

In my study,[4] when I examined the dynamics of the marriages of my patients' parents, I discovered that an unconscious emotional contract, most often never verbalized, had existed between the couples in which the mother allowed the father to distance himself from the home for whatever reason or interest, be it career, hobby, or other friendships, in exchange for the mother's getting the exclusive right to care for—and control—the child. The mother never complained about the inordinate amounts of time the father spent away from home. What I learned was that the mother didn't want the father at home, especially if he sought to play the normal role of a "rescuer" or savior to take the child out of her control and introduce the child to a larger reality that went beyond the mother's orbit and to give the child positive experiences of being able to cope successfully in that reality without her.

The effort to separate and individuate from the mother is a two-track process that involves the separation of the internalized self-image from the internalized mother-image and the parallel evolution of the capacities of the self. These capacities are strengthened and reinforced by the child's self-assertive explorations. Any events in the first three years of life that influence either of these tracks can be powerful determinants of whether or not the child completes this process. For example, a child with a congenital hip problem who wears a cast for the first 18 months will not be able to use his motility to explore his individuation farther and farther into the world beyond the mother, which is a crucial part of the process of separation.

In some families, a mother and child may become physically separated before the child is psychologically ready. A mother's death, a divorce, illness, or any event that takes her away from the child for extended periods of time prevents the child from relying upon her presence and support to negotiate her separation from her. Fate separates them, at a stage when the infant cannot understand what is happening. We have learned from child observation studies that separating from the mother is an important task for the child to accomplish on her own (with the mother and father's support, of course). It is not something that can be done for the child or to the child because it is the *process* of separating that is crucial for developing the real self and its capacities, not the existential fact of being separate.

John Bowlby's studies of children aged 13–32 months who were separated from their mothers (a complementary study to Mahler's work) filled in additional pieces of the puzzle of what goes wrong, preventing the emergence of a unique and whole self.[5] Bowlby studied the mourning process that children who were hospitalized for a physical illness went through when they were not able to have their mothers around them as they were used to at home. He discovered that mourning could take two courses. One type of mourning enabled the individual to relate to and find satisfaction in new objects. This is considered to be a healthy way to mourn. Bowlby also discovered a second kind of mourning that pathologically prevents a person from developing new relationships and outlets. This kind of mourning proceeds through three phases.

The first is the protest and wish for reunion phase that may last a few hours or several weeks, during which the child appears acutely distressed at having lost its mother and seeks to recapture her by whatever limited means he possesses. He entertains strong expectations and wishes that she will return. He tends to reject others, such as nurses and doctors, who offer to do things for him, although some children will cling desperately to a particular nurse. In the second phase hopelessness sets in. The child sinks into despair and may even stop moving. He tends to cry monotonously or intermittently, and becomes withdrawn and more inactive, making no demands on the environment as the mourning state deepens. In the third phase the child begins to show more interest in his or her surroundings, and this is usually welcomed as a sign of recovery. The child no longer rejects nurses, but accepts their care, food, and the toys they bring. He may even smile and be sociable. But when the mother returns to visit, it is clear that he has not recovered. The strong attachment to the mother typical of children this age is strikingly absent. Instead of greeting her, he may act as if he hardly knows her; instead of clinging to her, he may remain remote and apathetic; instead of tears when she leaves, he will most likely turn listlessly away. He seems to have lost all interest in her.

If a child has to stay in the hospital for a prolonged period of time, he will become attached to a series of nurses, each of whom leaves, thus repeating again and again for him the original experience of losing the mother. In time he will detach all deep emotional feeling from relationships and act as though neither mothering nor any other human contact has much significance for him. He learns that when he gives his trust and affection to a mothering figure, he loses her. He tries again and loses the next. And so on. Eventually he gives up taking the risk of attaching himself to anyone. He becomes increasingly self-centered and, instead of having desires and feelings toward people, he becomes preoccupied with material things that won't let him down such as sweets, toys, and food. He will no longer find gratification in relationships and will settle, instead, for immediate self-contained gratification. A child living in a hospital or institution who has reached this state will no longer be upset when nurses change or leave. He has constructed a defense against being hurt and disappointed. He ceases to show his feelings even to his parents when they come and go on visiting days. They, too, are swept into the orbit of disappointment and pain as they realize that the child is more interested in the presents they bring than in them as people.

Reflecting on Bowlby's findings and applying them to my adolescent and adult patients, I realized that there were strong parallels between the mourning process and the defenses it produced in Bowlby's subjects and what my own patients were going through. I came to recognize that when my patients go through a separation experience that they have been defending themselves against all their lives, they seem to react just like Bowlby's infants in the second stage of despair. The separation brings on a catastrophic set of feelings, which I have called an abandonment depression. To defend against this mental state, they retreat into the defensive patterns encouraged by the false self, which they have learned over the years will ward off this abandonment depression.

In adults without a sense of their real self, the abandonment depression symbolizes a replaying of an infantile drama: The child returned for support and encouragement, but the mother was unavailable or unable to provide it. The acknowledgment and approval, so crucial to developing the capacities of expression, assertiveness, and commitment, were simply not there. Years later as adults, those patients hear the same message from those they have selected in order to repeat the pattern. It is not okay to be the unique separate self you really are—or could become.

This is how Jane, 16, suffering from headaches and nausea and unable to sleep, struggled to describe her depression:

"I feel like I'm dying, powerless and sinking under five thousand pounds of self-hate. I feel like a rotten tree with total despair inside. Hopeless, drained, no strength, I can't do anything. I'm badly wounded and hurt as though I'm being squashed, and there's no way out. My own emptiness frightens me. If hemlock were sitting here, I'd drink it."

Bill, 25, tempted to quit his job as a computer analyst, put it this way:

"When I sit there trying to work, I feel hurt, stepped-on, crushed and want to give up. I never feel any support or connection with anyone. I'm completely lost, helpless, unable to cope with reality. I feel adrift, alone. I have no sense of worth or meaning. The feeling of being deserted kills me, and I can't work. Trying to work is tempting fate, risky, treacherous. I can almost hear voices telling me it's wrong to be myself. I have to block them out, or I think I'm dying. So I give up. I feel completely abandoned and I want to yell, 'Help me out! Where is everybody?' But the voices yell back, 'He's crazy!'"

Madge, a 30-year-old divorced woman, explains her inability to accept the fact that she is a grown woman:

"I've been frightened into thinking that growing up is wrong. I think I'm destined to die because I'm growing up. I can envision no life except the way I lived as a girl at home. I feel dirty and disgusting when I think about becoming a woman. Having sex, smoking grass, having a drink is throwing myself to the winds and anything can happen to me. I'm an empty shell that should be filled with grown-up attitudes, but I can't put any in without breaking it—breaking who I am. Growing up is like defying God. I feel guilty and frightened."

Scott, who idealized Mr. Spock because of his lack of human feelings and fantasized about moving to the Arctic Circle where he wouldn't have to interact with humans, wrote a composition about a statue in the park named Rich:

"Rich was different. He had no parents he could remember. He could not communicate to anyone and was never accepted but was just looked at and usually that look became a stare, an unbelievable stare.

"Nights were the worst of all. During the day he watched people doing what normal people do. Singing, dancing, dining, talking, and just enjoying life. In the day he could pretend he was one of those happy people. But at night his fantasies died. He was desolate, cold, and lonely; he felt like crying every night, but some unexplainable force held him back, saying 'Don't cry, don't give in to this world.' Many times he thought of suicide but it would not work for he was immortal—an immortal, lonely, rejected, and unwanted outcast who could not cry out for his lips were cement, too heavy to move. But one day he did cry out, although nobody heard him. And he said to this world, "I hate it, I hate it, I hate being a statue!"

What is the abandonment depression, as described by these four people, that can so impair the real self that it never emerges as the strong center of their lives it was meant to be? How can abandonment depression drive people into states of such unbearable loneliness, helplessness, and depression that they are unable to recognize themselves as valuable human beings? How can intelligent and well-meaning men and women buy the false self's bill of goods: that avoiding the abandonment depression at all costs takes precedence over leading a balanced, rewarding, and creative life?

Abandonment depression is actually an umbrella term beneath which ride the Six Horsemen of the Psychic Apocalypse: Depression, Panic, Rage, Guilt, Helplessness (hopelessness), and Emptiness (void). Like the Four Horsemen of the Bible—Conquest, War, Famine, and Death—they wreak havoc across the psychic landscape leaving pain and terror in their wake. No wonder that many people prefer the unholy alliance with a strong false defender that can ward off the psychic havoc these Horsemen strew in their path. The intensity and immediacy of these six feelings can become unbearable in people with a severely impaired sense of self.

To these people, the real self is under constant attack, and a siege mentality clouds their ability to perceive themselves and the world in realistic terms. In the eyes of the besieged self, the world, one's closest relationships, even one's own body can become the enemy. The world appears to be a hostile environment, so alien and threatening that the self is like a "stranger in a strange land," uncertain and ignorant of the standard techniques that others use to cope with reality. Relationships are stifling, engulfing, or always on the verge of breakup, leaving the self hurt and abandoned.

Everyone dominated by a false self knows each of these painful feelings to some degree. They create a panicky state of helplessness, of being out of control, and an inexorable need to feel protected and safe again, even in the pseudo-armor of pathologic pleasure the false self forges for the embattled self. The false self unfailingly comes to the rescue, but the payment for "feeling safe" is the failure of the real self to develop autonomy.

The lack of support for the emerging self leads to depression. We have all encountered the garden varieties of depression, either in ourselves or others: dejection, sadness, gloom, the blahs, "not feeling up to snuff." Different people describe feeling depressed in different ways, but in normal states of depression, we can usually sleuth out the causes and handle the depression by the successful tactics we have learned to use in the past. We do things to get our mind off it—take a walk, go shopping, read a book, turn on television, talk to someone else. We need "cheering up" and our real selves know ways to go about it. Sometimes we just have to wait it out, knowing it will pass. It is a mark of maturity that we can get through periods of depression either on our own or with the help of someone who understands us and has our best interests at heart.

The experience of the abandonment depression is far more serious and devastating than the forms of depression that come and go in the course of our daily lives. In the throes of the abandonment depression, a person will feel that part of his very self is lost or cut off from the supplies necessary to sustain life. Many patients describe this in graphic physical terms, such as losing an arm or leg, being deprived of oxygen, or being drained of blood. As one patient put it, "I felt as though my legs would not work so I couldn't possibly leave the house, and when I went to fix lunch I just knew that I wouldn't be able to swallow. And if I did I would probably throw it back up."

At the darkest level of this depression, a person can despair of ever recovering her real self, and thoughts of suicide are not uncommon. When one is brought low enough repeatedly, or for an extended period of time, it becomes increasingly harder to imagine oneself happy again or able to push through life with the strength and confidence with which the reasonably healthy go about their daily living. At this point a person can teeter on the brink of despair, give up, and consider taking her own life. If the separations they experience in their external lives are painful enough to reinforce their feelings and fear of abandonment, some will commit suicide.

In therapy, the first expressions of depression are usually not so grim. Patients often toss off their situation with statements like "Life is boring," "I'm numb," "There are no feelings in me," "I always feel down even when I'm doing things I ordinarily like doing a lot." The common characteristic is that they seem not to derive any satisfaction from their lives. They feel cornered by duties and activities that do not trigger enthusiasm or interest. Even when they have free time to do what they want, none of the plans or activities they occasionally dream about spark their interest. Things they thought they would do, given the chance, now seem unexciting, meaningless, or too threatening. The numbness is pervasive and unending; and they can't seem to break out of it. On the surface it appears to be a strong attack of the blahs.

But the blahs alone don't bring people into therapy. There are deeper rumblings than the patient or the therapist can detect in the initial sessions. The roots of depression push farther into the past than seems apparent. In time the true sources, eating away inside, make themselves known. But initially they are well defended by the false self.

"Life had no meaning for me," said Ted, 20, who had dropped out of college because of severe depression and an inability to apply himself to his studies or his part-time job. He was at a standstill. "I suddenly realized that I had no motivation to study; I began to wonder why I was in school. Was it just because I was conditioned to go? I had no goals. I looked at myself and realized I was so sensitive that I considered everything an insult."

As he put it, he would always look at things from other people's points of view, rather than his own, then wonder why he didn't feel that he was ever expressing his real self. Even sex had no payoffs for him.

"I could sleep with a girl, but it had no meaning for me except the physical kicks. I couldn't look a girl in the eye and be open with her." Eventually, in therapy, Ted realized why not. He had never been able to be himself.

It is the nature of the false self to save us from knowing the truth about our real selves, from penetrating the deeper causes of our unhappiness, from seeing ourselves as we really are—vulnerable, afraid, terrified, and unable to let our real selves emerge. Nevertheless, when the defenses are down and the real self is thrown into situations calling for strong self-assertion, situations that trigger the repressed memories of earlier separation anxieties and feelings of abandonment by the mother, the serious nature of the depression is glimpsed and felt. At this point it is not uncommon for the patient to panic and slide down to the very bottom from which he convinces himself he will never recover.

A successful 38-year-old lawyer whose wife of twelve years was leaving him because she was tired of being ignored (which came as a surprise to him!) described his sense of loss in very graphic terms. "It would be like my hand being cut off from my wrist. How would I be able to live with only one hand? How could it live without me? We need each other. I wouldn't be able to live without it." He admitted later that he had married to set up "another home like when I was a boy, so I could devote myself to my legal practice like I used to do my schoolwork when I was a kid." He showed little concern for his wife's needs, and his false self had persuaded him over the years to build up his life around busyness and self-centered activities that brought him gratification and praise from others. Needless to say, his wife had been a primary source of praise. And now she had had enough of it. Without her, he could not imagine living, certainly not in the style to which his false self was accustomed.

Depression and rage ride in tandem. As depression intensifies and comes to the surface of awareness, so does anger. At first, most patients cannot pinpoint the reasons why they are angry. The target of their rage is rather diffuse and projected on outside sources. People describe themselves as being angry at life or the world in general—or just angry. Contemporary life is filled with plenty of frustrations that breed justifiable anger and resentment. In fact, not to be angry at *something* in today's society would seem a bit strange. This brand of anger is quite normal; and with a little reflection, the specific causes are soon discovered—specific injuries, frustrations, put-downs, disappointments. A mature man or woman can recognize these and control the angry response in those situations where it would not be appropriate to indulge it. However in these patients, life's ordinary frustrations are used as a target upon which is projected a deep inner rage.

Anger that is part of the abandonment depression, however, has more damaging consequences. In the case of one young woman, anger led to physical and emotional collapse. As she put it, "I would get so angry, I just couldn't protect myself from it anymore. I'd start to shake and black out. I felt a craving, like heroin. I would convince myself that I couldn't make it, that I was totally helpless. I needed help, like alcohol or a drug. I just wanted to roll up in a rug on the floor like a baby. That's why I shake. I can't control that feeling, that anger. I'm afraid I'll act like a baby— either go home and drink to block it out or lie down on the floor and cry." In this patient the intensity of the anger caused bodily shaking. She was helpless in dealing with this anger and turned it against herself. Feeling like a baby, reliving childhood strategies for avoiding painful feelings, comes easily to her and to many patients trying to avoid abandonment depression. Their anger is long-lasting, building up from painful childhood experiences that may not be easily recalled because they are too solidly defended against.

Eventually, in therapy, the patient begins to focus this anger more specifically. Undifferentiated anger becomes targeted: at one's job, a colleague, a neighbor, one's mate, in the here and now. But this is just the beginning because the false self is still performing superbly, camouflaging the real target—the infantile feelings and memories—beneath a tightly woven network of self-destructive activity and thinking. It argues relentlessly that the root of the problem is minor and should be ignored, that "mature" men and women would not get so upset over something so trivial, that one's equilibrium should be maintained even if it means placing unreasonable limits on personal hopes and dreams and accepting life in a diminished form. And all the while, the hidden scenarios from early childhood that laid the pattern for the anger, now too painful to recall, are cleverly concealed.

The more depressed a patient becomes the angrier he gets, and eventually the real seeds of the anger are uncovered: incidents in the first years of life when the real self was trying to emerge and failed to do so. When the rage reaches a peak, a person can actually entertain homicidal fantasies. As suicide seemed appropriate for the bottoming out of depression, so homicide seems to be the only solution when anger and rage reach the levels beyond which they can no longer be endured.

An attractive 27-year-old executive secretary named Anne complained to me that her life had fallen apart in the last six months.

She was alarmed over her mounting anger at her husband who was becoming more and more involved in his work at a large electronics company. He seemed to her unfeeling and selfish and blamed his long hours on new contracts and foreign competition. According to Anne, he wasn't in the least concerned about her own needs. She was seriously questioning whether she wanted to spend the rest of her life with him. The more she thought about how bleak her future married to him looked, the more furious she grew at herself and at him. To assuage her feelings, she resorted to drinking and smoking pot.

Eventually she began an affair with a man at work. This man had several other relationships going, which she knew about, but Anne convinced herself that he really did love her more than any other woman in his life, even though he was not the type to get very close. In a way, that suited Anne just fine. She came to admit that she grew angry when anyone got close to her, and then she would withdraw. Overly sensitive to criticism, she assumed that no one could possibly like her if they knew how angry she was down inside.

Anne was trapped in the bind of needing intimacy but fearing rejection so much that she could not permit anyone to get close to her. She had an uncanny radar system poised to detect any real candidate for a relationship. Unable to tolerate the possibility of rejection, she would torpedo the relationship before it ever got a chance to surface.

Anne's situation is not uncommon. The false self has a highly skilled defensive radar whose purpose is to avoid feelings of rejection although sacrificing the need for intimacy. This system is constructed during the first years of life, when it is important to detect what would elicit the mother's disapproval. With the proper therapy, people like Anne come to understand their self-sabotaging patterns of behavior and change them.

Rage and fear lead to panic. We have all experienced it at one time or another. We get lost in the woods on a camping trip, we watch a son or daughter ride a bicycle too fast out into a busy intersection, we imagine we won't get an important report finished by the boss's deadline. These are all normal moments of panic, arising from the defense mechanism that warns us of danger so we can take the necessary steps to avoid it. Without such healthy fear—and caution—we would probably not have survived as a species.

As part of the abandonment depression, panic and fear operate on a more insidious level, arising not from legitimate and present dangers but from an abiding and unconscious fear. The false self plays its deceptive role, ostensibly protecting us but doing so in a way that is programmed to keep us fearful—of being abandoned, losing support, not being able to cope on our own, not being able to *be* alone.

Pam, the 19-year-old college freshman we met in Chapter 1, dropped out of classes because of depression and panic. Since childhood she had indulged in cannibalistic fantasies in which she was sometimes the victim, sometimes the cannibal. Part of her impaired self-image was that she was worthless, nothing more than a bug or insect whom nobody loved and who could be wiped out as easily as one swats a spider or steps on an ant. "I feel everyone's angry at me. I'm frightened that I'll be attacked. I feel like I'm an insect, a bug, unable to defend myself."

Panic feeds on the fear that we cannot express our anger over abandonment. It can be a claustrophobic strangling of energies, a tightening up of options: either we express our anger and risk losing the love of others or we deny the anger in order to remain in the helpless state of dependency and hold onto others. As the panic grows, patients report that it feels like facing death or actually being killed. Often this anxiety will be channeled into psychosomatic disorders such as asthma and peptic ulcers, each being a perfect metaphor for the underlying fear. The asthmatic experiences vital supplies of oxygen being cut off, and breathing understandably becomes strained and difficult. A person with a peptic ulcer is often hungering for emotional supplies that were lost in childhood or that were never sufficient to nourish the real self. As an adult, she is unable to find sources to supply the needed emotional support or to get through life without it.

Fear plays an important role in the lives of people dominated by a false self. In the early 1970s I was amazed at how many patients were mesmerized by the then popular novel *The Godfather*. Of course, as a best seller, the book appealed to many people who were not victims of a false self, but the degree to which patients were attracted to the characters and problems in the book was a clue for me to something serious going on in their own lives. The book, describing the Mafia's use of terror and fear of death to discipline and enforce compliance, portrayed in concrete terms a key theme that dominated the patients' own stories about their lives. Like the haunted and stalked victims of the Mafia's vengeance, my patients clearly understood the score: Comply, and you receive rewards. If you do not comply, you are killed.

A person living with a death threat, or what is perceived as a death threat, hanging over his head necessarily leads a fearful life in which every move to express himself, to allow his real self to emerge, is accompanied by the need to look over his shoulder in fear and panic. In therapy, panic can escalate as the patient slowly becomes aware of the depression and anger that have been bottled up over the years. The false self has blocked any expression of these feelings for so long that whenever they do manage to surface, even in the slightest way, the resulting panic can be paralyzing and terrifying. Fear of letting these feelings out in the open, even in therapy, can mushroom into panic proportions.

Guilt is the "fifth column" behind the patient's front line of defenses. The Horseman Guilt is not the "reasonable" guilt that a person feels when he genuinely does something he believes wrong—guilt that is appropriate for an injury or harm caused another. Appropriate guilt for the right reasons and in the right degree oils the wheels of society and keeps us civilized.

The Horseman Guilt is another matter. It is fed by the guilt we internalize in early childhood from the disapproval expressed by the mother for self-actualization or individuation. It is then reinforced later in childhood and in adolescence. As the 30-year-old woman we met at the beginning of this chapter described it, growing up is wrong. Becoming an adult is actually sinful. She goes on to explain, "When I assert myself rather than comply, I feel that I am nasty and impudent and that everybody will be angry with me. All the responsibilities and pleasures of adulthood are connected. If I choose one, I choose them all and lose my innocence. In other words, having sex is like lying, stealing, or rejecting the decent, wholesome little girl that I tried so hard to be for so many years."

Even after striking out on our own, a strong, reprimanding voice, fixed in the psyche, reminiscent of parents, teachers, and authority figures from the past, can echo down the corridors of time in our daily lives when we entertain those special thoughts and wishes we know would, in the past, elicit disapproval. The real self's genuine urges, however—starting a new career, beginning a relationship with someone, moving out of town, spending an evening away from the family, spending a little extra money on a new hobby or pastime—should not produce guilt feelings. When the false self is solidly in control, those harmless, natural desires for self-expression can trigger the voice of warning, the rebukes, the disapproval we have kept locked in our psyches over the years.

In people who have a strong sense of their real selves, such undertakings do not provoke guilt; or if they do, the real self calmly recognizes it as an echo of mother's or father's disapproving voice and perhaps even laughs at it for coming up inappropriately. Operating from their real selves, such people put aside the incipient guilty feeling and proceed as they wish. For people with an impaired real self, however, the guilt produced by this warning can be as paralyzing as it was when they were five years old. They feel guilty about that part of themselves that wants to individuate. Not being able to face up to the internalized guilt-trip, these individuals will suppress making any moves in the forbidden direction and resort to the old familiar clinging behavior that they remember made them feel safe and good years ago.

In some cases, especially among adolescents and young adults, clinging behavior may be directed to the actual mother, which reinforces all the more vividly a person's sense that she is not strong enough to carve out a healthy, independent lifestyle. In other cases, the clinging may no longer be to the real mother, but to another person who represents security and approval. In effect, we expect someone to take care of us like a parent whether that person wants to or not. In either case, the false self argues convincingly that clinging is the only reliable strategy to avoid feeling guilty.

Helplessness springs from the patient's inability to activate his impaired real self to deal with these painful feelings. Everyone is helpless at one time or another. We need other people for services, knowledge, and companionship. As members of society we come to rely on others in those areas where we have little or no skill or expertise. Ordinarily such experience reminds us that we are not in total control of our lives or totally independent. As healthy individuals we accept these limitations and balance feelings of help-lessness with confidence that in some areas we can and do support ourselves and satisfy our own needs. Healthy individuals evaluate the situation, recognize the extent of their own competence, and get the help they need, knowing that at other times they will be capable of handling things on their own.

Helplessness as part of the abandonment depression, however, is abiding and total. Although specific incidents can trigger it, it is not *caused* by specific incidents, but persists like a gloomy back-drop to life, casting a pall over most activities and life situations. Unlike a healthy man or woman who says, "Well, this is one of those situations at which I'm not very good," the false self says, "You are totally helpless and good for nothing."

Penny, a woman in her late 20s who had just found a good-paying job and moved out of her parents' home, described her feeling of helplessness to me this way:

"It's hard for me to manage myself. I never did anything com-pletely for myself before I moved to the city. In high school and college I had no responsibilities. This is the first job that I have had with any responsibility. I feel that now I have to show initiative and set my own goals. My life has been so structured, I never had to do it before. I never had to spend time alone. I think other people should plan for me."

Penny had a boyfriend at the time and hoped that by clinging to him she would be able to put some structure into her life. "I hate the idea of being responsible and taking care of myself. I don't think I can; it seems that I'll break down. That's why I need Rod so much. I can't take the pressure. I'm an empty personality. I'd rather be an extension of Rod. I've always structured my life for someone else to do it for me."

Penny's real problem of course eventually came out: she had an impaired real self. The way she put it was, "I've never been re-warded for being an individual, for being myself. I am also afraid of being depressed and alone with myself. I never developed any-thing in myself on my own. I did well in college and had lots of interests, but they were all for everybody else's approval."

Mastery depends upon self-assertion, but asserting oneself brings on the fear of abandonment. It becomes an inescapable cycle that can twist one's thinking patterns for the rest of one's life, even in therapy, where it becomes translated: "Getting well means taking charge of my life, but I can't take charge of my life until I can get over feeling so helpless, and I must be helpless or why am I still in therapy?!" And of course feeling helpless works—it is an essential feature of the abandonment depression which drives the person into a clinging relationship either with a mate, a friend, a family member, or a therapist.

Many people assume the passive, helpless role in relationships, looking for someone to take care of them rather than someone who will love and respect them as equals. The false self will keep a person playing the "little girl" or "little boy" who still needs to be told what to do and, in addition, needs a wiser, firmer hand to help him do it. At work the false self can prevent us from assuming more responsibility, applying for promotion, making decisions, standing up for what we think is right even though others around us disagree. Many people dominated by a false self stay in unrewarding jobs that neither challenge their talents and skills nor pay what those skills could command in a different job situation. To ward off feelings of abandonment, the prisoner of the false self will stay underpaid and underworked and then wonder why his or her job provides so little satisfaction.

The problem is much more serious than just the universal penchant for griping about work. It is part of the human condition to complain about jobs and the need to work for a living. A healthy real self recognizes frustrations and problems at work and either resolves them or accepts them as necessary deficiencies in an otherwise rewarding situation. For the false self, however, the lack of satisfaction has little to do with specific problems intrinsic to the line of work and more with the internal fear at activating the real self.

Peter, a 40-year-old president of his own large company, rose to the top because of his superior skills as a salesman, based on his need to please others—a case of the false self succeeding in business without really trying. Unfortunately, another side of Peter's false self—the helpless self—prevented him from managing the company efficiently and with any sense of personal satisfaction. Because of his need to please others, he found himself paralyzed in situations where he should have been confident and assertive. He could not face up to the inevitable risks involved in saying no.

Early on as he was founding his company, he established a board of trustees, as was proper, but his false self totally misused it. Convinced he could not make decisions on his own, he relinquished much of his authority to the board, which he considered a superior authority, rather than a sounding board. He constantly sought the members' approval and expected them to make decisions that were properly his responsibility. The board naturally resented this, since the members had accepted their positions on the assumption that they would not be involved in the day-to-day decision-making process. In time, they came to resent Peter and conspired to defeat him. Because he played the helpless child, hoping the board would take care of him, Peter found little genuine satisfaction in his work. But he had little hope of resolving the dilemma as long as he could not assert his real self enough to gain control over both his business and personal affairs.

A life ruled by the false self's defense against inner emptiness ends up truly empty. However, it is far from empty of pain, suffering, depression, guilt feelings, and elaborate schemes to deny one's own best interests. Many patients describe themselves, their thoughts and feelings, as "numb." They trudge through daily tasks as if drugged, unable to find anything but a looming void at the center of their lives.

As it emerges, the false self internalizes an unwarranted amount of anger and devaluation from parents, teachers, peers, and unlucky life experiences. In time those negative attitudes become the patient's own and come to dominate his way of viewing life and of approaching challenging situations, undermining or stifling positive attitudes and self-concepts and reinforcing the feeling of inner emptiness. Unable to recognize his strengths and creative abilities, the individual comes to imagine that there is really little inside but the faults, failures, and disappointments that he has come to expect since childhood. These self-destructive attitudes provide a poor foundation to build on, and people who view their entire lives as having never really gotten off the ground see no progress and imagine themselves still operating very much as they did when they were children. When they ask themselves, *What have I accomplished in my life?* their typical reply is, *Nothing*.

Jean, an editor of a women's magazine, felt that her life was totally empty even though she was a highly skilled writer, with a

long list of free-lance credits behind her and a job with a prestigious publication. But her days at the company were long and boring. She could do her work with her little finger. In her mid-forties,
she wondered if she should switch jobs or careers, or possibly go
back to free-lancing, which had given her so much satisfaction
when she was younger. The thought of free-lancing, however, terrified her. Jean's problem was that she took the staff job because it
gave her the security she needed with the highly structured authority system comprised of several superiors who could organize her
day, delegate her jobs, and keep on top of her to make sure she
met deadlines.

Clearly Jean was overqualified for her position, but her false self
convinced her that to satisfy her dependency needs she should
stick with it. Eventually she grew more negative about herself and
came to believe that her earlier success as a free-lance was due to
a fluke of good luck. She became convinced that she had very little
real talent and that she was basically good for nothing but the
unexciting job at the magazine.

When the false self calls the shots, as it did in the case of Jean,
we fail to recognize our own self-worth. We belittle our talents and
skills and we can easily come to settle for second best, overcome
by the gaping void within us, which we are powerless to fill with
meaningful activity or relationships. For such people, life seems
empty and worthless. They have too much time on their hands.
The hours and days drag on, and their lives go nowhere. How do
they fill this void?

Many adopt a self-destructive lifestyle similar to that of drug
addicts. The junkie uses the phrase "taking care of business" to
refer to all the activities involved in obtaining and taking heroin.
Getting money, obtaining the drug, avoiding the police, getting
back home safely, shooting up, and enjoying the "high." What those
of us who know little of this world fail to realize is how time-
consuming and self-absorbing these activities can be. An addict's
total daily activity is devoted to "taking care of business." People
with no real self are not as self-destructive as the heroin addict
since they can function in daily life, but they resemble the addict
in that "taking care of business" absorbs a large part of their day.
Hours are spent "acting out" in order to avoid the abandonment
depression. They have learned to engage in a long string of patho-

logic activities that function like a kind of armor to protect against the emptiness, helplessness, and depression that would otherwise consume them. Avoiding the abandonment depression in these self-destructive ways is their "fix." Their entire day is given to it. It's their "business."

Some people's false self will actually lure them into drugs, alcohol, or abusive behavior. Others sink into passivity or dead-end activities, such as excessive daydreaming, mindless shopping, overeating, or unfulfilling sexual liaisons. Some will cling to people, familiar places or objects such as furniture, clothing, art, or daily schedules and routines that do little to further the meaningful activities they are ostensibly engaged in. Their primary purpose is to avoid the fear associated with independence and self-expression—fear of the abandonment depression.

PORTRAIT OF THE BORDERLINE

NORMALLY, the real self and its capacities emerge allowing the child to mature into an autonomous adult capable of self-activation and self-expression, with a sense of entitlement and the self-confidence to live creatively in the face of challenges and disappointments. However, when the child experiences the abandonment depression during the first three years of life, the real self shuts down to avoid further aggravating the feelings of abandonment. This shut-down arrests psychological development and produces varying degrees of impairment in all the capacities of the self. Unable to tolerate feeling the abandonment depression, the child engages in a number of measures to protect himself from feeling depressed, at the cost of growth and adaptation. He avoids activities that would further the emergence of the real self, and consequently all the self's potential capacities are impaired. In addition, the need for defense causes a similar arrest of what is classically described as ego development so that it, too, continues to function on a primitive level.

Certain functions of the ego—reality perception, impulse control, frustration tolerance, and stable ego boundaries—can only develop through successful separation and individuation. The child who cannot separate from his mother will not internalize these functions, which she had performed for him, and make them his own. Consequently, he exhibits deficiencies in all these areas. When the ego suffers from poor reality perception, the child must continue to rely upon mother or someone else for an understanding of how the world works. His own skewed perceptions will leave him bewildered in situations that the child with a clearer perception of reality will handle more easily.

In normal development, the mother introduces the child to increasingly difficult levels of frustration so the child will learn that she does not always get what she wants. At some point, the child's ego realizes, accepts, and internalizes this, understanding that it is a normal, although disagreeable, fact of life. The child with an arrested ego, however, will have a poor ability to tolerate frustration. Similarly, in the course of normal development, the mother, setting limits for the child's behavior, instructs through appropriate reprimands so the child learns self-control. But when ego development is arrested, control will not be internalized and develop into a reliable ego strength.

Fluid ego boundaries render it difficult to distinguish whether feelings and mental states are external or internal. The impaired ego will be as likely to project an internal mood on the outside world as to confuse external circumstances with internal feeling states.

Because of the developmental arrests of the real self and ego functions, the child continues to rely heavily upon primitive mechanisms of defense: denial and clinging, avoidance and distancing, projection, and acting out. In order to prevent the abandonment feelings, the child denies the reality of separation. Although physically, he is a separate, autonomous self, he doesn't feel, think, or act that way. He develops a fantasy that by clinging he can act out his wish for reunion with the mother, making it seem in fantasy as if he and she are still a fused pair as they were before and immediately after birth. This fantasy is linked with and motivates the need to behave defensively and regressively rather than to encourage the real self to emerge. He projects onto the mother his need for her, which in his mind becomes her unquenchable need for him. Denial and clinging become reflexive responses, fixed in the child's personality, later to become primary means of dealing with similar separation stresses in adulthood, especially those involving intimacy and separation where he will expect an exclusive relationship with the loved one and will use clinging in the hopes of achieving it.

To further assure himself that he will not trigger the abandonment depression, the child learns to avoid opportunities to express himself, or assert his wishes, or activate what is most unique in his personality, all of which could threaten his emotional equilibrium by precipitating feelings of abandonment. Those early interpersonal interactions in which he experienced the devastating effects of the mother's unavailability become internalized, fixed intrapsychic images that act as a mold for his personality structure. This infantile pattern comes to dominate his perceptions and reactions to situations in later life—regardless of what actually happens in those situations. He learns that for him life is more tolerable when he holds himself back and avoids situations that would stimulate his own growth through self-activation and self-expression. Relinquishing growth seems a small price to pay in order to feel safe.

In relationships, the person will either cling or stay aloof and emotionally uninvolved out of fear of being hurt or rejected. He learns that many of life's challenges have to be avoided and other people have to be either possessively held onto or kept at an emotional distance in order for him to feel secure. For he remembers on an intrapsychic level that, when he was a child, mother was more rewarding when he avoided life's challenges and relationships with other people and kept his true feelings to himself.

Because the child has denied that he has separated from the mother and perceives that she is still the commanding half of his experience, problems and difficulties can be projected onto her. Pain, suffering, unhappiness, disappointment, frustrations are not merely facts of life, they are all in some way her doing, not his. Or, alternately, he may see them as being entirely due to his own inadequacies. The intrapsychic pattern is so set that the child, and later the adult, will have no realistic understanding of the causes— or the solutions—for his problems.

After psychically projecting the conflict into the environment so that he does not feel it internally, he literally "acts it out" in behavior. Typically, the individual, due to his hypersensitivity to rejection, will avoid facing up to and dealing with the abandonment depression by playing out the painful parental relationship with another person cast as the parent. In this way, what was internalized and caused pain in the past is externalized and dealt with as if it were an external problem in the present. The illusion is created that the person is "managing it" in the here and now. There are always two components to acting out, the psychodynamic aspect, which involves the internalized relationship with its accompanying pain, and the behavioral interaction with a contemporary in a replaying of the original rejection scenario.

Acting out does not always require a partner, however. The term is also applied to behavior, usually self-destructive, that one engages in as a defense against the abandonment depression. Alcohol, drugs, excessive work habits, and other addictive activities can serve as a distraction from depression.

In addition to the emergence of these primitive mechanisms of defense another consequence of the developmental arrest is that the ego remains driven by the pleasure principle to seek pleasure and avoid pain rather than develop the reality principle, the ability to deal with reality whether it is pleasurable or not.[1] Pain continues to mean the pain of the abandonment depression; pleasure remains the superficial "feeling good" that comes from *not* experiencing the abandonment depression. This myopic view persists as the child matures with the result that a large part of the ego bypasses the transformation from a pleasure ego into a reality ego. In time, the "pleasure ego" becomes a pathologic ego, quick to follow the false self's narrow guidelines for avoiding pain rather than dealing with reality. The reality principles upon which real self-activation and self-expression could be grounded are poorly developed.

The splitting defense mechanism, which usually recedes as the real self emerges, persists as a principal defense against the abandonment depression. The conflicting images of the good mother and the bad mother, the good child and the bad one, and the feeling states associated with them (being loved or being rejected) remain conscious but are kept apart so they do not influence one another. It is as if they were closed off in two separate closets. The widespread use of splitting fosters and deepens the other defense mechanisms as well as the ego defects. The bifurcated worldview created by splitting reinforces the primitive defenses because from the person's perspective the world is still structured as it was in the first months of life: The self-representation consists of a good self-image linked to a good mother-image and a bad, inadequate, or deflated self-image linked to the bad mother-image.

In psychodynamic terms, the child fails to achieve "object constancy," and will go through life relating to people as parts—either positive or negative—rather than whole entities. He will be unable to maintain consistent commitment in relationships when he is frustrated or angry; and he will have difficulty evoking the image of the loved one when that person is not physically present. He will never fully realize that mother is one, complete person who sometimes rewards and sometimes frustrates the child. He will continue to think of her as two separate entities, one benevolent, the other wicked.

Similarly, he will never create a single unified self-concept that he recognizes as himself in both good and bad aspects. Instead, he will continue to see a "good" self that engages in immature, clinging, passive, unassertive behavior and a "bad" self that wants to grow, assert itself, be active and independent. The "good" mother approves of the "good" child while the "bad" mother disapproves of the "bad" child. The "good" mother supports and encourages the regressive behavior while the "bad" mother grows hostile, critical, and angry when confronted with the child's assertive behavior.

Splitting fosters in the child's psychic structure a damaging leitmotif based on the themes of reward for clinging and withdrawal for separation. These twin themes repeated over and over as early interpersonal interactions between the mother and child become deeply internalized as stereotyped, fixated, and unchangeable intrapsychic images and feelings, and eventually become locked into the adult's entire personality structure. Reward and withdrawal, now intrapsychic, come to dominate his perception and response to life. He will be rewarded for regressive behavior, and he will be abandoned for self-assertion and autonomy.

To relieve the abandonment depression and the bad feelings about his self-image, he forgoes self-assertion in real life and substitutes the superficial "feeling good" that comes from clinging. It is this process that produces the "deflated false self," the basis of the borderline personality. Deflated because the bad self-image reflects weakness and insecurity, and false because it is based on a fantasy. The clinging behavior is based on a fantasy (modeled on recollections of childhood interactions) that people will provide support for clinging or avoiding self-activation. This fantasy is projected on the external world (even sometimes on people who are not supportive) and the patient feels good. It may seem paradoxical to "feel good" with people who are not supportive. But this situation serves to underline the fact that the patient can deny the real major theme to focus on the grains of support that reinforce his projection. The false self's self-perpetuating argument operates unrelentingly: any attempt to activate the impaired real self will lead to depression which requires further defensive behavior to avoid further depression.

Even as adults people with a deflated false self will feel as they did when children: bad, guilty, ugly, helpless, inadequate, and empty for never asserting themselves; and they will only feel good and actually "loved" when they are passive, compliant, and submissive to the person to whom they cling for emotional supplies. Caught in this vise that won't allow them to express or assert themselves honestly, their emotional lives are characterized by chronic anger, frustration, and feelings of being thwarted. The abandonment depression continually lurks just around the next corner, and the false self prevents the person from turning that corner.

To the deflated false self, "proof" of being loved is essential for feeling good. Fantasies of reunion with the mother are projected onto the environment and acted out for immediate gratification. The false self refuses to examine the dynamics of a present situation, which might require deferred gratification and self-denial to accommodate the needs of others or to satisfy his own needs in the most realistic way. The reunion fantasy obscures the reality of interpersonal interactions. Behavior becomes inappropriate to the actual circumstances, motivated only by the wish for the immediate gratification and fulfillment of reunion fantasies which, as they multiply, are accompanied by an ever increasing denial of reality. By the time the person reaches adulthood, a long pattern of fantasy and denial is so locked into his way of living that he has no capacity to discover appropriate behavior to fulfill his needs.

Nevertheless, the adult will manage to cope, convincing himself that his view of human behavior in terms of distinct rewarding and withdrawing segments actually works. And to a certain extent it does. He has learned to successfully stave off the withdrawing behavior of the people he loves by denial and rationalizations, for example, "He is attacking me because he's upset, not because he usually feels that way toward me."

Such feelings of being loved, no matter how strongly experienced, are not realistic or appropriate because they are based on a false portrayal of the self and the other. Only love based on honest self-expression and an acceptance of the other can sustain a healthy relationship. The person with a false deflated self remains perplexed and cannot see through the defensive structures of his life, his thinking, his ways of perceiving reality. He senses, but cannot understand, the hollow core at the center of his life. He has lived too long on deception, fantasy, and the myths of the false self.

As I have listened to patients express this dilemma in countless ways over the years I have been struck by how similar their stories are to the two classic folktales *Snow White and the Seven Dwarfs* and *Cinderella*. In relating their earliest childhood memories, they seem to be reflecting the archetypal pattern of these two tales, both involving a young daughter caught in the dilemma of expressing her real self or kowtowing to what could become a false self, offering her a pathological deal to save her from the abandonment depression.

In both stories there is literally a good mother and a bad mother. The good and natural mother is forever preserved in fantasy by her untimely death. She will never become the real mother engaging in frustrating activities that would threaten or alienate the child; she will never withhold her support, acknowledgement, or love. This role is clearly reserved for the intruding mother, the stepmother who is inevitably described as wicked or an evil witch.

Interestingly, the father plays no role at all in either story. Variations of the two stories differ, but the father seems either to be remote and uninvolved or off on a journey. The loss of the father is glossed over and rationalized. Many patients are so embroiled in the intense conflict with the mother that in the beginning of therapy the fact that the father was not around to play the crucial role of introducing the child into a world that is broader than the mother does not seem to occur to them. Of course, anger at the father is well defended against and will come out later in therapy.

The wicked stepmother is never a blood relation to the young girl; and in most versions of the stories, no effort is spared to paint her in the darkest, vilest colors. She is vain, haughty, proud, hateful, narcissistic, mean, self-centered, jealous, envious, and in the case of Snow White's stepmother, the wicked queen, a would-be murderess. In *Cinderella*, the stepmother's vicious characteristics are multiplied in her two daughters, who, in addition to sharing the stepmother's antagonistic qualities, are ugly. Thus in storybook form, we have the split mother image: a good mother who loves the young girl but who has died and an evil second mother intent on frustrating her stepdaughter's most heartfelt desires.

In *Snow White*, the queen cannot tolerate Snow White's beauty. She alone wants to be the fairest in the land. In place of "beauty" we could read "real self." Allegorically, the daughter's beauty threatens the mother because it represents the girl's real self that will emerge, separate, and grow into its own unique person. In the process, the mother—who does not have a real self—is abandoned.

In *Cinderella*, the wicked stepmother, wanting to exclude Cinderella from sharing the life of her own two daughters (i.e., extensions of herself), denies Cinderella any kind of satisfying or rewarding life. Condemned to a servant's role and forced to live in the attic with mice, Cinderella is allegorically depicted as being coerced into suppressing her real self's interests and desires by being required to spend all her time in menial tasks and physical household chores that require little ingenuity or creativity. Since these tasks keep her dirty and in rags, they, too, sabotage the young girl's beauty and so diffuse the stepmother's anger and need to idealize her two daughters, thus preventing her own abandonment depression.

The wicked queen in *Snow White* plots various diabolical methods to bring about her stepdaughter's death. Curiously, patients sometimes express the feeling that the only way they could please their own mothers was to kill themselves. In intrapsychic terms, it would mean the killing of the real self in the sense that it would never be allowed to emerge and develop.

Another similar theme that runs through the lives of many patients is the "return by midnight" warning in *Cinderella*. Patients universally have a strong sense of the impermanence of anything that is going well. It seems as if they are always perched on a razor's edge; although they may temporarily enjoy themselves, they expect to be plunged back into their feelings of abandonment.

Both stories use the device of a rescue fantasy and magical allies to solve the conflict. In *Snow White*, the seven dwarfs accept the young girl, give her a home in exchange for domestic services (which, in this case, allow Snow White to be creative, test her skills, and grow), and love her. Some psychologists point out that the dwarfs represent stunted aspects of Snow White's personality that were not allowed to develop and flourish under the influence of the wicked queen. In the end, Snow White is saved by the handsome prince. In *Cinderella*, the fairy godmother magically appears to help the girl go to the ball. In some versions of the story, this figure is the actual mother who reappears from the dead as a spirit helper come to assist her daughter. Cinderella fails to return on time, suffers the punishment, but is happily rescued by the handsome prince.

Such rescue fantasies have great appeal to the young child who has not yet learned how to cope effectively with reality, and the same type of fantasies appeals to patients whose ability to deal with life as it is is severely impaired by the false self. Some continue to hope against all odds that they will find the right man or woman, job, or lifestyle that will solve their problems; others no longer believe such a solution is possible for them.

The widespread appeal of these two stories (and others similar to them) does not imply that almost everyone suffers from a false-self syndrome and recognizes herself in the heroines who strive to break free from the poisonous home life that seems to be their fate. Nor is this interpretation of the tales the only one. Normally developing children, as well as healthy adults, can enjoy these stories for a variety of reasons, not the least of which is that they are entertaining tales. The reason children take to these plots and characters so avidly is that they often hear them for the first time at the age when these themes are most important to them. The story lines and developments rest on sound psychological foundations: the universal struggle over separation and individuation, over closeness with and separation from the mother. In children developing normally, as well as those becoming arrested at this early stage of life, the essential conflict with the mother is clearly and dramatically spelled out in all its parts: fear of abandonment, with defenses of splitting and denial; projection of anger onto the stepmother; and rescue fantasies.

The fairy tales, of course, have happy endings. The real life stories contain no Prince Charmings to resolve the conflict. So the child with a false self cannot look for a magic rescuer but must struggle through the childhood years constantly having to contend with the mother's repeatedly expressed negative attitudes towards the emergence of his real self. As the child gets older, the discrepancy between his chronological age and the level of his psychological functioning widens. He develops a "borderline personality disorder" which becomes progressively more entrenched over time as the individual encounters and struggles with the challenges of each life phase.

The abandonment depression is first experienced at an age when the young child cannot reflect on it or articulate what is happening. The child simply feels that the flow of life is cruelly disrupted and that he teeters on the verge of annihilation should the vital support of the mother be lost or withheld. As the child grows into adolescence and adulthood, he acquires the skills to reflect on how he feels and to describe the intensity of those feelings and what, at the time, appear to him to be their causes. In therapy the clinical picture presented by the patient is quite detailed and explicit, and in spite of the variations of age, sex, career, and stage of life, the picture is also rather predictable, for the borderline dilemma springs from a common dynamic patterned on early family circumstances and interactions sometimes combined with physical health problems.

The abandonment dynamic is always precipitated by an event such as separation or loss, or a situation requiring self-assertion and autonomy, which ruptures the line of defenses erected to prevent depression, leaving the person vulnerable to a full onslaught of the abandonment depression. In moments such as these, the person is brought to grips with how inadequately her false self prevents the painful feelings of depression. He feels deflated. The false and deflated self keeps his life empty, vulnerable, and driven by the constant fear that his defenses will be breached. And they are. Any separation stress analogous to the original traumatic separation experienced as a young child can trigger the abandonment dynamic.

The predictable events in the normal life cycle that represent further growth opportunities for the healthy child can precipitate a breakdown in the child with a deflated false self. The major passages and stages of life threaten his defenses and bring on the abandonment depression when he realizes he has insufficient strengths or resources to rely on.

The normal dependency expected and accepted in the preschool years and beyond helps to conceal the child's clinging defenses and the fact that the real self is not growing. At that time the parents are able to deny the failure to grow. These defenses may begin to fail when the child enters nursery school, kindergarten, or goes off to camp; however, unless the child is exposed to a severe separation stress during these years, he manages to struggle through with his problems unnoticed.

As the school years progress and the child grows older, he encounters more complex emotional and social tasks that tap his inadequate capacities to function autonomously, thereby revealing their deficiencies. Each advancing year poses its own unique challenges to which the child fails to respond in ways that promote growth and maturity. Eventually he leaves the local school and enters high school where his defensive patterns are even less able to prevent the abandonment depression.

It is not surprising that so many symptoms of the impaired real self are seen in adolescence when dependency is expected to recede and more rigorous social requirements for independence must be met. High school engages the child's time and energy more intensely than grammar school, often taking the child farther from home where he will meet a wider range of boys and girls from varied backgrounds. It is increasingly common for teenagers to hold part-time or even full-time jobs while going to school, which places even more stress on their ability to function independently, manage time, relate to adults, and fulfill obligations in creative, autonomous ways. Making friends, dating, and experimenting with sex also place demands on the adolescent's sense of self, testing his or her values.

For the borderline teenager these years can be devastating as the real world closes in and the youngster finds increasingly fewer places to hide. In order to defend against the abandonment depression, he may act out with forms of self-destructive behavior. The typical acting-out defenses include use of drugs and alcohol to drown or soothe the depression, sexual promiscuity, running away from home, truancy, abusive or provocative acts of disrespect to authority figures, stealing, reckless driving, or violent acts against persons or property that may provoke direct confrontation with the law. These symptomatic behaviors demonstrate the danger of depression and the tension associated with it. In terms of school work, a standard defense for avoiding self-assertion and self-expression is a passing but mediocre school record, which may label the student as an underachiever. Graduation from high school, of course, can breach the adolescent defenses completely as the teenager realizes that he will be thrown into the adult world of college or career. Often intimations of abandonment depression begin in the senior year, the symptoms intensifying as the commencement date approaches.

The first year of college can be extremely stressful for the student who has still not emancipated himself from the parents. The college milieu usually requires new defenses, although some students manage to survive by refining and implementing their former high school defenses. They continue to act out and settle for mediocre school work in a kind of extended adolescence, which merely postpones the inevitable rupture to the final year in college. It is not uncommon for some college students to flunk senior courses, with the semi-unconscious intention of staying in school another year.

In young adulthood difficulties with work and intimacy come to the fore. A common borderline defense is to stay home, claiming illness or other crisis in order to avoid the work situation that imposes too many demands for autonomy, self-expression, or self-activation. On the job, the borderline may perform perfunctorily, doing the minimum to hold, typically, a "safe" job far below his skill and interest level, since a more demanding job would require greater self-activation and self-expression. The typical syndrome presented in therapy is lack of satisfaction with the job or problems with coworkers or supervisors, often indicating that the patient is projecting the problem onto others to avoid facing up to it in himself.

These years of transition from adolescence to adulthood require increased self-activation or autonomy and therefore increase separation anxiety, which some people avoid by continuing to live at home, even though they could afford a place of their own. Usually this is not a happy or workable situation because it makes more obvious the young adult's avoidance of individuation and his inability to function as an adult with his peers. Nevertheless, the abandonment dynamic impels him to sacrifice adult life goals in order to maintain inner equilibrium. He may not be clinically ill, but he pays a high price for his comfort and remains vulnerable to all kinds of threats that can activate the abandonment dynamic.

Not all people with impaired real selves function poorly. Many are very successful at work. Some with artistic talent find a niche for themselves in such artistic fields as acting, writing, painting, photography, sculpting, or film making. They may use a high I.Q. and a tendency to intellectualize to enter a profession such as law, medicine, architecture, or accounting. Closer examination will probably reveal that the motivation for the work is not self-expression but meeting the expectations of others. For some there is a goal of attaining an illusion of personal closeness, or a closeness that is within very definite limits, such as the relationship of a lawyer and client or a doctor and patient. Examination of these patients will also show that they suffer a great deal of anxiety about their achievements and have very unrewarding personal lives.

The false self can dominate even extremely talented people who are likely to be drawn to careers where life can be lived vicariously, where within safe, protective limits they can deal with emotions and activities that they avoid in their personal lives because of the fears such emotions and activities would evoke. Any career such as reporter, photographer, psychiatrist, or minister which requires professional detachment places one in a position to project oneself into others' lives and identify with life dramas being played out there without fully committing oneself to the same emotions and activities in one's own life. For example, a reporter on the scene may feel as if he or she were really a participant. A minister or therapist with a deflated false self can experience in fantasy the joys and problems of a close relationship without the fear of self-activation and self-expression or of rejection that real commitment or intimacy would necessitate. Her readiness for projective identification, poor ego boundaries, and inability to perceive reality adequately all help allow her to experience vicarious gratification by interjecting herself into the lives of others.

The rebellious acting out typical of adolescence decreases when borderlines reach their 20s and 30s and major problems with the real self emerge in work and close relationships. A person who has been unable to establish a continuous intimate relationship by this time must confront the problem of loneliness. The alternative is to establish an intimate relationship but run the risk of invoking the fear of engulfment or abandonment.

When the borderline marries and has children, he has difficulty in parenting, as he is unable to support his children's attempts to assert themselves as individuals. Warning of the troubles to come are the children's nascent borderline symptoms and the adult's anger and disappointment as a parent. While still young, the children will probably accept being treated as extensions of their parents and will keep their own desires within the tight orbit of what the parents will allow, but when they reach adolescence the new pressure to become independent brings on rebellious acting out on the part of the children and rage and depression on the part of the parent.

The intergenerational conflict usually decreases in middle age as the need for parenting and caretaking diminishes, but depression can now be evoked when the borderline realizes that time is running out and youthful dreams and fantasies may never be achieved. It is interesting to note how often turning 40 precipitates a separation/individuation stress for borderline personalities, often severe enough to bring them into treatment. We have been told that life begins at 40, but the prevalence of midlife crises in so many healthy individuals attests to our realizing, either consciously or unconsciously, the fear that life begins to end at 40. We grow more aware that the basic structure of our lives has been built and there is not much chance left for major changes. Although these realities confront everyone, they are especially poignant and destructive for the middle-aged borderline who has spent his entire life substituting fantasy gratification for real-life fulfillment. As borderlines enter the second half of life, they find they can no longer avoid facing up to what they have been denying and defending themselves against all their lives. Hoped for achievements are unfulfilled; wished for relationships were never attempted or have gone sour; opportunities to recoup are either gone or fast disappearing. There is too much water under the bridge. Such realizations can trigger the abandonment dynamic and bring on a depression much more severe than the normal midlife crisis.

The senior years, which bring with them so much social and environmental change and loss, demand an emotional flexibility and adaptiveness not usually found in the borderline who has never been able to deal effectively with change or loss. The so-called golden years can be anything but golden for such people as they find themselves incapable of adjusting to their new circumstances.

In addition to suffering from the normal, predictable events of the life-cycle, the impaired real self is particularly sensitive at any time of life to accidental events that involve separation or loss and thereby threaten their clinging defenses. When the person to whom they cling withdraws, leaves home or town, becomes increasingly unavailable because of a new job or illness, or dies, the emotional reverberations for the borderline can precipitate the abandonment dynamic and bring the abandonment depression to a crescendo severe enough to require professional help.

6

PORTRAIT OF THE NARCISSIST

THERE is a second type of false self that, at first glance, seems totally unrelated to the deflated false self. In fact, it appears to be its polar opposite. This is the "inflated false self" of the narcissistic personality disorder. On the surface the narcissist is brash, exhibitionistic, self-assured, single-minded, often exuding an aura of success in career and relationships. Narcissists often seem to be the people who have everything—talent, wealth, beauty, health, and power with a strong sense of knowing what they want and how to get it. We have all known people like this, and it is not uncommon to wonder, perhaps even with a touch of envy, if underneath the grandiose style of behavior the person is not actually insecure, and perhaps miserable.

In fact, the narcissist's personality is based on a defensive false self that he must keep inflated, like a balloon, in order not to feel the underlying rage and depression associated with an inadequate, fragmented sense of self. If the balloon springs a leak, he can feel as miserable and insecure as someone with a deflated false self. Whereas the borderline's false self is preoccupied with fear of and vulnerability to the abandonment depression, the narcissist's false self is characterized by an imperviousness to depression. In fact, a common impression given by the narcissist is that depression is simply not a part of his life.

The narcissist's false self is more successful than the borderline's deflated false self, which is really not very competent. It talks a good game, but cannot consistently defend the borderline from experiencing the abandonment depression. Separation stresses occur, the defenses crumble, and depression moves in. In the case of the narcissist, as long as the false self is adequately inflated, it has the ballast to keep him floating high, oblivious to frustration and depression. Often the narcissist seems to be immune to life's vicissitudes, like a manic-depressive locked into the manic phase, much to the admiration or envy of those around him.

If, then, the narcissist is so well adapted to his environment and appears to be master of his life, how can we say that he has a false self? From a closer clinical look, the illusory quality of the defensive self becomes apparent in three respects: the content of the defensive self, its motivation, and the massive denial of reality it requires.

The defensive self is characterized by self-importance, grandiosity, and omnipotence. As we saw with Stewart in Chapter 1, he could not be happy unless he was the best; whether it was tennis, business, or the women in his life, he had to "score" and receive his trophies. For him life was a contest, not for the sake of winning itself but to use winning as a vehicle to prove his uniqueness and perfection and win the adulation of others. Both he and Daniel, the other narcissistic personality described in Chapter 1, admitted in treatment that they need control and perfection as a prerequisite to feel good about themselves. While most people value the admiration of others, that admiration is not their primary goal. Similarly, we all want to be in control, to succeed, and to do the best possible job. But healthy people value these objectives for their own sake and not merely as a means of obtaining admiration from others. To the outside observer, as well as to the narcissist himself who has not had treatment, these activities, such as spending an unusually great amount of time on one's work, appear to be realistically and appropriately motivated; that is, they seem to be engaged in for their own sake. However, this is an illusion. The motive is to use these activities to fuel the narcissist's need for perfection and uniqueness.

The narcissist is motivated by the continuous need for "supplies" to feed this grandiose conception of himself. "Supplies" here means quite specifically those activities and relationships that reinforce his grandiosity. The false defensive self is false in that it is based on a grandiose fantasy, rather than on reality, and it is defensive in that its purpose is not to cope or adapt to reality but to reinforce grandiosity in order not to feel depressed. Typically the narcissist is a restless person, pressured to keep moving to keep reinforcing his sense of grandeur. It's not uncommon for him to be a workaholic at a job that he does well. Having nothing to do is threatening, since it does not meet his need for reinforcement or fit in with his self-image of being an achiever. The narcissist has firmly adopted the old adage that "not to move forward is to drop behind."

The term *narcissist* comes from the Greek myth of Narcissus, a young man who fell in love with his own reflection, mirrored in a lake. Unable to pull himself away from the contemplation of his own beauty, he eventually starved to death and fell into the water, never more to be seen. The person with a narcissistic personality disorder reenacts in his own life two key themes of the myth: he becomes totally absorbed in his own perfection and in his striving for the narcissistic supplies that he needs to keep his image full-blown and intact. Beneath the grandiose false self is an impaired real self whose development has been arrested, as was the borderline's, in an effort to find protection against an abandonment depression. The grandiose self guides the patient's feelings and behavior, obscuring or hiding the underlying impaired real self with its abandonment depression. The latter will emerge in psychotherapy.

Narcissistic supplies come from "mirroring," or what we might call "reinforcing feedback." The narcissist looks to others in his environment, and to the environment itself—clothes, car, home, office—to reflect his exaggerated sense of importance and perfection. He must surround himself with the right people who will appreciate and advertise his best qualities, announcing to the world that he is unique, special, adored, perfect, right. Wealth, power, and beauty in himself and those who are part of his life— family, friends, colleagues—must also be perfect since their perfection highlights his own and justifies his grandiose image of himself. Many observers would rightly consider these attributes to be superficial and not accurate indicators of a person's real worth, but the narcissist takes them seriously, and as long as he has enough of them, he can continue to believe in his omnipotence. Many people may seek perfection, knowing it is impossible to achieve and that they can only strive for it. The narcissist, however, not only believes it is possible but *claims* it rather than seeking it. In other worlds, he *is* perfect and is entitled to have his activities and relationships reflect it. He doesn't have to work or struggle for it. Should he not receive enough supplies to justify this claim for himself, or if the mirroring from the environment is inadequate, his grandiose self is frustrated and the anger and depression that underlie it emerge.

The successful narcissist—successful in the sense that his perception of the world and his place in it manages to prevent him from questioning his importance—must be creative and imaginative, and often quite talented, to develop a lifestyle that will resonate to his grandiose projections of himself and fuel his narcissistic needs. Creating this self-contained system of reinforcement and refueling techniques is a major accomplishment in itself, requiring enormous energy and diligence; and when done well, it too becomes a source of gratification, contributing to the narcissist's grandiose sense of himself. As he basks in the comfortable habitat that he has constructed, an air-tight cocoon of narcissistic enjoyment, life can seem pretty good. In fact, he does feel good; he feels secure, and as long as nothing punctures the closed circle, he will not be aware of any serious personality problems. He thinks he has it all, and those who know him would agree, since he has carefully selected and enlisted them to be part of his world and thereby buttress his view of himself. For example, there was a widespread notion among General Douglas MacArthur's top staff that his role in post-war Japan was the equivalent of the Second Coming of Christ. The fact that very few people outside his staff thought so suggests the very real possibility that MacArthur carefully hand-picked his staff to mirror his own grandiose image of himself and his role in history.[1]

Underneath this pursuit of mirroring and narcissistic feedback lies a massive denial of reality, different from the borderline's inability to deal with reality but sharing similar self-destructive habits that prevent the real self from emerging. Whereas the borderline denies his real wishes and goals in order to avoid self-activation that would bring on the abandonment depression, a reality the borderline knows only too well, the narcissist denies weakness in himself and the reality of depression altogether. Since the narcissist will not admit that his well-constructed environment can frustrate him, he cannot allow himself to be deflated by feelings of depression. He denies problems and setbacks, writing them off as something wrong with the world in general or with other individuals, never considering that they might spring from a weakness in himself or a flaw in his self-concept. The narcissist's utter conviction that he is special and omnipotent blinds him to any evidence that contradicts this conception of himself. For example, when a narcissist's wife leaves him, he does not get depressed; he gets angry. If he got depressed, he would be admitting to weakness. Anger, on the other hand, implies that he has been wronged, and hence is in the right; it can be viewed as a strength.

But should a severe enough crisis occur, one in which anger cannot displace depression, the narcissist may end up in therapy where he will have to step out of his cocoon and try to activate his real self. It then becomes painfully apparent how impaired that self is in dealing with reality. All the real self's capacities are as impaired as the borderline's. When the narcissist forgoes the seeking of narcissistic gratification and tries to activate the real self to undertake an activity for its own sake (rather than for mirroring) or to enter a relationship to care about the other person (rather than for mirroring), his facade crumbles and his real self impairment is revealed.

There is a healthy, appropriate narcissism without which we could not invest our unique self-representations with the positive feelings necessary for self-esteem or self-assertion, and for pursuit of our own unique interests, ideals, and ambitions. Normal narcissism is vital for satisfaction and survival. All the capacities of the real self come under the heading of normal narcissism, which in effect is the capacity to identify what you want and need, get yourself together, and go after it, while also taking into account the welfare of others. This is the healthy way to feel good about yourself. This important distinction between healthy and pathologic narcissism has been blurred by the tendency to see all narcissism as pathological.

The difference between healthy and pathological narcissism can be illustrated by the difference between a healthy and a narcissistic relationship between a speaker and his or her audience. People who really enjoy public speaking or lecturing claim it makes them feel good. They are asserting their real selves by presenting their ideas to a group of people. Their motive is to present their ideas, to stimulate and educate their audience. The source of their feeling good lies in their success in achieving this goal. But if the motive for lecturing or teaching is merely to exhibit the speaker's greatness, and the audience's role is not primarily to learn but to mirror the lecturer's greatness and importance, then it is a narcissistic motive.

And not just lecturers are narcissists; members of the audience can be narcissistic, too. It is appropriate to go to a lecture or take a class with the desire to learn or increase your knowledge and understanding. It is narcissistic to take a course from an important professor because it enhances your greatness to be in her class and you expect the professor to acknowledge how special you are to have gotten into the class.

A revealing example of the perfect mirroring needed by narcissists occurred several years ago when I was quoted in a *New York Times* article about the major symptoms of the narcissist personality disorder. Within days I received 12 phone calls from individuals who had read the article and suspected that they might have the disorder. Each came to see me for an evaluation, which as it turned out, proved them right. They were narcissistic disorders, and on finding out, they each asked if they could come for treatment. I agreed, but since I didn't have time in my schedule to take on 12 new patients, I suggested they see one of my associates in the Masterson Group. Not one returned to begin treatment, which indicated that they were not truly interested in treatment for its own sake, but rather were looking toward me as a narcissistic supply. Because of my reputation in the field and because I was quoted in the *New York Times*, being in therapy with me would reinforce their grandiose images of themselves, whereas being in therapy with anyone else would be seen as weakness.

The parable of the 12 narcissists who never returned clearly contains an element of humor, and in fact, the common tendency to make light of the narcissist provides some insight into the narcissist's problems and into the healthy individual's relationship to the narcissist and to his own narcissism. In early development—during the practicing phase—we all existed in a union with our mothers, in a condition of narcissism. The mother and child make up a perfect unit that rules the world, albeit the narrow world of the nursery. But to us it was the only world and because we perceived ourselves as part of the mother who was supreme master of that world, we experienced an all-powerful sense of control.

None of us really wanted to leave that heady state, even though it did finally come to an end. Parts of it, however, we never gave up, and whatever vestigial memory of that time remains reminds us that we have never had it so good since. The narcissist, on the other hand, never gave it up. He presents the illusion of having it all, and for that there is a natural tendency to envy him, and a certain delight in seeing him lose it. We enjoy watching the narcissist get his due, be one-upped, reveal that he is not immune to frustrations. The narcissist, however, would not share the joke because he cannot admit his vulnerability. The emperor must not be told he has no clothes. In therapy I often use humor with borderline patients who respond well as it helps them to gain an observing distance from their problems. Humor also serves as a respite, a much-needed island of amusement in a situation that is like a sea of depression. But humor will drive the narcissist away. He gets angry and aggressive. His omnipotence and grandiosity are not joking matters.

To illustrate further how the sense of entitlement can skew the narcissist's perception of reality, consider the impact the rejection of a doctoral dissertation would have on three different Ph.D. candidates: a person with a real self and its proper sense of entitlement, a candidate with a borderline personality disorder who has no sense of entitlement, and a narcissist with an exaggerated sense of entitlement. In most cases, a student with a healthy real self, told that his thesis lacked sufficient information, was not well argued, and in some places lacked clarity, though perhaps disappointed, would realize that the purpose of submitting the thesis at that time was precisely to learn its deficiencies so that they could be corrected. The candidate would then return to the project with creativity, commitment, and self-assertion to find ways to obtain the necessary information, improve the writing, and resubmit the thesis. Her adequate sense of entitlement and self-esteem, together with the capacity for self-assertion, would fuel this process. Then as the student realistically mastered the task, her self-esteem would be reinforced.

Because the borderline student has difficulty with self-activation, assertion, commitment, and creativity, he might procrastinate and delay submitting the dissertation way beyond the deadline. He would feel that the critical comments were a rejection not of the paper but of himself, a confirmation of inadequacy. This would precipitate the abandonment depression to which the candidate would respond by helpless clinging to a teacher or other authority figure or by backing out of the program altogether. This, of course, would further reinforce the inadequate sense of self and the notion that he was not entitled to a doctoral degree.

The narcissistic student would confidently submit the thesis to the advisor convinced that it would get a glowing report. She would view the criticisms as a personal attack, and the situation would trigger her underlying anger. The candidate would defend by seeing the committee as harsh and unfair or devaluing their ability and right to criticize, or both. She might contest the decision or withdraw from the program. The reality that the paper was defective and in need of more work would be denied.

Not only are the narcissists' work lives and sense of self distorted by their need to bolster the false self, but their relationships always have hidden agendas, too. On the surface is the illusion that the individual is friendly and sincere; but underneath, the relationship exists for one primary purpose, namely to keep the narcissist's grandiosity reinforced. Other people exist in the narcissist's life to gratify her, to be used and exploited, to mirror the narcissist's image of herself as being unique, special, and important.

Because she understands her own narcissistic needs so well, the narcissist is extremely sensitive to the narcissistic needs of others (everyone has them although not to a pathological degree) and she manipulates them by gratifying their narcissism so they will then gratify hers. She knows that we all like to feel good about ourselves and that a narcissistic wound not only hurts but is hard to accept. Knowing this, she can easily exploit the narcissistic urges of others to get what she wants. Often others cannot see through her ploy, since she comes across as clever, charming, charismatic, and, on the surface at least, like a friend who makes them feel good by complimenting, cajoling, and admiring them. For example, an aspiring actress might use all her personal and physical charms to get the attention of a director in order to get a part in a play. Their affair will continue for the length of the play's run, but when the production closes, so does the relationship. The actress will then leave the director because the narcissistic goal of the relationship is fulfilled.

The reason the narcissist finds it impossible to commit herself emotionally and sincerely to another human being is that to do so would activate the underlying emptiness, rage, and depression of her impaired real self. There is little in her that is not self-absorbed and self-centered. To become emotionally involved would be to direct her feelings and interests to another, and as far as she is concerned there is no "other" in her life.

We have all encountered people with inflated false selves in social settings where they appear warm, interested, and open but only when they are talking about themselves or their own interests. They do not ask us about our interests or life, except in an obviously formal way out of deference to social norms or in order to manipulate us into becoming a source of narcissistic supplies. A further indication of their true motivation is that if we stop asking them about themselves, the relationship quickly disintegrates and they find ways to avoid us. When the narcissist shows his true hand in these situations, it reveals a real lack of empathy for others.

To demonstrate this lack of concern for others to my classes, I often ask all those who think they have a substantially genuine interest in others in addition to their interest in themselves to hold up their hands. Everyone holds up his hand, which I suppose is to be expected in a class of students hoping to become psychotherapists. Then I tell them that this is why they will have trouble understanding how the narcissist ticks. He or she has absolutely *no* interest in others for themselves. Narcissists are completely foreign to most of us in this regard. They do not realize or accept the fact that the world contains other human beings who are emotionally involved with each other and with their own legitimate needs and interests, which are just as important as the narcissist's. And yet the narcissist has craftily learned how to survive in this world because it is only through other individuals that he will obtain gratification and maintain his inflated sense of self. Consequently, his narcissistic antennae are always extended to seek out possible sources of feedback that will confirm his notion of his own superiority and importance.

So the narcissist is in a peculiar and threatened position. He needs others to supply his narcissistic needs, but he must cultivate his relationships carefully so that they don't require too much emotional involvement or commitment. To invest his emotions in a relationship would activate a real self too impaired to follow through on the consequences of those emotions, one of which is the possibility of being hurt.

At work the narcissist needs the same mirroring he needs from personal relationships, usually in the form of praise and admiration for the great job he is performing. The narcissist expects this praise from supervisors as well as from colleagues and coworkers. Anyone who has ever worked for or with a person with a narcissistic personality disorder knows how frustrating and stressful the situation can become. In spite of the fact that the narcissist usually does a good job, he is not always pleased with the work of others. Since he can do no wrong, any difficulties have to be due to others.

It is relatively easy to spot narcissistic personalities in politics, business, and social movements. The limelight that goes with leadership is a strong magnet for narcissists, and even though success requires long hours and grueling work schedules, the payoff is worth the effort to them. Frequently, their staffs are overworked and are expected to produce perfect or near-perfect results. The narcissistic leader or boss elicits martyrlike devotion from followers by manipulating their desire to be part of his achievements. With rhetoric and ritual the narcissistic leader creates a sense of excitement and purpose and draws on his workers' sense of mission. He is often fulsome in his praise of their devotion. In the end, however, the shrewd observer can see through the empty praise and the facade of concern for supporters, for ultimately the narcissistic leader is only concerned about praise for his own achievements, and values others only in so far as they fulfill their role in promoting his own glory.

The narcissist tends to be a workaholic, as we have seen in the cases of Stewart and Daniel, and perfect mirroring for the workaholic requires that he be surrounded by other workaholics who can match his drive and enthusiasm for industriousness. If you

have ever worked for a boss who was a workaholic, you may remember the open or implied pressure on you to show as much
commitment to the job as he did and the disappointment when
you didn't. One often gets the impression that no matter what you
do, it isn't good enough, and on those occasions when it is good
enough, the narcissistic boss manages to deflect the credit to himself.

A patient of mine who was the third-ranking officer of a large
company was expecting to be made president. When he was by-
passed for the position, he asked why and was told that his own
work was superb but that he had miserable relationships with employees. They complained of his incessant pressure for performance, his unawareness of their needs, and his intolerance of mistakes. This took him by surprise. That night he went home and
related the story to his wife who, to his further amazement, confirmed the company's evaluation of him, pointing out that his relationship with her and their children was just as terrible. He was
rarely home, was cold and aloof when he was, and paid no attention to the needs of others in the family. At his next appointment
with me, he wondered what was wrong with so many people that
they couldn't see how wonderful he was!

There are three levels or types of narcissism, high, medium, and
low, each referring to the degree to which the individual is a successful narcissist, successful from the narcissist's point of view, that
is. The successful narcissist is the one who can make the environment continuously resonate to his narcissistic needs. People respond with praise and admiration; work provides a stunning show-
case for the narcissist's talents and abilities; his possessions,
hobbies, and pastimes keep him buoyed up emotionally and help
him sail through life.

The high-level narcissist rarely comes for treatment. Everything
is going too well for him and he manages to rebuff disappointments
in his usual self-centered manner. Often he is in a profession that
has considerable narcissistic supplies built right into it. If the narcissist finds the right niche in life, he can go for years without
realizing that his life is empty at its core and that beneath the
narcissistic glitter there is an impaired real self. Acting, modeling,
politics, and other professions that are by nature exhibitionistic
can be very protective environments for the narcissist since they

offer continuous feedback and keep the narcissist's balloon well inflated. (Of course, not all people in these professions are narcissists.)

It is remarkable what serious problems a high-level narcissist can tolerate or ignore as long as his balloon is full. We are all aware of some politicians, for example, who are terrors to work for, whose families lead lonely and miserable lives because of the incessant campaigning, and yet who rarely appear concerned about the very people on whose efforts their careers depend. Nothing seems to bother them, because campaigning 16 hours a day is a turn-on. A work and travel schedule that would exhaust the average person is an elixir for the narcissist.

The medium-level narcissist has to work harder. She has not found the knack for creating a life environment that will provide the vital supplies and narcissistic feedback. She manages mainly through denial of these difficulties until a truly serious separation stress occurs against which she has no defenses. An unrelenting marital conflict, a painful setback at work, or a serious health problem is usually necessary to deflate her balloon and bring her to seek professional help.

Lower-level narcissists have extremely poor defenses and tend to oscillate in and out of depression much like the borderline, and in fact may be mistaken for borderlines because of the symptoms they present on beginning therapy. It is only after the therapist probes the patient's intrapsychic structure that the difference is apparent. Whereas the borderline complies with others and avoids self-assertion to gain approval, the low-level narcissist seeks adulation, praise, and perfect mirroring.

The developmental roots of the inflated false self have not been studied as thoroughly as that of the borderline's deflated false self. There is still considerable speculation on how the narcissistic personality develops. It appears, though, that the narcissist suffers a developmental arrest prior to the emergence of the real self, between 18 and 36 months. How and why this arrest occurs is not always clear.

In some cases the mothers of narcissistic personality disorders are emotionally cold and exploitive narcissistic personalities themselves. They ignore their children's separation and individuation needs in order to mold the children to fit their own perfectionistic standards and serve their own emotional needs. The perfectionist mother needs a perfect child to act as a mirror for her own perfectionist self-image. The emotionally cold mother needs a child able to function as perfectly as possible on his own to minimize the amount of time and emotion that she needs to invest in him.

The child's real need to separate and establish his own individuality suffers as he resonates with the mother's idealizing projections. Repeated and continual identification with the mother's idealized image of the child preserves the grandiose self-image typical of the early exploratory phase, when the crawler/toddler feels the world is his oyster and nothing can get in his way to frustrate him, or cause him pain or dissatisfaction. In reality, of course, the mother is not perfect and neither is the world, but the child is blinded to the mother's failures and imperfections which, were he to acknowledge them, would cause depression.

For the narcissistic child, the fused symbiotic image he holds of himself and the mother is never split. Mothers of normal children teach them about the realities of life by introducing them to frustration experiences in carefully measured doses that gradually dispel the notion that the fused "grandiose child-omnipotent mother" entity can go on forever. They deflate their children's feelings of grandeur and bring them down to earth. The mother of the future narcissistic personality never dispels this notion.

Thus, the fused, symbiotic relationship endures, and the child grows to adulthood perceiving himself just as omnipotent and grandiose as he was as a child. He identifies on the surface with the grandiose omnipotent mother image who can do anything. However, underneath this defensive, fused, grandiose self is the inadequate, fragmented, impaired real self with its rage and depression and the intrapsychic image of the angry, attacking mother who disapproved of his emerging real self when it sought self-expression along lines other than the perfection and grandiosity that she required. When the child grows up, both of these intrapsychic feelings and images are activated and form the basis of his relationships with others: When others mirror his grandiosity he likes them; when they frustrate his need for mirroring, he attacks or devalues them.

A second possibility for the origins of the narcissistic personality disorder may be in identification with the father. When a child experiences the emotional unavailability of a mother who is particularly emotionally empty and unresponsive, he can use his experiences with the father as a corrective to rescue him from the resultant depression and the mother. The child transfers his fused, symbiotic image of the mother and himself, together with all the associated feelings and yearnings, onto the father in order to deal with his abandonment depression and preserve his sense of omnipotence which he doesn't want to lose. If the father is a narcissistic personality himself and the transfer occurs while the child still believes himself to be part of the omnipotent parents the child's grandiose self will be preserved and reinforced through identification with the narcissistic father. A healthy father, on the other hand, may help to limit the evolution of the child's narcissism.

Over the years I have discovered a variation on the narcissistic personality disorder that is difficult to identify and can easily be overlooked or misdiagnosed as something else. The closet narcissist does not feel that he can express grandiosity and self-centeredness directly and openly as the brash, exhibitionistic narcissist does so well. The closet narcissist must find another person, group, or institution through which he can indulge his narcissistic needs while hiding his own narcissistic personality. The closet narcissist has the same intrapsychic structure (a grandiose self-image fused with an omnipotent parent-image) as the exhibitionist but the major emotional investment is not in the grandiose self but in the omnipotent other. Therefore this patient does not actively seek the mirroring of his grandiose self; rather he idealizes the other and hopes to receive their admiration, or simply "basks in the other's glow." This is how he defends against his underlying abandonment depression. There are several possibilities as to how this happens. Either one or both parents are exhibitionistic narcissistic personalities and the child is required to idealize them to survive, or in some cases, the mother might initially idealize the child's grandiosity in the earlier stages and then attack it as the child gets older and comes into conflict with her wishes.

As an example of a closet narcissist, consider Frances, 47, who came to me after a long history of therapy beginning when she was 27. She had been treated twice a week for two years by a psychologist, she had seen a psychiatrist for a number of years, and tried gestalt therapy for two more years. Nothing seemed to work. She noted that she was constantly absorbed in other people and things outside herself and had to have a structure of daily activity as well as a constant supply of friends. Otherwise she felt empty, angry, and depressed. As she said, she needed "constant connection with and continuous stroking from other people."

Frances was the second of three children from an economically deprived home. Her father was a quiet, withdrawn, self-centered, perfectionistic clergyman who spent most of his time with parishioners. Her mother totally supported and idealized the father. In the family, his perfectionistic views were always "right," and as a child, Frances felt he knew everything but for some reason was not sharing it with her. She claimed to receive even less emotional or intellectual support from her mother, whom she described as also self-centered but demanding.

As an adult, Frances frequently felt helpless and alone even when she received positive feedback from her friends and activities. She was quite aware that she contributed to these relationships only because she enjoyed the positive feedback. When she was with others, she found herself engaging in behavior that would elicit their praise and admiration, even though it required activities for which she had, in fact, little interest or enthusiasm. One of her real interests was the piano, and her talent was almost concert quality, but she tended not to practice or take her interest in it very seriously. She admitted to being overly sensitive to criticism herself and yet constantly criticized her office help for not providing perfect mirroring.

She had had two ongoing relationships with very successful but self-centered men, and experienced a severe separation when each man broke off the relationship. She fell into a deep depression and remained isolated for long periods of time. Frances thought that she loved each man and was surprised to hear from them that the reason they wanted to end the relationship was that they didn't believe Frances was capable of love.

Frances was a closet narcissist, unable to forcefully express her narcissistic self; she avoided self-assertion and expression of the exhibitionistic, grandiose self. Instead she assumed a defensive posture of inhibition and passivity and allied herself with friends, men, and employees who she hoped would mirror her own grandiose self-representation. When they failed to mirror her perfectly, Frances grew depressed.

An examination of the roots of the narcissistic personality disorder today would be incomplete without considering the role of broader cultural trends and themes commonly blamed for, or equated with, this form of individual psychopathology. Recently, narcissism has been associated with all that is wrong in American society, beginning with the revolution of the sixties and ending in the self-fascination of the Me Decade. In fact, the sociocultural swing toward a narcissistic society began much earlier. American society was born in revolution against what was perceived, at least from this side of the Atlantic, as authoritarianism, or the principle that the individual should submit to and obey authority simply because it is authority, not because it is right. The American revolution was fought against the authoritarian attitude of the British government over taxes, property rights, land use, and economic development; and so was born a society which in theory would champion the rights of the individual over the established powers. Nevertheless, authoritarianism continued to flourish in child-rearing patterns, in the schools, in the courts, in business, and in many social customs, particularly those governing relations between men and women and with minority groups.

One of the principal benefits of the activism of the sixties was the change in standards in all these areas—a change from authoritarianism to a greater emphasis on individualism and entitlements. These changes ostensibly created a better environment for the flowering and expression of the real self—in other words, healthy narcissism. But to what extent, then, does the sense of individual entitlement, now woven all the more tightly into the fabric of our society, also open the door for pathologic narcissism? Or to put it another way, does the resultant narcissism contribute to a unique and healthy American character, or is it a pathological national flaw?

The narcissistic disordered self will exploit opportunities for freedom and independence to gain narcissistic, not real, self-gratification and will fiercely battle any authority that would infringe on the individual's sense of entitlement. Christopher Lasch in *The Culture of Narcissism* has chronicled how the pendulum of sociocultural values may have swung too far in this direction. There are elements in society, similar to the traits in the narcissistic self, that have gone beyond healthy individualism to pathologic self-centeredness, which results in an erosion of realistic, adaptive social standards in favor of exclusive, obsessive self-gratification. This inevitably leads to inner emptiness, isolation, and loneliness even if the individual does not have a narcissistic personality disorder. If one behaves as a narcissist, one experiences some of the narcissist's isolation and loneliness.

7

The Challenge
of Intimacy

INTIMATE relationships are the *bête noire* for the person with an impaired real self, calling as they do for self-expression, self-revelation, and the ability to function independently while sharing with another human being. Invariably borderline and narcissistic individuals are unable to enter into and sustain healthy relationships. For them intimacy is the ultimate stumbling block since they must enter into a state (as Webster defines it) "marked by very close association, contact, or familiarity," engaging "one's deepest nature." This is the kind of intimacy we expect from healthy individuals who are able to reveal and share what is deepest, truest, or most real about themselves. I would define intimacy, therefore, as the capacity of two people to offer each other's real selves affection and acknowledgment in a close, ongoing interpersonal relationship.

Consequently the emerging of the real self is of vital importance to the capacity to love another person successfully in a sustained, mutually satisfying relationship. The dividends of establishing one's autonomy from the mother and being able to activate and express oneself freely, assured of her support and approval, are crucial for the development of an ego strong and secure enough to maintain a loving relationship. Particularly necessary are the ability to perceive the loved one as a complete human being with both good and bad traits; the capacity to be alone and feel genuine concern for—as opposed to a neediness for—others; the capacity to tolerate anxiety and depression; and the capacity to commit oneself emotionally to another without the fear of engulfment or abandonment. Also important is the capacity to mourn the loss of a loved one in such a way as to free oneself emotionally for a new relationship.

Since the preservation of the human race depends upon men and women relating to each other sexually to produce offspring, and since it seems that in human societies, a stable, enduring relationship between parents facilitates the survival and development of the children, it would seem that biological design would have mapped out an easy route for developing the capacity for intimacy. However, the truth is very different: whether biology has failed to provide easy means for achieving intimacy or the means exist but are diverted by societal customs and expectations, it has become extremely difficult for human beings to develop a strong capacity for intimacy. As family life is constituted today, there are two important developmental thresholds to intimacy, neither of which is easy to cross: the separation/individuation phase of development and the oedipal stage.

The first important threshold to the capacity for intimacy is crossed as the child separates and individuates from the symbiotic union with the mother during the first three years of life. If this individuation is accomplished successfully, a relationship of mutual trust emerges between the mother and child providing the basis for the all-important sense of entitlement to the support and encouragement that one needs for healthy development. Here the child first learns—or fails to learn in the case of an arrested development—that the caretaking partner can be relied upon to nurture the emerging capacities of the real self for self-activation and self-expression. Whether the seeds of trust planted in the child's psyche continue to grow depends upon whether the environment provides or fails to provide support. The affectionate interplay that takes place between the mother and child during this period establishes the pattern that will become natural for the child in later intimate relationships. Since we all emerge somewhat wounded from this stage, most of us grow up with less than perfect capacities for trust and intimacy, just as we do with the other capacities, such as autonomy and creativity.

The oedipal threshold to intimacy occurs when the child with an autonomous self and the capacity to view the parents as whole, separate persons in their own right develops a sexual dimension to her relationship with the parent of the opposite sex and a rivalry with the same-sex parent. The child invests the parent with sexual feelings and importance that take precedence over the parent's formerly one-dimensional role of caretaker. Now the relationship becomes sexualized. During the latency period prior to adolescence, these feelings go underground to be revived at puberty, at which point the remaining residue of the unconscious oedipal conflict is worked through by turning to peers for sexual emancipation. The infantile sexual attachment to the parents is transformed and directed to sexual figures outside the home in the experimentation that comes with dating. The teenager's affectionate style will still resemble that established during the early years of separating from the mother, while the sexual quality of relationships will derive from the oedipal stage. It is a primary psychological task of adolescence to integrate affection and sexuality in a way that is workable for the individual.

The purpose of teenage romances, then, is twofold: to establish a confident sexual identity in relationships with others; and to experiment in order to identify the type of person that attracts one and evokes one's affection. By dating and meeting a variety of individuals, the adolescent sorts out various types of people and relationships. If the adolescent has a healthy real self, the feedback from this experimentation will help determine his ultimate choice of partner, and it will be an appropriate one, with the mutual give-and-take that reinforces and enhances the real self of both partners.

From a developmental point of view, it is really quite a tribute to the human instinct for preservation, to the drive to assuage personal loneliness, and to the drive for sexual gratification, that so many individuals are able to surmount these obstacles with sufficient success to be able to pair up as adults, albeit with problems. The strong bonding instinct attests to the importance of intimate relationships for both the individual and the human species.

Although there are many definitions and styles of love, from the perspective of the real self and its development, love is the capacity to acknowledge the other's real self in a warm, affectionate way, with no strings attached, and to enjoy the sexual passion

Definition of Love

that energizes the relationship in such a way that the welfare of the partner, in every sense of that term, becomes as important as one's own welfare. In fact, we could say that true love is a union of two people, each for the *good of the other*, where the other's best interests become at least equal to one's own. In light of what we have been saying throughout this book, to love is to like, approve of, and support another's real self and to encourage the other to activate, express, and nurture that real self. This investment in the other enlarges, enriches, and completes the experience of the self.

Building an intimate, loving relationship with another is the way we overcome the essential aloneness and isolation of the self as an adult. Without such a relationship, the real self will always remain to some extent unfulfilled and incomplete, since the vestiges of that first intimate symbiotic relationship with the mother will always remain in our psyches and memories. Only by risking genuine intimacy are we likely to find a partner who will reinforce and promote a healthy kind of relationship similar to that given up so long ago but never entirely forgotten. In contrast to the relationship of the dependent child seeking nurturance from an omnipotent other, however, the adult relationship is characterized by balance, based on mutual sharing of two independent selves, acknowledging and reinforcing each other.

There is more confusion and rationalization about the capacity for love than about any other human ability. No man or woman is perfect, and therefore none of us can live up to what we might envision as the perfect relationship or the perfect way of loving. In our own ways, we each fall short and are reluctant to admit our failures and accept our limitations. The desire to love and to give often exceeds our capacity to do so, and we are prone to assuage our disappointment with rationalizations.

Each type of pathology produces its own confusion and its own distorted version of loving and giving. The borderline patient defines love as a relationship with a partner who will offer approval and support for regressive behavior, usually in the form of taking responsibility for the borderline. The narcissist defines love as the ability of someone else to admire and adore him, and to provide perfect mirroring. To extend this perspective further, the schizophrenic would seek a lover who could enter his psychotic world and form a symbiotic relationship based on the patient's psychosis.

Psychopaths seek partners who respond to their manipulations and provide them with gratification. The schizoid—a disorder caused by the lack of support in the early years of childhood akin to that experienced by borderline and narcissistic patients—finds love in an internal, autistic fantasy.

Genuine intimacy begins to develop in the early overtures two people make to each other, based on self-activation and self-expression. As we sift and test the responses we get in these first encounters, we look to see how the other person appreciates or fails to appreciate our real selves. When the feedback is positive, affectionate and sexual feelings usually intensify along with a growing willingness on the part of the two people to become more intimately involved with each other on all levels. The rate and depth of the involvement depends on how each partner responds to this experimental process. If it works, each person spontaneously and harmoniously begins to like, acknowledge, and respond to the expressions of the other's real self. In time, the combination of the two becomes greater than the sum of the individual parts; and the real self of each experiences a sense of wholeness and completeness. The couple has achieved genuine intimacy.

There are all kinds of illusions that make it appear that intimacy is working for a couple, even when, on closer inspection, what we find is not a healthy interchange between two real selves expressing and reinforcing their capacities but a pathologic contract between two false selves which, although it may seem to survive for the moment, inevitably falls apart. A good illustration of this is the couple who always fight in public to the extent that friends wonder why they even stay together. The answer is simple: they stay together because they fight so much. It works for them. The classic example is the case of two borderline personalities who project the withdrawing, disapproving parental image onto each other so that they do not have to feel and be aware of the associated depression. As long as they are angry at their partners, they do not have to feel depressed. For them interpersonal conflict is preferable to feeling intrapsychic depression. If you ask them about their relationship, they are always "having difficulties"; but actually in a pathologic way, it is a relationship that works for them and satisfies the needs of their false selves.

A proof of the pathology behind this kind of "working" relationship is seen in treatment of both borderline and narcissistic patients. When a patient announces that she has found a new lover and that the relationship is comfortable and easy-going, I strongly suspect that the new partner is inappropriate for the patient and is providing a kind of defense against the patient's painful feelings. On the other hand, if a patient relates that the new relationship is fun and exciting, but also causes a lot of anxiety, I know the new partner is more appropriate and better for the patient in the long run because he is challenging the patient's old defenses and stimulating the patient to relate in terms of the real self. Anxiety is present because borderline and narcissistic personalities cannot relate on a realistic level without giving up the defenses of the false self, which in turn makes them feel exposed and vulnerable to the anxiety and depression that they are struggling hardest to avoid.

In the case of the borderline, relationships, dominated by the need to defend against the fear of the abandonment depression, will be unreliable, vulnerable to frustrations, and heavily dependent on the mood or feeling of the moment. The borderline lover will have trouble sustaining relationships because the loved one will be seen as two entities, one rewarding and satisfying, the other withholding and frustrating.

There may be no continuity in the way the borderline views his partner. It shifts moment to moment and is either totally good or totally bad. In any event, the lover is never perceived as a complex, richly ambiguous person embodying faults and virtues simultaneously. Consequently, the borderline becomes a kind of "fair weather" lover whose emotional investment in the partner will wane in times of disagreement or when tempers flare. An exception, of course, is where both partners need to fight with each other.

Without the ability to perceive other people as whole and constant objects, it becomes difficult to evoke the image of a person when the person is not physically present. Feeling bereft of the loved one brings on the fear of abandonment, conjuring up the possibility that the person has actually disappeared or ceased to exist or is never to return. Such feelings may become so powerful that the borderline cannot imagine otherwise. Conversely, when a relationship does in fact end, the patient will not be able to mourn, in the sense of grieving over the loss or separation in a healthy, cathartic way that puts the loss behind him and allows him to get on with life and form new relationships. Since as a child the person never fully separated from, and so "lost," the mother, he never developed the capacity to mourn and recover from a loss.

Most people suffer at least some minor trauma in separating and individuating from the mother which later shows up as some kind of minor difficulty in relationships, for there are no super-mothers who are able to respond one hundred percent positively to every act of the child's unfolding individuality. But for the person with a severely impaired real self, the conflict over intimacy revolves around a single, major theme: A close emotional involvement with another person activates and reawakens his fear of being engulfed or abandoned. If he gets too close the feelings of being pulled back into the symbiotic whirlpool become too intense. If he gets too far away, the possibility of being abandoned looms before him.

On the interpersonal level, the borderline is afraid of being engulfed or abandoned by the other person. From the intrapsychic perspective, he is afraid of losing the image of himself on which he relies for a sense of identity or losing the image of the maternal object which is also a major component of his identity.

Every borderline patient has both fears; their relative strengths depend on how far along the patient was before his attempts to separate and establish his own individuality were arrested. If the arrest occurred early in the process before the ego boundaries were secure, fears of engulfment predominate; if later after the child has established a sense of himself, even though weak and unsubstantial, fears of abandonment will predominate. Borderlines may use the principal defense mechanisms of clinging and distancing either exclusively or alternately at different times. Whichever style of defense was used as a child to deal with separating from the mother becomes the dominant pattern in dealing with close interpersonal relationships.

The adult who uses the clinging mechanism is projecting and acting out his wish for reunion with the mother onto the loved one. The wish contains a fantasy of being the exclusive center of attention and receiving undiluted and constant approval from the other person. Usually in therapy, the initial complaints will focus on the other person's shortcomings in being able to fulfill this impossible demand. The borderline, however, usually doesn't realize how intolerable the demand is and will tend to deny that what he really hopes for is to be the center of an impossibly exclusive relationship. The adult who favors distancing as a defense mechanism often picks out a partner whose personality traits make any kind of relationship difficult if not impossible. The prospective partner may be aloof, self-centered, too busy or inaccessible, unresponding, or even physically or psychologically abusive, all of which encourages or justifies the distancing behavior on the part of the borderline.

Most intimate relationships require too much give and take, and are too fluid and unpredictable, to allow the borderline's defenses to remain undisturbed. A Great Wall of China cannot be built on the emotional plains of intimacy; the love object cannot be held at bay or encircled and trapped like an enemy. Eventually the inevitable closeness threatens those defenses and confronts the impaired real self with the need for a genuine emotional involvement to sustain the relationship, and the impaired real self discovers that it lacks the capacities for dealing with it.

An intimate relationship is a separation/individuation stress in its own right because it requires self-activation and autonomy; and a patient will respond to the anxiety it creates just as she would toward any other separation or individuation stress—by utilizing the defenses. The clinical manifestations of this are protean, and a few examples will help to flesh out the portrait:

A typical, unconscious strategy for many borderline individuals is to marry a childhood sweetheart, in effect postponing adulthood by trying to preserve childhood patterns with which they feel safe. These marriages usually occur immediately after high school or around graduation from college, when the person would normally go off into the adult world where more individuation and more adult responsibilities are required. Marrying a childhood sweetheart provides a way of clinging to old patterns associated with childhood and family and seemingly camouflages the need to grow out of them and establish an adult life on one's own. (Of course, not everyone who marries a childhood sweetheart does so for this reason.)

The case of Becky illustrates this well. Because of her bad feelings about herself and the need to find someone who could take responsibility for her life, Becky thought that meeting John, an old high school boyfriend, again in college was the answer. They fell in love and got married in their sophomore year. John was a narcissistic type, and Becky was able to feel better about herself because she had such an idealized object. In the course of treatment, she realized this arrangement was at the heart of most of her marital problems, and in time she decided to separate. The stress of divorce was excruciating for her, and she plunged immediately into an intense round of sexual acting out as a defense against her feelings of abandonment. She could rationalize this behavior easily because she had not dated widely in high school or experimented sexually. She felt she was owed this period. So instead of clinging to her narcissistic husband to handle her anxiety, she clung to a series of men without establishing any real relationship with them beyond the sexual. Eventually she decided to live with a man who also had borderline problems and was unable to take responsibility for himself or Becky. Over time she became aware of this and began to act out her rage on him. Throughout she was able to hide her own anxiety about intimacy. Interestingly, all of the men that Becky became involved with had sexual problems of one type or another, of which Becky was extremely accepting and tolerant—another cover for her enormous anxiety about her own capacity for intimacy.

Another illustration of the borderline's problem with intimacy is Rachel, a beautiful woman from a socially prominent family, who harbored extreme feelings of inadequacy and ugliness about herself. I am always initially surprised (even though it is such a recurring pattern) to discover how easily the most beautiful, intelligent woman with a borderline disorder is incapable of realizing her beauty, talents, or other positive qualities. It attests to the power of the false self to distort self-perceptions, the power of the inner self-image over the outer appearance. As Rachel, sophisticated and well educated, began to move away from her parents in late adolescence, she fell in love with a poorly educated man from a different ethnic group and much lower social class. This was in part a rebellion against the upper class values of her parents but also an avoidance of her anxiety about intimacy and a confirmation of her low self-esteem. They moved in together, and soon Rachel was pregnant. Rachel left her lover after the baby was born, taking the child with her as an object of her own to cling to. She dated other men, but the pattern was typical: When she got involved with an appropriate man (who activated her real self), she would grow anxious and stop seeing him. When she found someone who resonated with her negative feelings about herself and treated her as poorly as she treated herself, she felt comfortable and wanted to continue seeing him. (The epitome of this type of relationship is the sado-masochistic alliance in which both parties receive pathologic gratification.)

In many borderline relationships, the patient prefers a partner who is only partially accessible, such as one who lives a considerable distance away or is only available on weekends or works a lot or is married. In fact, borderlines have antennae a mile long listening for the subtle clues dropped early in chance meetings with potential lovers that indicate they are not available for a full-time relationship. At the first mention of the fact that he works a lot, lives out of town, or is married—conditions that would discourage a normal person from getting her hopes up for a lasting relationship—the borderline grows interested. This is just what she needs. Borderlines seem to find each other and begin their affairs of convenience, unconsciously blinded to the fact that they have embarked on a dead-end course.

I often tell this type of patient that they could walk through a room with 20 potential partners, 19 of whom are eligible and one of whom is ineligible, and they would spot the ineligible one immediately. Knowing the relationship has no future makes it uniquely attractive to borderline lovers because both partners know that they are freed from having to relate to each other on a realistic level, and hence they are freed from the separation anxiety that activating their real selves would entail. What they are left with is freedom to indulge in romantic feelings and fantasies about the other. Borderline patients can also indulge in intense rounds of sexual activity. The sexual intensity masquerades for real intimacy and usually succeeds in seducing the borderline into thinking that the relationship is really working. Needless to say, the borderline patient is usually shocked and devastated when the partner ends the relationship.

A typical example of the borderline's preference for self-limiting relationships is Cynthia, who was married and having an affair with a married man. While they were both married their rendez-vous with each other were exciting, stimulating, and fulfilling. But the man divorced his wife, got serious about Cynthia, and eventually asked her to divorce her husband and marry him. As soon as the man was free and available for a serious, full-time relationship, Cynthia began to have her doubts about him. In treatment, she noted that "something was wrong" with the relationship. When I asked her what she thought it might be, she found personality and character faults with the man, and for a long time projected the problem onto him, rather than seeing it for what it was, namely, her inability to continue the relationship now that it meant facing up to the fact that it had a future, if she were willing to have it.

There are endless variations on this theme. Some can respond sexually only to partners they are not emotionally involved with, while others get serious only about those with whom they are not having sex. When the relationship turns sexual, they lose interest. Some individuals function well only where there is no continuity at all, such as with one-night stands.

Consider the situation of Eileen, an attractive woman in her early 40s who could pass for early 30s; her initial complaint in therapy was that she had been worried recently about growing older. She was not happy with how her life was going; she easily grew depressed, felt lonely, found it hard to concentrate, noticed she was drinking more than usual, and in general was beginning to feel panic over not having a permanent man in her life. She had a successful job as an editor at a New York publishing house but found the work boring. She stayed on for the security and financial benefits, sometimes wondering, though, whether she shouldn't return to freelance photography, a career she had found enormously rewarding as a younger woman.

Eileen's track record with men left much to be desired. She had had no sexual experiences with men until her last year of college, when she became involved with a classmate, got engaged, graduated, and quickly broke off the engagement because of anxiety. Her next affair was in her late 20s with a married man a good deal older than she, a domineering, narcissistic individual who served as a clinging object for her. She continued to live at home until her father died and then moved out when she was 31. She married for the first time a salesman who was rarely home and not interested in maintaining a viable family life. The marriage ended in divorce a year later, and Eileen moved into her own apartment.

Since then Eileen's relationships have consisted of serial affairs with men living or stationed in distant parts of the world: Moscow, London, California. They fly into New York for a week or ten days, and get together with Eileen for theater, drinks, sex, and living out romantic fantasies; then they go. In contrast, whenever she has met a man in the city who was available for a more permanent relationship, she has suffered such severe anxiety that she has been unable to relax, think, or act appropriately.

Eileen's life was motivated by the paradox of the clinging/distancing defense. In order to avoid the anxiety provoked by the thought of a relationship with a man who lived in town, she resorted to distancing by picking men who were seldom around and to clinging by initiating instant intimacy. Immediate, casual sex does not lead to greater intimacy as we have defined it in terms of the real self. Although sex is a powerful emotional experience that can propel people into closer relationships, the relationships are not based on intimacy in any profound or meaningful way. They do not acknowledge and support the real self, or place the other's best interests equal to one's own. Instead, people in such relationships tend to be self-serving, using the other person to gratify their own needs. In fact, a relationship that turns sexual early on, or even begins as a sexual relationship, can abort the experimental process so crucial to building genuine intimacy. Sex has the power to blind the couple to the realities about each other and how they function together, so that the sifting and sorting out of positive and negative qualities in order to make an honest commitment based on knowledge and understanding never takes place. This testing process can rightly cause anxiety and worry, but healthy individuals can tolerate it, knowing that as time goes by they are learning more and more about their potential partner and themselves.

It is important to keep in mind that the beginning of any relationship can be exciting and romantic precisely because we know so little about the new partner. The vast unknown can provide an arena for exploring all kinds of exciting personal fantasies, all of which is heightened by the excitement of sexual discovery. In time, as we get to know each other, this excitement fades and the rela-

[handwritten marginalia: phases of relationship]

[handwritten marginalia: Romantic — turn to discovery of the real self in person — Move from fantasy to reality]

tionship moves from fantasy to reality. At this point, if it is to endure, it must be based on real-self involvement and commitment or it will deteriorate into a pathologic relationship motivated by false-self defenses.

I confronted Eileen about her distancing defense by saying, "It seems to me that for a man to qualify for your bed he has to come by plane and be holding a return ticket." I asked her why she could not find an eligible man in New York City. Shortly after this confrontation, she met a man in the city and began dating him, but she would dissolve into anxiety and, as she put it, "start to act like a schoolgirl again," unable to think straight, decide what to wear, wondering if he liked her, not knowing what to say to him on the phone. True to form, she found relief from the anxiety through instant intimacy in bed. Nothing came of the relationship, and it ended a few months later.

The distancing defense can be crucial for a borderline's success at work or school. In many cases, patients perform well and enjoy notable achievements in their professional or scholastic endeavors. But when they meet someone and fall in love, they also fall apart in terms of their careers. What happens is that while they are able to hold would-be lovers at bay, they feel minimal anxiety or depression. But when a close relationship materializes, it activates their real selves, which lack the capacities to make the relationship work. They give up their distancing defense, but unable to participate in a relationship without some form of protection, they resort to clinging dependency which, in effect, is a form of helplessness. In a short time, helplessness comes to dominate their entire lives, including their work lives. Their performance suffers. Usually when the relationship breaks up, they pull themselves together again and return to their careers, fully capable as they were before. Being in love for healthy individuals can be a catalyst for even better performance, since feeling good about themselves carries over into their work. In the case of the borderline, feeling bad carries over, and their work suffers.

Another variation on the borderline's inability to conduct appropriate relationships is the exclusive clinging behavior which manifests itself shortly after the relationship is established. The person becomes excessively preoccupied with the new lover, vulnerable to every word or gesture or slight. The borderline patient demands exclusive and constant attention and resorts to rage at the partner if she cannot provide it. The borderline suffers enormous anxiety if this intense contact is interrupted for any reason, legitimate or illegitimate. Women frequently express this by obsessive wondering about why a man hasn't called or dropped by.

Borderline men also have problems with intimacy characterized by clinging and distancing. Since in our culture, men have traditionally initiated sex, borderline men are often free to use instant intimacy to relieve the anxiety of getting to know a woman on other levels. Eric, a good-looking, successful 35-year-old businessman and a member of the jet set, dealt with his fears of engulfment and abandonment by a series of short, transient relationships with women who, as he explained it, "have to be beautiful and admire me. Then I'm always turned on and eager to get to know them. But generally after a few months, the excitement wears off, I grow bored and lose interest." In other words, as the relationship grows more intimate on psychological levels, it grows too close for comfort. As relationships move beyond the glamor of fantasy toward reality, Eric's fear of engulfment leads to depression, the causes of which he projects onto his partner, and then he breaks off the affair.

A certain type of borderline man will marry a woman or set up a live-in arrangement to satisfy his passive, dependent needs. The woman agrees to support or take care of him, and he becomes the "house husband" who usually cares for the house, cooks meals, and attends to other domestic chores. In effect, he has turned responsibility for his life over to the woman. These arrangements tend to break up as the woman realizes that the man's inability to take responsibility for himself implies his inability to really care for her or shoulder any responsibility for her needs.

In all these pathologic contracts, the relationship may have the semblance of working and may provide the illusion that all is going well, when in actuality the partners are relating to their own fantasies rather than to the reality of the other person. They strongly deny the reality of their situations and use whatever compliance their partners offer to fuel their fantasies. While their fantasies are still intact, they can avoid anxiety and depression because they are living in an impermanent world of sexual and romantic excitement, grounded in their illusions rather than in reality.

A close neighbor of the borderline is the schizoid personality disorder. The schizoid personality is characterized by symptoms of emotional coldness and aloofness, indifference to praise or criticism from others, and close friendships with no more than one or two persons including family members. Although not as much research has been completed on the schizoid personality, substantial clinical evidence suggests that the schizoid's development is similar to that of the borderline's. What distinguishes the schizoid from the borderline is the primary defense of distancing and isolating the self from the internal object.

The schizoid personality's intrapsychic structure contains split images of the other person. The powerful rewarding image demands total obedience as the price for relatedness. The self representation linked to this rewarding image is that of a compliant, victimized, manipulated slave or object. Unlike the borderline relationship of a powerful, omnipotent parent to a helpless, regressed child, the schizoid's relationships resemble a master and slave. Dominance and submission are the major themes. When this dynamic is activated, the individual feels related to the other but at the price of feeling like a prisoner—always deceiving, hiding, fearful of entrapment. The overriding anxiety centers around being controlled and, ultimately, engulfed with a total loss of self-identity. These feelings are largely defended against and only appear when the schizoid person takes up the challenge of a real relationship in the external world.

The predominant and almost continuously activated withdrawing image of the other is seen as dangerous, devaluing, and depriving. The self representation linked to it is therefore one that must be largely self-contained, self-sufficient, and self-protective to ward off the danger of attack, criticism, ridicule, and abuse. The feelings linked to this image also have the "not free" quality; but unlike the prisonlike quality associated with the rewarding image, these are of the self-in-exile: isolated, marooned, abandoned.

The schizoid dilemma or compromise is to be neither too close and precipitate fears of entrapment and enslavement, nor too far away and trigger feelings of alienation and exile. To defend against these fears the schizoid person will most frequently substitute fantasied or imagined relations for real relationships as a defense. These revolve around caricatures of real relationships—romance that reads like a Harlequin novel, sado-masochistic fantasies, or gross distortions of real relationships that render them nonthreatening through role reversals. For example, the person who becomes obsessively infatuated with another will often harass the other in a sadistic, ritualistic, and controlling manner, and in so doing identify with the intrapsychic aggressor.

The inflated false self causes enormous problems with intimacy. In fact, narcissism and intimacy problems are practically synonymous. The narcissist is unable to relate to other people except in terms of his own inflated self-image and his unrealistic projections of himself onto others. Every relationship involving a narcissistic personality requires adulation and perfect responsiveness from the partner or an idealization of the partner so that the narcissist can bask in the other's glow. Whenever these requirements are frustrated, or appear to be lacking from the narcissist's point of view, he resorts to rage which is always externalized and projected onto the other.

The next step is to devalue the partner since she is not living up to the narcissist's wishes. The narcissist's overblown sense of entitlement makes it almost impossible for him to see what he is doing in these situations since he cannot imagine that his own projections onto the partner are causing him such severe dissatisfaction in the relationship. He feels entitled to the narcissistic supplies and automatically responds with rage and devaluation of others when he doesn't get them. The narcissist's ability to appear charming and sensitive to others acts like a Venus flytrap for the unsuspecting lover who can often be at a loss as to how to extricate herself from the tangle of rage and blame that results from narcissistic disappointment.

The more reinforcement that life provides the narcissist in terms of success, money, power, or prestige, the more the narcissistic personality feels entitled to a mate who will provide the same. This may be one of the reasons that the divorce rate runs exceptionally high among people with wealth and power; they grow so accustomed to getting what they want from others in life that they expect the same in their close relationships.

The most common arrangement is the narcissistic husband whose clinging borderline wife idealizes him and uses his sense of superiority to shore up her own inadequate self. She is usually very compliant, subservient, and eager to give him what he wants, but she always fails to meet his standards. Then her husband turns on her, attacks her for her inadequacies, and in so doing, reinforces her negative feelings about herself. It is often only in treatment that she realizes how little she is getting out of the relationship.

The case of Frank, the closet narcissist we will examine in Chapter 10, is a classic example of the vicissitudes narcissists endure trying to find the perfect mate. Because he had difficulty activating himself, it would all be up to the woman to establish the relationship, which Frank would interpret as her worshipping him. Obviously, this would make him feel good, and he in turn would idealize her and think he was in love. But when the first fervor of romance and fantasy ended, the reality would set in, and he would come to realize (without being able to admit it to himself) that she did not worship him, no matter how much she still loved and admired him. He would get angry and depressed, project it onto the woman, and conclude that the relationship was not working out. As he explained his own entrapment, "I'm constantly falling in love with women who aren't right for me. In the beginning, we get along well and it's exciting, but for some reason things fall apart. Then I go through long periods of loneliness and isolation where I can't find anyone."

It is very common for narcissists to have sexual difficulties, often severe ones, varying from premature ejaculation to impotence in men and inability to experience orgasm in women, because sexual gratification is not high on a narcissist's hidden list of priorities. Narcissistic gratification comes first, and the threat of two bodies and two sets of emotions coming so close requires them to activate their defenses to protect their narcissistic vulnerability. With their defenses up, they are not in the most sexually receptive state for satisfying love-making. Nevertheless, when narcissists are not in an ongoing relationship, they can engage in a lot of sexual acting out, which may create the illusion that they can function sexually quite well. As one male patient put it, "When I have sex with a woman, it's important that she climax or else I feel like I'm a lousy lover. In fact, I'm always more concerned about her response than I am about my own satisfaction because her enjoyment is a measure of my performance, and I'm never happy with one woman for very long if I'm not at my peak sexually. Then when I finish with one, I have to go after another."

To be engaged in a never-ending pursuit for a woman who will spontaneously fulfill the narcissist's unexpressed wishes is typical of the closet male narcissist. The exhibitionist narcissist would see the woman's sexual response as part of his entitlements and would say openly that he expects her to devote herself to his needs. He would manipulate her in such a way that she would have to accept his entitlement or he would leave her. Both the male and female narcissist lack the most fundamental knowledge or instincts about how to go about realistically establishing and nurturing a relationship; and not only are these ideas and skills foreign, they are threatening.

Two narcissists who marry or continue an ongoing relationship always run into trouble. They begin by mirroring each other and enjoying the mutual narcissistic glow they provide for each other, but this cannot be maintained indefinitely. When one or both fail and disappointment sets in, they are faced with the dilemma of separating or tolerating a situation that frustrates their narcissistic needs. Judy, a narcissistic woman in her 40s with a five-year-old daughter, is a very successful department manager for a communications company. Her narcissistic husband is basically angry and devaluing and withholds affection from her. In addition, he will not provide her with money (he manages their combined incomes) nor help with domestic responsibilities. Despite the fact that she comes to treatment and complains about what goes on in their marriage, she tolerates it. The bottom line for her is that she prefers to blame her misery and distress on him, than to see her own part in the problem.

Ralph, in his late 50s, has had many acting-out relationships with women and for years preferred one-night stands or prostitutes to committing himself to any one woman. Finally he found the "perfect woman" and married her. She, too, was narcissistic. When she decided to have a career, she became less available to tend to his needs. He became furious, accused her of gross inadequacies, and they divorced. He returned to his pattern of one-night stands, which he then found unsatisfying as his loneliness and isolation increased.

Bill, a 27-year-old man with a schizoid disorder, in his last year of graduate school, felt increasingly paralyzed when faced with having to make important decisions about his future which included leaving home and finding women to date. Previously, relationships of all kinds had been difficult for him to initiate and keep going. He had always been a loner and unhappy because of it. He had never verbalized these feelings to anyone else in his life. Rather, he often felt that people were making fun of him and humiliating him. The prototype of these feelings was a memory of lying in his room at night when he was nine or ten and imagining that a toy clown in his room was sticking his tongue out at him. Powerlessness in his relationships was woven into these feelings of ridicule and humiliation.

He traced feelings of powerlessness back to his mother, from whom "all power and efficiency flowed to me like through a huge umbilical cord." He felt that without her he could not function successfully. A further "condition" of their relationship was that he be what she wanted him to be, which meant "asexual." The visual symbol for these feelings about his mother was the fact that the only photo of him that she kept at home was a portrait of him at age five sitting on her lap which reminded him of a puppet sitting on a ventriloquist's knee.

Bill was caught in a phase of life that always exacerbates the typical schizoid dilemma: the need to make career decisions and the wish to risk getting closer to another person on an emotional level. He stated repeatedly that he was in constant fear of being controlled by his mother and forced to pursue a job that he would not want. Even to discuss various options with her or to answer her questions would mean that his ideas were no longer "his own"—they would become hers, and he would have to reject them. On the other hand, moving away from her, physically and emotionally, would leave him feeling "like a stranger in a foreign land, an alien, totally losing contact and being cast out into endless, empty space—a real life man-in-the-moon." Once Bill was consciously aware of the dilemma, he began to understand the need to evolve a better compromise. He had to—and wanted to—take up a new position between enslavement and alienation, one that left him closer to others, yet not too close.

He was finally able to make decisions about his future and to act on them, but he was able to do so only by the extreme defense of refusing to discuss any of his future plans with his mother. He was able to manage the resulting anxiety and "fear of exile" by discussing these feelings with me and by slowly building a network of social contacts. For a long time these were in highly structured group settings, where he could more easily adjust the distance he could tolerate between himself and others.

He had been in treatment for two years when he got a job in another state. He decided he was ready for the move. One year later he called me to report that things were going well at work and with his colleagues. He had terminated all contact with his parents, which he felt was necessary, and had been able to pursue his own interests which included a marginally successful social life with women. He doubted, however, that he would ever marry since he "enjoyed his independence too much."

Another schizoid patient was Lillian, 32, single, who complained of chronic and increasing loneliness and feelings of futility. She was successful in her career, although she had made several job changes, each one bringing her into less contact with people but also increasing her economic independence. Control, fear, and fantasy were the central themes of her life. Control was the overriding concern, as she felt that her life had been a continual struggle to escape from the sadistic, intrusive, and domineering influences of her family. She saw her family relationships as a battle of wills. She felt that if she were to try to be close to her parents she would have to totally give up her "self" and literally become their live-in slave. Lillian feared her inability to maintain a separate and individuated life. She would despair and attack herself with thoughts that she was worthless, hopeless, too damaged, and so forth to ever be able to have her own life and her own relationships.

Typical ways she would express this were: "I have difficulty relating to people. . . . I am limited because it's always been hard to share myself with others. . . . If I depend on you, that implies control. . . . If you are important to me and you know it, it's like giving in to you. . . . When I'm relating to people there is a gap between what I'm saying and feeling, or not feeling, I'm just talking; it's not part of me. . . . I need a lot of approval, but I don't feel worthy of getting it because I don't accept myself."

In order to deal with her fear of enslavement and alienation, Lillian had developed over a lifetime a rich, internal world, a fantasy life that she could control and which she did not have to fear. She recalled that as a young child of four or five, she would most enjoy playing alone with her many dolls. Also, by that age she could read very well and began a lifelong habit of creating close and tiny places for herself, such as in a closet or under a desk, where she curled up for hours to read. She would evolve elaborate fantasies of being a "superwoman"—powerful and perfect. All her fantasies served either to provide her with an escape from painful self-perceptions or from threatening interaction with others.

Her core self-image was that of being retarded and defective. She felt worthless, of no use to herself or anyone. The best she could strive for was to be competent and self-sufficient and, therefore, not a burden (and hence inevitably a slave) to anyone. As she became aware of the defensive purpose of her fantasies, she would explain: "I don't know if I use day dreaming whenever I don't want to relate to people or vice versa. . . . I've kind of decided that my fantasies and day dreaming are a major part of my problem. . . . I use fantasies to escape being with people—to be alone—it's less painful, more exciting, more fulfilling. . . . I think my feelings toward you are basically representative of what the problem is. There are two parts to it—one is I need and fear your approval; secondly, I sexualize what is not sexual."

In fact, Lillian had only acted out once on her sexual wishes and fantasies in a brief relationship with a therapist she had seen earlier in her life. For the rest of the time, she had maintained complicated and predominantly sado-masochistic fantasies in which she was the master and men were the slaves. She used these sado-masochistic fantasies to replace more primitive romantic fantasies whenever she felt especially disappointed, rejected, frustrated, or futile.

All three personality disorders—borderline, narcissist, and schizoid—produce distorted intrapsychic images of the other partner in a relationship. The borderline and narcissist manage to maintain an effective link with that image. The schizoid, however, is compelled to maintain a rigid defense by distancing from the other to such an extent that the intrapsychic link is disrupted and the patient substitutes autistic reveries about the relationship which become a surrogate for any attempt to establish a real relationship in actual life. The schizoid's feelings of vulnerability should he or she allow an attachment to take place are so great that continued isolation in reverie is necessary as a defense.

Because the stakes are so high and the feelings run so deep, anxiety about intimacy is almost universal. The early period of a relationship places one's self on the line where it is vulnerable to rejection. We tend to handle the resultant anxiety by minor clinging and/or distancing defenses in the early experimental stage of a relationship. As the experiment succeeds and the relationship solidifies, the anxiety subsides. Although these anxieties are similar to those in the borderline patients we have looked at, the emotional pendulum in normal individuals does not swing as wide, and anxiety is relieved by the successful interaction between the two people.

Even with reasonably successful development through childhood and adolescence, it is not easy to reach adulthood fully prepared to establish an intimate relationship based on sincere interest in the other person—and make it work. And yet if we keep our partners' welfare paramount and support and encourage them in the activities and desires that spring from the real self, we will be truly loving them by acknowledging their deepest needs and wishes. To whatever extent we still carry the anxieties about intimacy (even though we are not borderline or narcissistic) we can, with awareness and effort, limit their influence on our behavior. For example a person who becomes aware that his possessiveness is a protection against anxiety about rejection can limit those actions that are impelled by the possessiveness by seeking assurance from the other. In ways like this we can strive to curtail their effects so that they do not harm our loved ones and destroy our relationships. When anxieties become so intense that they, or the defensive strategies deployed to defend against them, threaten to prevent or destroy relationships with others, psychotherapy can provide the insight needed to change underlying borderline, narcissistic, or schizoid patterns.

8

PSYCHOTHERAPY WITH THE BORDERLINE

FOR years the patient with a deflated false self was considered incurable. The borderline personality disorder, which the Freudian schools labeled a "narcissistic neurosis," was unable to respond to classical Freudian analysis because the borderline patient was not able initially to form a tranference relationship with the therapist, a prerequisite for successful Freudian therapy. Despite the projections that the patient transfers onto the therapist from his own background, he must also be able to see the therapist as she is—a separate, complete individual with both positive and negative qualities. In this setting, the therapist uses free association and interpretation to bring the patient's unconscious conflict between the id and superego into consciousness, where the patient's ego can then redistribute the emotional forces that were the source of his problems. The powerful feelings that were buried in the unconscious and caused symptoms gain access to consciousness and to the functions of the ego, where they are partially discharged and partially redirected into more adaptive channels. A prerequisite for success in this approach is the "therapeutic alliance," an explicitly conscious understanding that the patient and therapist are working together to help the patient achieve mature insight into the nature of his problems and the means to alleviate them.

At the beginning of psychotherapy the capacity to form a therapeutic alliance is minimal in the borderline patient because he lacks a mature ego with its fully developed capacities. Because of the ego's arrest in the pre-oedipal stage, the borderline has limited capacities to tolerate anxiety and frustration, to accept certain reality limitations, to distinguish between fantasy and reality, as well as to differentiate the past from the present, all of which are necessary for classical Freudian analysis. He has little basic trust and does not relate to the therapist as a real, whole human being with positive and negative attributes. Furthermore, the borderline's problem does not arise from a conflict between the id and superego but rather from the developmental arrest of the ego and from defenses constructed against the abandonment depression that ensues when the real self emerges. Establishing the therapeutic alliance, therefore, becomes a goal of psychotherapy for the borderline rather than a prerequisite; and it is a difficult goal at that, since the patient's inclination is to retreat from such an alliance when faced with the separation-individuation stresses that arise in treatment sessions.

Unlike the transference of classical psychoanalysis, the borderline transference is not transference per se but "transference acting out," in which the patient projects onto the therapist feelings towards parental figures from his past without any awareness of their true origins and also without any perception of the independent existence of the therapist in reality. Instead the patient sees the therapist as literally being that projection. This allows the patient to replay earlier scenarios in the present without feeling or remembering their links with the past. He alternately activates and projects upon the therapist each of the split representations of the self and the mother or other significant figure from his childhood. During sessions in which the patient projects the withdrawing image upon the therapist, he perceives therapy as necessarily leading to feelings of abandonment and will deny the benefit of therapy and continue to act out the withdrawing image or activate the rewarding image as a defense. When the patient projects the rewarding image with its reunion fantasy upon the therapist, the patient "feels good" but falls under the sway of the pathologic false self, concerned with immediate pleasure rather than long-term recovery, and reverts to regressive behavior whose self-destructiveness is denied.

Both projections are forms of transference acting out in which the therapist is not treated as a separate person upon whom the patient displaces infantile feelings for the purpose of understanding them and working them out but as the actual maternal figure on whom the patient can engage in a kind of instant replay of the abandonment scenarios imprinted in childhood. Without realizing it, the patient drags the past into the present and projects it upon the therapist. The therapist's task is to help the patient convert the transference acting out into a real transference and therapeutic alliance by skillfully executed confrontation. "Confrontation" is used not in the sense of aggressively opposing, as characterizes the relationship of the United States with the Soviet Union, but rather in the sense of bringing to the patient's attention empathically but firmly the denied, maladaptive, self-destructive aspect of his defenses.

The patient begins therapy feeling (again without being aware of it) that the behavior motivated by his split perception of reality and the pathologic false self is ultimately good for him because it has been his usual method, tested over many years, of avoiding the abandonment depression, which is to say, it has been his method of not feeling bad. He feels good, in the sense of an inner equilibrium, unaware of the damage being done to him by the denial of his self-destructive behavior and distorted views of reality. The initial objective of the therapist is to confront the patient with this destructiveness. Insofar as this encourages the patient to control his behavior, for example, to stop drinking or avoiding situations that call for self-activation, the therapist is then perceived as the withdrawing, disapproving maternal image. This perception causes the patient to resist controlling his behavior and to revert to the false self-compliance and submissiveness that will activate the rewarding responses from the therapist, since that is the patient's only strategy for preventing the ensuing abandonment depression. As this interaction progresses, a circular process results consisting of resistance, confrontation, working through of the feelings of abandonment, further resistance, and further confrontation, which leads to further working-through. This circular pattern may continue for several years of treatment.

Borderline patients are extremely sensitive to the unconscious rewarding and withdrawing responses of others, which enables a skillful therapist, who can maintain control over her responses, to elicit this circular working-through process. Eventually an alliance develops between the therapist's healthy ego and the patient's embattled reality ego, an alliance formed when the patient internalizes the therapist as a positive figure whose constructive attitudes, once they become internalized as an image in the patient's intra-psychic structure, battle against the patient's pathological pleasure ego for control of the patient's motivations and actions.

At the beginning of therapy, the patient will resist allying his emotions with the therapist because it means giving up his usual method of avoiding painful feelings of separation anxiety and abandonment depression. At this point he is inclined to rely upon the familiar strategy, which he thinks works, rather than one still unknown and untested. But the more he invests in the therapist, the more he will give up these old defenses and turn to therapy to work through these feelings of abandonment. First, however, he must "test" the therapist with his habitual self-destructive strate-gies to answer two vital questions: Is the therapist competent? Can he trust her? Thus the first phase of therapy is the testing phase.

It is necessary for the therapist to patiently and consistently con-front the patient with the genuine destructiveness of his behavior and of his distorted perception that a real therapeutic alliance or involvement in therapy is equivalent to the painful state of being engulfed or abandoned, which up until now has been the patient's experience when activating the real self. At the same time, the therapist must demonstrate by actual dealings with the patient the necessity and value of trusting the therapeutic relationship. A host of therapeutic attitudes and actions contribute to achieving this objective: the therapist's thoughtful concern for the patient's wel-fare, the accuracy of her confrontations, her reliability, her refusal to exploit the patient or to permit the patient to manipulate her. Only when the therapeutic alliance is established will the patient be willing to give up his lifelong dependence on the false self's ploys for emotional security. This is a momentous turning point in the therapy for the borderline personality disorder, as it means the transference acting out is being converted into a therapeutic alli-ance and transference and the patient is passing into the second or "working-through" phase of therapy, where it now becomes possible to work through, attenuate, and overcome the depression. This turning point is signaled clinically by the following develop-ments: (1) Patients give their now-recognized false selves a disparag-ing nickname, such as "creep," "queer," "baby," "devil." (2) Envi-ronmental conflicts subside and depression occupies the center of the therapeutic stage, bringing with it memories, fantasies, and dreams.

The depression fuels the recall of memories, which return like a motion picture projector run in reverse; that is, the most recent separation stress comes first followed by successively earlier ones until the patient reaches the "bottom" of the depression where he feels that mother's unavailability occurred *because* his real self wanted to emerge. When this level is worked through, most of the depression weighing down the real self has been discharged, and a dramatic change occurs—the real self starts to flower. The patient develops new thoughts and ideas as he continues to work through the remaining depression. He now enters the last or separation stage.

At this crucial juncture in treatment, when the abandonment depression has been attenuated and the difficulties with real self-activation emerge, patients often explore new interests and activities, some of which have lain dormant over the years. These might include a hobby, a new career, an athletic activity, or some line of reading and studying that had always appealed to the patient but which he could never muster the self-activation and individuation necessary to pursue. During this stage, he must work through, in the transference, his expectation that the therapist will function as the mother the patient had always wished for to provide approval or encouragement.

Based on Mahler's notion of the mother's role in "refueling" the infant as it attempts self-activation and self-expression, the therapist begins a strategy of "communicative matching" in which she shares with the patient whatever knowledge or interest she has with the subject or activity and incorporates these discussions as integral aspects of the therapy sessions. In effect, the therapist sharing the interest provides the support and encouragement that was denied the patient in the past whenever he attempted to engage in activities and interests expressive of his real self.

Because of the developmental arrest, part of the patient's personality has been left in the closet, locked away, as it were. He has never learned even the very basics about how to pursue successfully what he is really interested in whether this be a career, hobby, or relationship. The therapist deals with this immaturity by providing a learning experience through communicative matching responses which also often serve as confrontations. He offers the patient through his confrontations what may seem as obvious and commonsensical information to the average mature adult who has learned it from experience and incorporated it into her psyche. However, these responses are not obvious to the patient.

Such "lessons in life" can be divided into those pertaining to work and those pertaining to relationships. Work considerations include: the more work fits what you want, the better you will be at it; experiments are necessary to find out what you want; successful work requires initiative, self-assertion, repetitive effort, honing and refining of skills, picking up after failures, learning from mistakes, and trying again. In relationships, the patient must learn that: it takes time and experimentation to establish a good relationship; the other person's personality must be tested to see how naturally the two people will fit together; the degree of emotional involvement should be monitored and governed by what is learned in these experiments; the closer the relationship, the more caution, time, and experimentation is needed; one has to mourn the end of one close relationship before being able to undertake another.

Patients experience these responses from the therapist as an acknowledgment and refueling of their real selves, which encourages them to pursue the new interests with persistence, continuity, and equally important, a new sense of spontaneity, entitlement, and vigor. The real self gradually overcomes the difficulties and achieves its true capacities. Slowly the person learns to identify his real individuative wishes and articulate them in his daily life; he learns mastery and coping skills and builds self-esteem so as to continue his search for a real self. Throughout, the therapist must refrain from acting like a cheerleader for the real self. He cannot direct, force, seduce, or intimidate the real self into activation; he can only respond to the patient's initiative. If it is going to happen, the patient must make it happen on his own. The therapist can only create the conditions that make the patient's self-activation possible.

In the course of therapy, the patient will again experience the abandonment depression brought on by these new efforts at self-expression. He will vacillate between enthusiasm for the new interest and the fears that come from attempts to activate the real self. There will be peaks and troughs in which the therapist must utilize communicative matching only when the patient is expressing the real self and refrain from it when the patient goes back to the defensive behavior of the false self. Eventually, the patient will internalize the communicative matching, similar to the way the healthy adult internalized the mother's ego functioning as a child. Of course, the therapist is not "parenting" because she is not the patient's mother; she is not sharing personal emotions but is meeting the patient's therapeutic needs. Through successful treatment, the patient will work through the transference fantasy that the therapist is the mother the patient always wished for and realize clearly that the therapist is not a substitute parent.

There are three types of therapy beneficial for the borderline patient: shorter-term, intensive analytic psychotherapy, and counseling. (The word *shorter* is used to distinguish this therapy from "short-term" therapy, which usually lasts a matter of weeks.)

Shorter-term therapy, which is the most common form of therapy, consists of once or twice a week sessions that usually last anywhere from 6 to 18 months. The goal of shorter-term therapy is not to work through the abandonment depression but to repair the defects in ego functioning and improve self-activation. The ego defects and the primitive defenses all interfere with reality perception. In this sense, the ego of the borderline is perforated with holes. The therapist's task is to plug the holes and thus provide the patient with a more complete and solid perception of reality. The therapist's confrontive remarks about how the patient perceives and handles real life situations provide an alternative view of reality that the patient eventually internalizes. Shorter-term therapy often results in dramatic improvement in the way patients function in daily life and conduct their relationships, and the patient usually wants to terminate therapy when the immediate problems that brought him into therapy clear up.

The patient's self-image and self-assertion improve, along with her perception of reality, but the impaired real self is not fully overcome and the abandonment depression is still present. However, the patient can now meet it with a new sense of vigor, optimism, and control. Instead of resorting to her old self-destructive defenses, the patient now calls on her capacity for self-assertion to contain the depression. Each patient finds her own unique style. For example, a patient who was anorexic or bulimic turns to jog-

ging to deal with periods of stress, or a patient who had been alco-
holic finds that playing a musical instrument helps to contain feelings during stressful times. Should a severe separation stress occur,
a patient may have to return for additional treatment.

Intensive analytic psychotherapy, a longer-term treatment with
sessions at least three times a week for three to five years or longer,
has as its primary goal to remove the defenses against the abandonment depression and to reactivate the real self in order to bring
on the abandonment depression in full force for the purpose of
working it through in the close therapeutic relationship. The pre-
liminary objective is to create the therapeutic alliance and transference and remove the pathologic defenses that prevent the depression. This is followed by interpretation of the past through
memories, dreams, and fantasies. As the patient goes back deeper
and deeper, the abandonment depression occurs, with all six psychic horsemen. The patient realizes in this final working through,
however, that it was not the separation stresses that caused problems over the years but the unavailability of maternal support at
his initial efforts to separate and express his real self.

In both shorter-term and intensive analytic therapy, the therapist establishes a therapeutic alliance and facilitates the emergence
of the patient's real self through the use of confrontation as illustrated in the following two cases.

Fred, a 19-year-old college student, dropped out of school because of a severe abandonment depression. "Life has no meaning
for me. I can't study or even think," he announced on beginning
shorter-term therapy.

The third of three children, Fred recalled his mother and father
never being home or doing anything together. He obeyed his
mother, who was domineering, never wrong, never able to admit
faults or accept criticism. Father was a lawyer who worked all the
time and was rarely home. Although "kind," he tended to avoid
trouble or conflict with the mother, and his support for Fred (when
Fred would submit to the mother's demands) was never expressed
with any genuine feeling.

In therapy Fred projected the rewarding parental image (based
not on the reality of how the father acted but on the father's empty
verbalizations) onto his father and the disapproving, withdrawing

image onto me. Fred acted out by massive passivity in the sessions, expecting that I would take over for him and suggest topics, direct him, and give advice. He was often stonily silent, reenacting the passive role he played at home, where he would not confront the mother in order to receive the father's love and support. He felt he had earned that support by his behavior. When I didn't take over and direct him but instead confronted him with his passivity, he would grow angry and accuse me of "not helping." He acted out his anger by missing or being late for sessions, by blocking, silence, and accusing me of not being interested in him, of being rigid, having a monotonous voice, or being bored. Our financial arrangements led to his criticizing doctors in general for being greedy and interested only in money. If my attention lagged or I accepted a phone call or was late, he would burst out in rage.

As the intensity of this projection mounted, Fred would attempt to get revenge on his father for his failure by acting out against me and the therapy. I emphasized for him the *reality* of the arrangements necessary to provide a framework for therapy. I couldn't always be available, regular hours had to be kept, I had to charge a fee to make a living but this fact did not preclude my genuine interest in his problems. Whenever I pointed out the reality of these considerations for him, I met deep silence. Fred was intensively acting out in the transference with me his profound disappointment and rage at the father for failing to fulfill his side of the unconscious contract beneath which lay the abandonment by the mother. There was little room for a therapeutic alliance.

Slowly, gradually over the course of the first ten months of therapy two times a week, my refusal either to reinforce his wishes to be taken care of or to reject him because of his projected anger, and my continual, firm reinforcement of the limits of reality began to establish a beachhead of a therapeutic alliance. He stopped criticizing and attacking me, began to see me as a therapist, not his projection, and to start exploring and investigating the sources in his past of the very angry feelings he had previously projected onto me. His avoidance and passivity abated, and he became self-assertive enough to return to school.

Penny also came for therapy twice a week. In the early sessions she dramatically elaborated on her panic, her symptoms, her fear of physical expression, and her inability to manage. I confronted her helplessness by saying, "Why do you feel so helpless?" This led her immediately to describe her feelings:

"I don't think I can manage it myself. My mother was my worst enemy. When I was lonesome in college and called home, she encouraged it. I was totally taken care of, overindulged. It makes it hard for me to manage myself. I never did anything completely for myself before I moved to the city. In high school I had no responsibility. This is the first job that I have had with any responsibility. I feel that now I have to show initiative and set my own goals. My life has been so structured. I never had to do it before. I never had to spend time alone. I think other people should plan for me."

After a few confrontive sessions, the acute symptomatology subsided; Penny became depressed and began to intellectualize about the difficulties between herself and her mother. For example, she would say, "I dislike the idea of being responsible and taking care of myself. I don't think I can; it seems that I'll break down. I can't take the pressure. I'm an empty personality. I'd rather be an extension of someone else. I've always structured my life for someone else to do it for me. When I turn to my mother and she doesn't do it, I get furious at her, then I get depressed."

At the time, Penny had a boyfriend to whom she clung for relief of anxiety and for support. "I've never been rewarded for being an individual. I am afraid of being depressed and alone. I never developed anything in myself on my own. I did well in college and had lots of interests, but they were all for everybody's approval." I confronted this defense by asking her why she had so much difficulty managing on her own.

The next level of confrontation dealt with the lack of continuity between sessions caused by Penny's avoiding thinking about them because they made her "feel bad." She reported after one session feeling "bad and empty, like I'm losing something, like I have to be on my own and independent, and then I get anxious and—forget about it."

I confronted her about her appeals to her mother for reassurance which encouraged her to stop calling her mother and to manage the feelings herself. Throughout these first three or four months of treatment, Penny described her symptoms and interpreted her situation intellectually but showed little genuine affect. She would become overwhelmed with guilt, depression, and anger when she spoke about her parents and would block out her thoughts in order to deal with the guilt. When I confronted her blocking, she articulated the borderline dilemma by saying, "I don't want to admit I'm competent or in control. I have to pretend I'm helpless. If I'm competent, I will be cutting mother off, or she will cut me off. I wouldn't need her anymore. She'd have no duty to perform."

As Penny continued to delve deeper into the conflict with her mother, it was necessary to confront her denial of feelings in general, as well as her denial of anger and guilt at the mother. At one point, when she turned down her mother's request to spend some time with her, she said, "Mother uses me as a tool for herself. She put in my head the one thing I can't do is separate and that I would be punished for it. She was the original power. I was empty."

Following this, she had a nightmare that she was losing her mind and going crazy; she would not be able to speak or move her feet to walk. Throughout this time she was clinging to her boyfriend, and it became necessary to challenge and confront the clinging. I questioned why she needed him to provide her internal security, pointing out some of the destructive aspects of this behavior to the relationship. Throughout the first year of treatment, she attempted to deal with our sessions by intellectualization, denial, avoidance of individuation, blocking, and suppressing of affect, acting out in the transference, and clinging with the boyfriend. The confrontation of all these defenses gradually brought about a therapeutic alliance and transference.

The establishing of the therapeutic alliance changes transference acting out to transference. For example, in the case of Fred, before the alliance was established he was angry and attacked me for not being interested in him or taking over the sessions for him. When the therapeutic alliance was formed and he could see me realistically as his therapist, it became clear to him that those feelings of disappointment and anger in the sessions were not due to me. Once this was established, he could begin to explore the sources of those feelings in his past. Similarly, with Penny when she felt the need to be cared for in early sessions she would ask me to give her advice. Later on when the therapeutic alliance was established, she realized that these feelings of needing to be cared for in the sessions had nothing to do with me but were an expression of her difficulty in not being able to manage herself and so turning the job over to her mother or a mother substitute. Intensive psychoanalytic psychotherapy differs from shorter-term therapy in that the goal is more complex: resolving the abandonment depression, freeing the impaired real self to emerge and assume its capacities and complete his development through the oedipal stage and beyond. As a consequence, the patient must be seen more often and for a longer period of time. In the first phase of therapy, the therapist utilizes confrontation to establish a therapeutic alliance, as in shorter-term therapy. But then a marked difference occurs. Rather than just helping the patient to face and express the depression, the therapist embarks on a systematic, in-depth, analytic exploration of the abandonment depression through the patient's memories, dreams, fantasies, and transference. As the patient works through the depression, the real self emerges, and the patient develops to the stage where he can view others and himself as whole objects, thus overcoming splitting and the vulnerability to separation stress.

The dynamics of intensive analytic psychotherapy for the borderline patient are clearly seen in the case of Lynn, a 30-year-old librarian and free-lance writer who first came to see me for the problems she was having with her husband. Lynn was born in a large city on the East Coast to a mother whom she viewed as cold and unfeeling. She was subtly terrorized by the mother's threat of abandonment: if Lynn did not obey, her mother would withdraw. Over the years the mother coerced her daughter into becoming a writer, something she herself had wanted but never accomplished. Lynn complied, studied hard, and did well throughout her years of schooling. Lynn's father was an irresponsible Don Juan who attempted suicide when she was 26. Her younger brother, four years her junior, had been chronically ill with asthma since age three. The brother had been clearly the mother's favorite.

Lynn had suffered three major abandonment depressions: the first at age eight when she went to summer camp ("the most miserable summer of my life"); the second when she left home for graduate school (she eventually transferred to a university closer to home and began an affair with one of her professors); the third when her mother divorced her father after his suicide attempt, and

Lynn left home to take a job as an assistant librarian in a college in eastern Tennessee (where she was depressed, lonely, and frightened, and married in order "not to feel alone").

Lynn's husband was the focus of the first year of therapy. Lynn described him as cold, insensitive, stingy, selfish, and depriving—the same description she gave of her mother. He objected to her working but demanded that she pay more than her share of the family expenses. They had one daughter, Margaret, age five-and-a-half. Lynn could not respond to her husband sexually, although she was able to reach orgasm with her lover, a fellow librarian. She functioned compulsively well at her job but found little satisfaction there. Lynn reported that her chief sources of satisfaction were her daughter and the affair with her colleague.

During the first year of treatment, as a result of my confrontations of her allowing her husband to use her, Lynn faced up to his abusive, devaluing ways. As she came to realize that he rarely supported her and continually attacked and fought her whenever she brought this up, she began to trust my confrontations of the reality of her marriage, and the therapeutic alliance, necessary for further progress, was established. She decided on a divorce.

At this point, her clinging to her daughter Margaret increased, and I began confronting Lynn with its destructiveness to Margaret's welfare. I asked her how and when this need to cling began. She reported, "When Margaret was born I felt like a woman fulfilled. I loved being up with her at night, even though I was tired. I resented others' efforts to care for her. I loved her needing me; I thrived on it. Obviously I was satisfying myself as much as her." When I asked Lynn how she felt when Margaret learned to walk, she replied, "I hated it. I remembered how she crawled out of her crib. I felt she had 'moved on.' I was not happy about her advancing out of babyhood. I wanted her infancy to last forever." Lynn remembered that when Margaret first started school she would often have to stay home in the morning because she didn't feel well. Lynn would occasionally go with her to school. "When she walks out of the apartment I'm never sure she will return. I try to go with her every chance I get. I want her to know that I love her so that she'll love me back. I was determined not to treat her as my mother had me."

This last comment is typical of borderline patients with children. Initially, they enter therapy convinced that they are not going to treat their own children as they had been treated by their parents, and yet, without realizing it, they are engaged in equally destructive behavior that prevents their children's real selves from emerging. As treatment progresses, they begin to see the truth of this, and their initial desire to be better mothers or fathers than their own had been is a great motivation for healing their lives.

When Margaret began day camp, she put up a fuss each day, clearly testing her mother to see if she would keep her at home. At first Lynn's inclination was to give in to her daughter, since her apparent reluctance to go to camp played right into Lynn's need to cling. That was its purpose. The daughter needed the mother's permission to go. I confronted Lynn on this, pointing out that keeping Margaret home was destructive since it showed no confidence in Margaret's capacity to manage herself. I said, "Margaret must feel that she can't grow up without losing your support." Lynn then encouraged her daughter to go to camp. Later when Lynn checked with the camp officials, she found that Margaret was actually having a great time each day in spite of the morning complaints at home about having to go. Consequently, Lynn insisted that Margaret continue.

At one point, Lynn admitted, "I can't see our relationship through her eyes." This theme is the heart of the problem, since the borderline is too entrapped by the demands of the false self to prevent abandonment feelings to try to view relationships through the eyes of another separate person. All of Lynn's psychic energies were aimed at preserving her clinging relationship with Margaret rather than providing what was best for her daughter and for her real self.

Lynn reminisced that when Margaret left for camp, she herself felt as she had when she went to camp at age eight. As she gave up the clinging and let go of Margaret, the child flourished, and Lynn's depression deepened. In other words, she had overcome the defense. Further memories of being abandoned in graduate school surfaced, and Lynn recalled how she was unable to work, flunked exams, and had fantasies of starving herself to death in order to make her mother worry. She was saved from all of this, she remembered, only by beginning an affair with one of her teachers. These two themes dominated the content of Lynn's sessions over the next summer months: Margaret's flourishing at day camp and Lynn's reliving in psychotherapy the period of abandonment at age 21 when she went away to graduate school.

In the fall when Margaret resumed school, Lynn was in better control of her impulses to cling. "For the first time I can't wait for Margaret to start school," she reported. "I'm realizing that having Margaret around is not helping anymore, maybe because I'm letting go. I'm beginning to see that she will grow up and have interests of her own." But when Margaret caught a severe cold, the old worries returned. Lynn confessed, "When Margaret coughs I'm afraid she will die! As she grows up, I feel I'm losing my last support. I think I'm digging my own grave."

But Lynn continued to make progress, slowly releasing her grip on Margaret's life. When her daughter's birthday rolled around, she reflected on the changes over the last year. "Last year on Margaret's birthday I felt like commiting suicide. This year I had a marvelous time. Margaret decorated for her party and was proud to not really need my help. I was proud, too, that I could accept that fact."

As Lynn's clinging behavior lessened two predictable trends began: Margaret's development mushroomed and, without her usual defense of clinging, Lynn's abandonment feelings intensified. To compensate for this, she began to cling more to me in the transference and to a very self-centered man whom she was dating. Accompanying these developments were two new themes in therapy sessions: Lynn's anger and anxiety about being on her own and her fear of being engulfed or abandoned if she should allow a real close relationship with a man to develop.

"I'm furious at you," she said to me, "because I have to be on my own without any advice." She did, however, start to work on a book dealing with women poets that she had been considering for some time. As a demonstration of support (communicative matching), I shared her enthusiasm for the project and my own throughts about the subject.

When Lynn contemplated going to Europe on her own, she asked, "Why is this so painful? When does it get easier? I'm afraid of being over there with nothing to do." These feelings are typical for the borderline patient; being without a systematic work schedule can produce separation anxiety because constantly having to make choices requires too much self-activation and self-expression. But Lynn did go to Europe by herself and came home feeling very pleased. "I was proud, pleased—and scared to death! But I did it!"

Soon after her return, the man she had been dating proposed marriage. The proposal made her a nervous wreck, and she projected her guilt onto Margaret. "I feel guilty about telling Margaret, but it is really my mother I felt most guilty toward about marriage. She is lethal. When she hears about my marriage, she'll do something awful." As it turned out, the man she intended to marry was unable to follow through on his proposal due to his own difficulties with intimacy and commitment. The breakup led to our discussing in depth Lynn's acting out defense of picking inappropriate men with whom a close relationship was not possible.

"Because of my mother's lack of confidence in me, I have never expected a man to love me, and I fulfill this by the kind of men I choose. I'd rather be taken to dinner at the Plaza than have a real relationship with a man. My father was charming, but I could never rely on him. I've always been attracted to that type of man, and I never expect more than words and empty promises." I pointed out to her that because she picked men who were unable to love, she was in fact settling for arrangements rather than relationships, for dates rather than genuine intimacy, and she was therefore caught in a destructive self-fulfilling prophecy.

This led to a dream in which Lynn saw herself being mugged and assaulted by her ex-husband and her last boyfriend. In her free association she realized, "I was enjoying the misery of those two relationships. I expected to be rejected and hurt and picked men who would hurt me." I interpreted this for her to mean that she was an "injustice collector" in that she had acted out her mother's prophecy of being rejected by picking men who would reject her. This was her way of taking revenge on her mother instead of being able to accept the fact that her mother did not support her emerging real self. Lynn admitted, "I would murder her in cold blood if I knew for sure that I could get away with it."

In a subsequent session Lynn talked about her projection of the mother image onto men. "I don't feel good about a man unless he finds me inadequate but overlooks it and is nice to me. I feel the same way about you." In other words, this is the way Lynn defended herself against the hopelessness of her wish for unconditional love from her mother. She acted out her predicament with men. I stressed the fact that she would just have to give up the wish for reunion with her mother and face the hopelessness of that past situation in order to have a real relationship with a man in the present.

These considerations led to a dream in which Lynn, lost in the subway, called her mother and grew angry when she wouldn't come. I pointed out how this dream reflected her "lifelong search for a mother." Lynn recalled how she had hoped that her mother-in-law would become her mother, but I suggested to her that that was a variation on the Cinderella solution in which the mother-in-law would become the good mother to replace the real mother who was evil. Lynn replied, "I can't stand to face the fact that she just didn't care. If I accept that, I feel no one will care." But I explained to her that the opposite was more likely to be true; namely, not until she faced the hopelessness about her mother would she stop pursuing men to fulfill the fantasy of the mother loving her and perhaps find one who could truly care.

This led to a dream that recalled a real life event from her childhood: going out on her first date and seeing her mother scrubbing the floor on her return. I pointed out that the mother's message seemed to be: "You can't have a man and me." Lynn remembered how her mother attacked any boy she dated and made her feel bad before dates by talking about how ugly she looked. "At my PhD graduation mother took a picture of my head from the rear and had it framed."

Then a significant dream occurred in which her mother died and the family was angry because Lynn didn't go to the funeral. "I fought with my brother over mother's clothes." With this dream the force of the mother image was beginning to weaken in Lynn's psychic life. She also expressed the fear that she would end up like her own mother, leading a miserable, desolate life. I pointed out the potential truth of this. Her mother persistently and stubbornly treated Lynn like an object for her own use and lost her. Her mother had been unable to invest emotionally in her own person as a separate self. Lynn could possibly be heading in the same direction. This confrontation led to more self-activation on Lynn's part. She began to do volunteer work at a hospital and began writing a second book of short biographies about women novelists.

After several years of working through her abandonment depression and supporting her emerging self, she was ready for a relationship, and fate stepped in with kindness and the promise of new hope—Robert. As she realized that she found Robert attractive and that he also liked her, Lynn reviewed her past relationship with men. "I'm afraid I'll wreck it with him like all the others. He's the nicest thing that ever happened to me. I feel like a bowl of whipped cream. I expect him to leave me. I don't deserve him."

Around this time she had a dream that an old woman on the subway asked her for a copy of *The Hobbit* and Lynn refused. She saw this as standing up to her mother and went on to say that she had only recently realized that in her fantasies her mother was always 35 and beautiful and resentful of Lynn's own beauty (remember Snow White). I pointed out the confusion in her feelings of wanting revenge against the real mother and her need to separate from the psychic image of her mother.

A few sessions later she announced that she was falling in love with Robert. "It's like drinking champagne all the time. I can't believe it will last. If I had met him before this treatment, I would have run away from him—too threatening." She announced excitedly that she was really enjoying being alone and pursuing her relationship with Robert. She also considered the fact that perhaps her mother didn't like her because she *was* okay, something her mother was not. I pointed out the truth of this, suggesting that because she had mourned the loss of the mother and separated herself, she was able to invest her own self-image with the positive feelings it deserved. Now freed from the emotional ties to her mother/daughter image, her fears of engulfment and abandonment subsided, allowing her to take a chance on a real intimate relationship with a man who seemed good for her.

She dreamed of being led down the street by an old crone of a woman. The street was filled with snakes. She had to jump over them to escape. Lynn's interpretation was, "I feel I've changed, that it's all slipping away from me—Margaret, mother, and you. I don't care about mother. I'm frightened, but underneath I'm sure of myself. It's painful to go on without her but not impossible. Not only have I survived her but I am more intact than I ever was. When I'm with Robert I'm happier than I've ever been in my life."

Later she had another dream about her mother in which the

mother came closer and closer, finally to announce, "Lord & Taylor is closed." Lynn laughed at her free association. "Eight or nine years ago I saw mother in Lord & Taylor, but she didn't see me. Shopping and clothes are a perfect metaphor for our relationship. Mother never approved of the clothes I bought, and I used to be caught between buying what mother liked or what she despised, neither of which *I* wanted. Clothes were a symbol of mother's onslaught. The day I saw her I just wanted to get out, and knew I was going to." I reminded Lynn that she used to say that she could spend all day shopping in Lord & Taylor with her mother, and I felt the dream suggested that she was putting an end to the wish for reunion with her at long last. Lord & Taylor was truly closed.

Eleven years later Lynn was living a meaningful and successful life at work and in a relationship. She had internalized the work of treatment and made it her own. The change in her psyche was deep, stable, and had endured. All the struggle and effort had been worth it.

Lynn's history illustrates how the developmental failure in childhood stunts the capacities for love and work and inevitably leads to an adult life that becomes a horrifying repetition of the emotional deprivations of childhood. Every effort to change the difficult and painful life situation produces only further failure and frustration. There is no easy way out. The borderline adult's metaphor for his childhood as a concentration camp becomes a prophecy for an entire life. The chains formed so early and bound so firmly prevent any effort to escape.

Psychotherapy can enter this dismal scene and slowly, tediously, sometimes tortuously, bring change. In Lynn's case, she divorced her husband, controlled the acting out of the wish for reunion with her mother on her daughter, and finally, she mourned the loss and thereby allowed her real self to emerge. With an emotional investment in her real-self image, fears of engulfment and/or abandonment diminished. Self-activation and self-expression began to flower and, with it, creativity at work. A true, loving, intimate relationship was possible. Lynn could now love and work.

Counseling is indicated for those patients who do not have sufficient ego strength to benefit from psychotherapy: if required to give up their defenses they would become psychotic. Counseling does not require the therapist to maintain therapeutic neutrality, so that a wide range of activities become possible, such as advice, suggestion, guidance, medication, and environmental manipulation. One caution is that if the patient does grow as a result of counseling, and his ego strengthens sufficiently to make him a candidate for psychotherapy, the counselor should refer him to someone else since her counseling activities have eliminated her therapeutic neutrality.

9

THE BORDERLINE SYNDROME IN ADOLESCENCE

THE crucible of adolescence makes its own imprint on the clinical picture of the deflated false self. The adolescent is still dependent on the family externally as well as internally while he or she struggles with the problems of emancipation, sexuality, and identity. These features create special difficulties: conflict with parents and severe acting out behavior due to the intensity of the internal emotional turmoil. I identified the borderline dynamic—activation of the self brings on depression, which, in turn, activates the defense against the depression—first in adolescents where the control of their destructive behavior revealed the underlying depression.

It is not easy to become a teenager in our complex society, considering the daunting tasks that need to be accomplished over the long years from puberty to adulthood. Unlike youth in less complex cultures who walked a clearly defined path toward adult status—a path marked by unchanging rites of passage and rituals of acceptance—modern young people must make the transition through a series of loosely defined milestones spread over many years. Although most teenagers meet and pass the external milestones in family life, school, and the world at large, not all of them manage a smooth passage across the intrapsychic milestones that complete the emergence of their real selves.

The challenges of adolescence are indeed formidable, especially learning to integrate sexuality into the self-image, which entails resolving the oedipal conflict, lain dormant since childhood. In addition, adolescents must emancipate themselves from their parents by leaving home, accepting work and social involvements outside the family, and defining their own values and goals apart from those of their parents. They need to come to terms with their own consciences, separating their values and standards of behavior from parental strictures. Once they have gained greater independence and autonomy and a comfortable sexual identity, they must then experiment with expressing these adult characteristics in the world beyond the family while still maintaining harmonious ties with parents and siblings.

Not many years ago it was thought that adolescence was by its very nature such a tumultuous, strife-ridden period that all teenagers would develop serious problems. The terms *teenager* and *problems* were almost synonymous. Parents and teachers routinely dug into the trenches for the long battle ahead. Teenagers who caused relatively little turmoil were considered rare, and their parents lucky. Common professional advice suggested that it was difficult, if not impossible, to discern whether a child going through adolescent turmoil was psychiatrically maladjusted or just a typical teenager.

My own studies exploded this myth by showing that those with severe symptoms of maladjustment were not healthy teenagers, soon to "get over it," but teenagers in need of psychiatric help.[1] Parallel studies of healthy adolescents indicated that they did not resemble adolescent patients.[2] Healthy adolescents embark upon the tasks of these years with a fairly well-consolidated autonomous self with access to all the capacities and functions needed. Therefore, despite the enormity of the struggle and the number of social and psychological tasks confronting them, healthy adolescents can emerge from the teenage years with a minimum of scars and symptoms, fully prepared for further development in young adulthood.

Adolescents with a deflated false self, however, enter their teenage years with enormous handicaps. They cannot rely upon an autonomous self and its capacities because the self has been arrested in the earlier stage of development and they are fully defended against the abandonment depression, which their impaired real selves are unable to face. Many borderline adolescents manage to go through chronological adolescence without overt borderline symptoms if their defenses remain intact and separation stresses are not too severe. But this always comes at a great cost to further self-development, with serious repercussions later in career, work, and relationships. Indeed, there are two crucial separation stresses that most adolescents cannot avoid: emancipation from their parents by consolidating their own standards and values and mastering the sex drive (which is also a drive away from the parents). In many borderline adolescents these two stresses alone are enough to trigger a clinical breakdown; but often they are accompanied by other traumatic events, such as the parents' divorce or the death of a parent. When a separation crisis brings an adolescent into therapy, the symptoms can be extremely broad and varied. They include some of society's most widespread and severest problems: juvenile delinquency, truancy, teenage alcoholism and drug addiction, sexual offenses, and the inability to tolerate discipline or responsibility at home or school.

Another more subtle group, not always recognized for the serious psychological problems that motivate them, are those teenagers who drop out of society to "find themselves" or establish their identity. While some teens do drop out or leave home for a period of time to engage in this task and return unharmed, many are borderline patients whose "search for identity" is a smoke screen to conceal their need to avoid commitment and responsibility because of the abandonment depression this would entail.

A third group consists of those teenagers who give up the struggle of resolving the abandonment depression altogether by throwing in with an authority figure who will relieve them of the task of taking responsibility for themselves and who provides them with an alternative authority and system of beliefs and values to guide their lives. Blinded by the exuberance of their new lifestyle, their initial impression is that they have "found themselves" or "arrived," but the relief they experience is merely a stopgap which impedes the development of their real selves. This type of teenager makes up a significant proportion of those who join religious communities, such as the Jesus Freaks and Hare Krishna, or join cults and communes based on one antiestablishment theme or another. It is not America's social values they reject as much as the need to establish and take responsibility for themselves.

A fourth group of adolescents may function better, but they pay a terrible emotional price: the phobic, the anorexic, and the many, many individuals who never come to a psychiatrist but spend their entire lives in a regressed style of living—continuing to live at home with parents, holding jobs far beneath their abilities or interests, avoiding the opposite sex, spinning out their lives by tending to complaints for which their doctors can find no physical cause: headaches, constipation, and the like. Of course, there are other causes for these symptoms, but many are borderline.

The human tragedy that faces both parents and children when a borderline adolescent does not receive treatment and must fend for herself in the struggle to grow up, with the depression it triggers, can be enormous. Years ago I saw a mother and father in consultation regarding their only son. The father had amassed great wealth; the mother was a successful artist. The son, a shy, inhibited boy, had great difficulty with self-activation, could not sustain any interests, and having no friends, led a lonely, isolated life. When he failed his senior year in high school, his parents sent him to a boarding school, which he left to join a religious cult. A year later the boy wrote his father a letter that made him fear that he had lost his son forever. It glowed with exuberance and satisfaction over his new life. The boy was overjoyed at being permitted to kiss the guru's toe. The parents were overwhelmed with guilt over what had befallen their son and depressed at the thought of facing their bleak future without him. They pleaded with me for ways to get him to come home. I could only woefully confirm their worst fears that it was probably too late and that pressuring him into returning would only alienate him further. Since this incident occurred long before the idea of "deprogramming" was developed, the only consolation I could offer them was that despite the negative aspects of the cult, he was at least leading a healthy and relatively disciplined life.

Failure to attack the fundamental causes of the adolescent's difficulties leaves the young person in a situation where the price exacted by the unresolved emotional conflict increases exponentially over time. The adolescent who has not separated from his mother cannot later face the challenges or tasks that life opens to him; that is, he cannot express himself in a chosen field of work, cannot love a mate, and when finally married, cannot be a nurturing parent. The passage of time presents these unfortunate individuals with inevitable life tasks and with truly a Hobson's choice: to avoid the challenge of growth, marriage, and parenthood with the consequent loneliness and suffering that this entails or to take on the challenge though emotionally ill equipped. Should they opt for the latter, they run the risk of witnessing their own unresolved problems manifested in their children.

Because their emotional conflicts are due to the failure of the real self to emerge and develop, their resolution requires confrontation of the false self and growth of the real self. Efforts merely to "patch up" the borderline adolescent result in the abandonment depression's continuing to smolder until it causes further breakdown or the defenses against it are transformed into pathologic character traits. What had been fluid becomes fixed. What had caused suffering, thereby producing motivation for change, becomes comfortable, reduces anxiety, and eventually becomes a barrier to treatment. Much of the individual's ability to derive emotional satisfaction by expressing his feelings in reality is lost in the unceasing efforts to maintain pathologic character traits. The more these traits are reinforced over time the more rigid they become making the individual less able to respond healthily to future stress. It is therefore essential that adolescents with borderline symptoms obtain effective psychotherapy as soon as these problems are identified.

Therapy for the borderline adolescent differs from that for adults in several significant ways, but the basic dynamic of the treatment process is similar, since both suffer from the same developmental arrest. On the one hand, the teenager is still unmolded and in a stage of development that supports flexibility and change, all of which can contribute to overcoming old patterns, not as firmly rooted as in adults. On the other hand, the early testing phase is much more difficult because the borderline's natural mistrust of others is compounded by the adolescent's mistrust of all adults. Furthermore, the adolescent is still dependent upon parents so it becomes necessary to engage the parents in therapy as well, even if the patient is hospitalized. The parents' participation is crucial because their teenager's problems are often reflections of a more involved family psychopathology, the teenager serving as a kind of lynchpin for the family's system of communication. When the cornerstone of their communication system is removed, parents may become anxious and take their son or daughter out of treatment.

The research that led to the discovery of the form of treatment for borderline patients began with the treatment of adolescents in an inpatient unit of a psychiatric hospital. One of my major discoveries at the time was the need to utilize the hospital as an auxiliary ego to control the adolescents' acting out, which is an almost uncontrollable problem of teenage patients. This is not to say that they cannot be treated as outpatients, but often treatment is enhanced by an early stage of hospitalization, followed by outpatient care.

Hospitalization for any patient is usually for protective purposes: the person is severely disorganized and cannot function safely, or the person is homicidal or suicidal. There is an additional, more positive reason to hospitalize a borderline adolescent, that is, to provide a structured environment to monitor all the patient's behavior 24 hours a day and channel all the patient's thoughts, feelings, and actions toward the psychotherapeutic interview. So doing makes it extremely difficult for the teenager to maintain his or her characteristic defenses of splitting, clinging, denial, avoidance, projection, and acting out. This is particularly indicated for those borderline adolescents who cannot overcome their defenses while they are being reinforced in the home.

The salient characteristics of the borderline adolescent are similar to those of the adult. They are motivated by the pleasure principle to the extent that they are compelled to seek immediate satisfaction and immediate relief of tension. They have a low frustration tolerance, poor perception of reality, poor ego boundaries, and cannot hold onto their feelings or keep them within themselves, and therefore act them out. They resort to fantasy rather than reality for gratification and deal with emotions and life situations passively or by irrational acting out, splitting, denial, and avoidance. Controlling acting out is a vital prerequisite for therapy since acting out discharges feelings and emotions in such a way that the person is not conscious of them for what they are and hence cannot recognize and discuss them in therapy sessions.

The borderline adolescent has no basic trust and tends at times to be withdrawn, isolated, provocative, manipulative, and hostile.

He deals with people as reproductions of his parents, who he believes are going to abandon him, rather than as distinct individuals who may be potential friends. Relationships with others grounded in these projections of his parents become further divorced from reality. Lastly, the borderline adolescent lags far behind his or her peers in achievement and social skills—the tools for mastering the environment that most children learn between the ages of six and twelve. Borderline teenagers have not learned these skills because their lives have been too unstable, often complicated by drugs and stymied by their inability to assert themselves.

We designed a therapeutic environment to deal specifically with these characteristics. The inpatient facility had a high staff-patient ratio and a carefully thought-out philosophy and methodology for setting limits to control acting out. As a result, frustration and aggression tapered off and the patients slowly realized that we were interested in them and their problems. For some of these adolescents, it was the first time in their lives that they received any positive discipline intended to help them deal with the anarchy of their impulses. For others, the firm rules allowed them to experience for the first time the satisfaction of coping successfully with an environment and establishing social relationships based on reality rather than fantasy.

The staff set up a standard of consistent expectations of realistic, healthy behavior, and when a patient deviated from this standard, it was brought to her attention. The penalty might range from a simple remark all the way to a graduated series of room restrictions, lasting from 15 minutes to 24 hours, during which the patient was asked to consider her behavior, knowing it would be the main topic of discussion in the next interview with her therapist. The confrontation focused the patient's attention on the meaning of that behavior, as the therapist attempted to relate it to the patient's feelings. In time, patients came to understand that we were sincerely interested in their behavior and possibly able to help them control their impulses. In effect, we were doing what their parents were unable to do for them and what they had never learned to do for themselves.

None of this was easy for the patients to go through. As we interrupted the patients' acting-out defenses, the abandonment depression came to the fore and they no longer had an escape valve.

We could then deal with the painful feelings in therapy sessions, where they could be discharged constructively through discussion aimed at insight, rather than through disruptive acting-out behavior. Patients did not start out with friendly attitudes toward the staff, but the ways that a patient distorted our intentions and goals could then become grist for the psychotherapeutic mill. Simultaneously as the patient was externalizing his old, negative assumptions and views, he acquired newer, more positive ones based on the attitudes and expectations of the staff. These eventually replaced the patient's maladaptive defenses and became the basis for new ego techniques of self-mastery and adaptation to the environment.

Meanwhile, in school or in occupational or recreational therapy, patients began to learn, for the first time, new social and achievement skills that were left by the wayside or never acquired in earlier developmental periods. The staff confronted the patient with his deficiencies in dealing with reality and emphasized the necessity of dealing with reality constructively. For example, a girl might prepare for an exam inadequately but, not perceiving either her inadequate preparation or her poor performance, think she did quite well. The teacher would point out her poor performance and then question her preparation, stressing the need for her to prepare realistically to meet real challenges, suggesting that this required effort and the ability to delay immediate satisfaction. We would also emphasize realistic achievement, as opposed to fantasy gratification, in responding, for example, to a boy who designed a cabinet poorly in occupational therapy, built it impulsively, and then asserted that it looked better than it actually did.

The goals of these policies were to provide an environment that demonstrated our competence to treat the adolescent and relieved him of the need to test our intentions, to undo the pathology of early developmental years, to prepare the patient for interview therapy, and to provide constructive learning experiences. We anticipated that patients would learn to develop self-control, the only basis for self-respect and true autonomy. As it turned out, our expectations were correct: adolescents stopped being slaves to their impulses and achieved an ego structure strong enough to enable them to decide which impulses they would express, when, where, and in what manner.

The stories of borderline adolescents are clinical versions of the ancient struggle of mankind against fate, as seen in both tragedy and triumph. They tell of human beings condemned by birth, poor parenting, and accident to be victims rather than masters of their own fortune; they are emotionally attacked and impaled before they have developed the resources and weapons with which to do battle. They cannot seek, for they are blind; they cannot fight, for they have no weapons. Unable to face their fate, they make a virtue of their incompetence and passivity. Their chains become a refuge; their way of life in all its human misery is defended as their pathway to salvation.

The therapeutic process presented here and sketched in its barest outline in the following four cases is in actuality a wearying and traumatic one for therapist and family. The resistance to separation on the part of both parent and adolescent is intense. The therapist must be patient, tolerant, vigilant, and persistent. He or she must make the necessary confrontations to enable both parents and patient to give up their resistance and seek a more lasting solution.

Once the therapist has unmasked the family's emotional compromises, numerous feelings are unleashed which throw the family members into emotional disarray but at the same time prepare them for the necessary change. The therapist must have a well-defined, embracing therapeutic goal in order to make the necessary confrontations and to deal effectively with the unleashed emotions. The therapist must have courage and persistence to ferret out the necessary information, no matter how turbulent the process may be.

In the beginning therapy may appear to be a battle, therapist against family, family members arrayed against each other. The underlying family conflict is similar to a painful boil or abscess that has drastically limited their ability to communicate with one another. As the therapist probes for the symbiotic ties that prevent the adolescent from separating from the parents and becoming an individual, the abandonment depression emerges. Along with it comes intense resistance to the therapeutic process as family members desperately try to avoid separation anxiety. The therapist, the most objective person in the group, is the only one who can guide the family to the center of the problem. As he gets closer and closer, the resistance of patient and parents increases. When the "abscess" is reached and the abandonment depression is laid bare, the family members re-experience their original pain and suffering. The resulting emotional catharsis drains the "abscess," relieves the anxiety and depression, and frees the family to repair the damage. The emotional climate of the treatment undergoes a marked change as the aura of battle is replaced by a joint therapeutic consensus.

This sequence occurs in those borderline adolescents and their families who have enough emotional strength to handle the anxiety and depression produced in order to bring about change. There are, however, some borderline adolescents and families who do not have sufficient strength to handle the stress, and with them, such a rigorous approach as this would be harmful. In these cases a counseling therapy, in which the therapist helps the family address its current problems without probing too deeply into their origins, is recommended.

To illustrate the problems of treating borderline adolescents, we will consider four patients whose histories and treatments cover both inpatient and outpatient settings. In addition, I will present follow-ups after discharge to show the range of outcomes to be expected for the borderline adolescent.

Fred had a domineering mother who tried to oversee and control his every action and a distant, compulsively overworking but successful father. He responded to them with silent, sullen, withdrawn behavior. He did poorly in school, had few friends throughout childhood, and suffered such severe separation anxiety when he first went to summer camp that he had to return home early. Shortly afterwards, he developed a fear of the dark that lasted for a brief time. Fred's school performance was always fraught with difficulties, despite his relatively high I.Q. In the 1960s, when he was 17 and in his senior year at a boarding school, Fred was hospitalized because of a radical personality change. Even though his school work had begun to improve at the beginning of the year, Fred underwent a drastic change from being extremely quiet, compliant, and conservative to engaging in rebellious, hippielike behavior that included a sudden obsessive interest in Russia, Communism, and the Beatles. His behavior included truancy, running away from school, and scratching his wrists in a token suicide attempt.

On being admitted, Fred denied having any feelings whatsoever, including depression. He also denied any significance to his suicide attempt, but explained that the razor blades found in his luggage were there "just in case this hospital stint doesn't work out." Fred's pathological defense mechanisms consisted of avoidance and denial of feelings, avoidance of any aspect of individuation or self-expression, intellectualization, and emotional withdrawal. He also exhibited a facade of overcompliance that made a mockery of any expectations the staff might have for him. For example, when the therapist confronted Fred with the destructiveness of his behavior, he would deny any feelings about that and, as a resistance, he would comply with what he perceived as the therapist's instructions, caricaturing what the therapist suggested but without emotional involvement or feeling.

Eventually the therapist was able to confront Fred with his terror of expressing himself honestly. When he was able to admit that and understand its significance for his behavior, he was able to relate it to the fear he had of expressing any anger for fear his mother would abandon him. From time to time, when the acting-out defense was blocked by the therapist in order to manage Fred's depression and rage, he would resort to the splitting defense by turning to the nursing staff, who he hoped would fuel his need for approval and take care of him. When his therapist confronted him with this, he resumed working through his depression and anger. He managed a series of family conferences extremely well, despite the fact that his mother attacked him rather bitterly and savagely for his attempt to assert himself. Nevertheless, he continued to improve and, after 18 months of hospitalization, was discharged to attend college where he continued in therapy with the same therapist for another four years. The parents were seen weekly by a social worker and also attended a parents' group once a week. The goals were to make the parents aware of their negative projections on Fred, to teach them how to parent, and to help them learn to substitute direct, verbal means of communication for acting out.

The parents viewed their involvement in treatment as ancillary and felt their major purpose in the sessions was to provide the social worker with information; in turn they expected him to keep them up-to-date on Fred's progress. The father was particularly affected by the parents' group therapy, viewing other parents as poor excuses for adults and feeling that it was no wonder they had children with problems. He would often leave feeling that he was healthier than he thought—seeing how "crazy everyone else was." Though he now viewed Fred as a competent adult, he felt it had nothing to do with his own involvement in therapy. "Fred grew up—that's the only difference," he said, assuming the hospital was responsible for Fred's improvement. Fred's mother believed she had changed for the better, less likely to "fly off the handle with Fred" than before treatment. Afterwards, she felt more in control of her own anger. Both parents thought Fred was overly touchy about his new independence to which they grudgingly acquiesced.

Fred saw no change in his mother and described her as rigid, controlling, and intolerant of his independence. He tried for the most part to avoid her company. He felt that he had changed because of treatment but his parents had not. However, he grew more relaxed with his father and enjoyed working and discussing business with him. "His strength doesn't scare me anymore."

At 25 Fred returned for follow-up, about eight years after terminating treatment. He had made considerable progress. He had graduated from college cum laude and had been working as an executive in his father's business for several years, living in his own apartment, and totally supporting himself financially. He had coped well when two love affairs broke up and his father suffered a stroke. There was no recurrence of the abandonment depression. He had many interests—camping, tennis, bicycling, arts, music, ballet, and creative writing. He hoped to publish some short stories he had written. He had a close relationship with his father and his brother but felt that he had to avoid his mother, who was still trying to run his life. He had taken charge of his life, was able to assert himself, act upon his thoughts and wishes in reality, maintain his self-esteem, and pursue his objectives in work and play. He was creative and autonomous; and his real self seemed to have emerged. He still had problems moving towards intimacy, admitting that he preferred to date and play the field rather than settle down in a close relationship. It also seemed that he was avoiding commitment by keeping himself busy.

Five years later, he wrote his therapist that he was happily married with two children and had had no return of his symptoms.

Fred is a good example of the real self trapped in the need to satisfy the rewarding image of the mother by nonassertive, non-self-expressive behavior that masked his deeper anger. Only when Fred was able to sense in therapy that his therapist could tolerate his anger was he able to express it and work through the depression that resulted. As the anger and depression abated, the real self emerged and began to direct Fred's life.

Scott was hospitalized at age 15 for violent behavior that escalated when he was around 11 or 12 and included smashing his favorite items and other household objects such as the phone and television, and even destroying some of his father's possessions. He had fantasies of living at the North Pole where he would not have to interact with others, where he could lead a life with no emotional content, like a machine, his hero being Star Trek's Mr. Spock who was devoid of human feelings. Scott's mother lacked firmness and self-assertion; and his father, a successful businessman, was often out of town for lengthy periods of time. At one point Scott talked about killing his little brother or his mother, and actually fractured her finger in the outburst that led to his hospitalization. The poignant thing about his behavior is that it was a desperate plea for help. A psychiatrist diagnosed Scott as a paranoid schizophrenic.

Despite his history of acting out, Scott's basic defenses were obsessive, schizoid, and paranoid. His obsessive pattern, for example, might take the form of spending hours working on a science project on which he could have done quite well even without the meticulous attention to detail that he felt it required. The schizoid quality of his character could be seen in his having to be the class clown to get attention or having no friends at all. He had difficulty relating to his peers. His fear of being attacked and rejected led to his desire to retreat to the North Pole to escape all human involvement. It was also seen shortly after he was admitted to the hospital where he adopted the same clinging, demanding relationship with a nurse that he had with his mother. The fact that his aggressive acting-out behavior disappeared once he was hospitalized suggests that it was motivated more by a plea for help than by the need to defend against the depression. In other words, it was not an essential defense mechanism.

In his 15 months of hospitalization, Scott projected the rewarding maternal image on certain nurses who would permit him to cling and from whom he angrily demanded attention. He projected the withdrawing image upon his therapist, whom he would constantly attack for not taking responsibility for interviews with questions and advice and for not giving him enough attention. He also handled his rage through a fantasy that his peers would attack him. Throughout Scott intellectualized, withdrew socially, and cut off all emotions. He entertained fantasies of becoming the commandant of his own concentration camp and torturing inmates. At the same time he had dreams of the Holocaust and his own death. His therapist increased sessions to four times a week instead of the customary three and continued his firm, consistent confrontation of Scott's projections in order to help him get in touch with his anger and depression, much of which he successfully worked through over time.

After he was discharged, Scott lived at the local YMCA and attended a private high school for his junior and senior years. At the time of his discharge, his father was receiving psychiatric treatment, as was his mother. His 12-year-old brother was exhibiting the same symptoms Scott had shown earlier. Scott continued therapy on an outpatient basis for six months, three times a week, until his therapist moved out of town, at which time he was transferred to me.

Scott's defenses against the abandonment depression that he suffered on being discharged (a predictable and inevitable reaction) consisted of excessive activity—running all over the city, going to plays, attending the opera, trying to find people to do things with, and forming brief, dependent, clinging relationships with girls. In his therapy sessions, he handled his feelings at first by denial and taking the rage out on himself. He would say, "The past is over and I don't want to talk about it. I don't have any character. I'm junk. I'm an ape. I'm subhuman." At this point he might delve into three subjects, any one of which would have previously produced panic—anger at the therapist or his mother, depression, and fear.

Near the end of his therapy, he reported a fantasy which he had first reported right after he was hospitalized: "A little kid in knickers, four years old, is shoved out the door. He turns around looking back at the door slammed in his face, feeling very alone." But this time the fantasy had changed; the door was closed behind the kid but now he turned around and looked out at the world, knew he had to go out there, and wanted to, even though he was afraid.

Here is how Scott described his six months of outpatient therapy after he was discharged and the positive change in his fantasy:

"One of my biggest feelings is a sort of fear. I've been getting more independent in facing the outside, doing more and more things on my own, but I've always felt that my therapist has been able to understand what's been happening inside my head and I could convey my thoughts when I had to and he could always grasp what I was trying to say, which I never felt anybody else could do. Now that he's leaving, I feel I'm going to have to deal with all these thoughts a lot more on my own, and I need to be a lot stronger and handle them and face the outside. I'm scared. Next year, you know, I will be living on my own. I'm going to school in the city, and it is frightening to be alone, and I have a terrible sense of aloneness. It's very hard to say goodbye to my therapist because a lot has happened. I got very close to him."

Scott spent the summer traveling through Europe on his bicycle, staying at youth hostels. He had a brief love affair which he terminated without an abandonment depression when he found out the girl was deceiving him. He enjoyed his summer thoroughly and returned to New York City in the fall to live alone in an apartment and attend school. I saw Scott three times a week in treatment. When we resumed therapy, he first worked through his feelings of abandonment at leaving his previous therapist and then his clinging defenses against further individuation. Eighteen months after hospitalization, he graduated from high school at the top of his class and was accepted at college. At that time, he ended therapy with me, spent another summer in Europe, and then began college in the fall. Two years after discharge, he was doing well in college and seeing a therapist only once a week. The depressive and paranoid features were gone.

Scott attended college for four years, graduating cum laude. During college, he saw a therapist on campus who did not confront him to enable him to continue to work through the rest of his abandonment depression. Rather, as Scott reported, "We worked on every-day issues; he became a father to me; he was fulfilling my fantasies of being taken care of." Under this approach, as might be expected, Scott's depression and anger decreased, and he seemed to flourish, with many outside interests and several short-term relationships with girls, who, however, dropped him because of his demanding and possessive behavior.

After leaving college Scott entered professional school, where he became quite depressed, lonely, and angry. Much of his anger was projected and acted out on the school. During his first year in professional school, his father died, which deepened his depression. He felt that he dealt with his father's death "pretty well." Afterwards, however, he reentered treatment where he again tended to project and act out his anger on his new therapist, who according to Scott's description of him, resembled the withdrawing parental figure: cold, quiet, distant, not giving.

"The anger, depression, and wish to be cared for are still there," Scott said, "although I cope with them much better." Mastery and coping were indeed much improved, considering the two separation stresses of his therapist's leaving and his father's death. He still used avoidance, denial, splitting, projection, and acting out; however, he was no longer paranoid nor did he resort to intellectualizing and detaching himself from his feelings. His self-image was dramatically improved. "Before I felt blind about myself—blind, angry, scared. I would grasp at anything to avoid feeling and would have killed myself without treatment." He could identify feelings, liked many parts of himself, thought he had great potential and was able to do more and cope better. In addition he had a more realistic perception of his parents and did not project as much on his peers, although he never became "one of the boys." He did, however, have several close friends with whom he socialized.

Relationships with girls continued to be difficult. He had had sexual intercourse with quite a number and, in addition, had two long-term relationships which were terminated because of his demanding and possessive behavior. Scott had more or less been living on his own and managing his own life since his senior year in high school. He was dealing with the external world fairly autonomously, but he still had difficulty achieving autonomy on an intrapsychic level, as reflected in his intense fears of being abandoned by girlfriends, which triggered his demanding and possessive defenses. Scott had always been creative and since discharge from the hospital pursued many interests avidly—marine biology, classical music, scuba diving, motorcycles, and travel.

Scott had shown a dramatic improvement in his self-image and his ability to take charge of his life. Even though he still tended to view others as either completely positive or negative, especially his therapists, and handled anxiety by transference acting out, his defenses against the abandonment depression were much less intense and much more adaptive. He did not retreat into detachment, paranoid projections, isolation, or withdrawal. In spite of the fact that some impairment persisted, this was no small improvement for a boy who, at age 15, was diagnosed as having paranoid schizophrenia and planned to move to the North Pole.

One day, years after the follow-up study was completed, Scott suddenly dropped in to see me. He was 26. He was in the last year of professional school, had changed his specialization from ecology to marine biology, and had been going out with the same girl for a year and a half. His depression and acting out had disappeared, and his perspective had considerably improved with treatment. He was now aware of the regressive effect of his college therapist's treatment and of how he had acted out to defend against the depression on leaving for professional school. He felt more "grown up," had a "better sense of reality," still got depressed on occasion, but felt he would be able to conclude his treatment in the near future.

Today Scott is 33, married, and a successful marine biologist.

Jill was admitted to the hospital, admitting, "All I want to do is drink, take drugs, and have a good time." She was 14. Her illness began around age ten when her 17-year-old sister began to rebel against their parents and Jill's stepbrother attempted to sexually molest her. The mother became more and more preoccupied with the sister's problems, and Jill began to cut classes, take and push drugs, steal and have sex with older boys. Eventually she became involved with a 19-year-old drug pusher for whom she ran interference because he convinced her that if they were caught, her young age would get her off. Jill was first placed in a reform school and then hospitalized.

Jill's developmental problems began in the severe disruption of her early childhood. When she was two and a half, she and her older sister were adopted from an orphan home. Her adopted mother died when she was four. From four to six, she was cared for by her grandmother and several housekeepers. When she was six, her stepfather remarried, and she became a model child. At seven her sister became involved in drugs and taught Jill how to hold the tourniquet for her while she "shot up." Prior to age ten, her school and social activities were good; but then she matured rapidly before her peers and felt embarrassed about it.

In the hospital, Jill's acting out was readily controlled. She began to work through her anger and depression, and finally started family sessions where both she and the family showed great resistance to her need to separate from the family. The discharge planning was complicated by Jill's reluctance to give up her fantasy of reunion with her parents and the parents' resistance to supporting Jill's growing independence. This resistance was further reinforced by a local psychiatrist who saw Jill as well as her family. Nevertheless, Jill was discharged to a local boarding school near home to continue in outpatient treatment with her hospital doctor.

Jill did well her first semester, continuing to see her hospital therapist as an outpatient twice a week. Claiming to be miserable, she then stopped therapy with her hospital doctor, dropped out of boarding school, and returned to live at home. Her condition deteriorated. Her depressions were acute and recurrent, her mood swings intense. She engaged in temper outbursts and overeating and increased her drug use, smoking marijuana every day. Occasionally she stole from her stepmother and, when confronted about it, said that she was entitled to the money. She got involved again with the same drug pusher and their relationship became sado-masochistic with his beating her. She became pregnant by him and had an abortion. She was on the honor roll at school but dropped out of school altogether after a fight with her mother; she resumed smoking marijuana and started tripping on LSD while trying to hold down part-time jobs. Throughout this period, she was seeing another outside private therapist once a week. He finally terminated treatment when he realized Jill was unable to control her behavior.

When Jill was interviewed, her self-representation, although a little better, was still quite unrealistic. For example, at age 17 she thought she might go to college to study to become a teacher, even though at the time she had no high school diploma. Part of her improved status at follow-up was due to a relationship with a new boyfriend whom she idealized "because he doesn't want to have sex." She continued to handle separation stress poorly, using destructive acting-out behavior to defend against the abandonment depression.

At the time of the follow-up interviews with the parents, Jill's father said in retrospect that his family had been like "an amalgam" when Jill was hospitalized—"a lot of people living together with very little communication." Everyone was on his or her own track and incapable of hearing anyone else or taking much of an interest in the others' activities. He also believed that both he and his wife tended to deny the existence of problems and viewed the world through "rose-colored glasses." He felt that much of the time he wanted to preserve a view of Jill "as a child, to protect her and to see her only as a completely loving daughter."

His individual treatment forced him to consider Jill more comprehensively and realistically. For the first time, he sat down and talked with her about her adoptive mother's death. Previously, his efforts had been "to spare her, hide all remembrances of her mother so that she wouldn't have to suffer." He also felt that he had subsequently become more comfortable in expressing and acknowledging his feelings with his second wife. In spite of this, he continued to have a blind spot when it came to setting limits for Jill. He allowed, even encouraged, her to quit boarding school and return home. Later he made it even more appealing for her to stay home by buying a car for her. Looking back on it, both parents and Jill viewed this as a mistake. The father continues to have difficulty setting appropriate limits for his daughter, now 18. Jill describes him as being easy to manipulate to get what she wants. Whenever he overindulges her, however, she gets furious because she knows he shouldn't give in to her and she also realizes that she shouldn't ask.

The adoptive stepmother is grateful for her experience in Jill's hospital treatment. "I learned that I had to look out for my own happiness and not to expect it to come completely from what my children could or could not do for me."

Perhaps Jill said it best: "After I left the hospital, I felt better about myself. Things were different. Then things started to overwhelm me, and I didn't care about myself. When I get close to anyone, I get bitchy and angry, and I get afraid they will leave me or die."

Jill still suffers from the severe trauma of her early life, the early onset of her acting-out behavior, and the terribly conflict-ridden family she grew up in. Her wish for reunion with her family at the time of discharge, coupled with her parents' resistance to her further growth, impelled her to give up in the face of the abandonment depression that is part and parcel of the discharge experience. She reverted to her old ways and is still today caught in the destructive trap of the false self. Although the family made some gains, particularly the mother, the father still cannot set limits for Jill and thus interferes with her development. Whether or not he or Jill will be strong enough to sustain the separation and work it through, only time will tell. Treatment does not always succeed, and Jill's case illustrates the combination of factors that can reinforce the defeat. The early years in the orphanage, the death of her adoptive mother when Jill was four, several caretakers when she was between the ages of four and six, and her adoptive father's remarriage created an enormous amount of separation stress at a very tender age. The continued attitudes of the sister and father as shown by the sister's introducing her to drugs and the father's inability to set limits continued to reinforce a resistance that she could not overcome.

Outpatient treatment for adolescents takes the same course as inpatient treatment, with several salient qualifications. First, in order to profit from outpatient treatment, an adolescent must be able to control acting out once a relationship is established with the therapist. The teenager must also be able to stabilize the way she performs in school and not be addicted to drugs. Similarly, the parents in their treatment with the social worker have to demonstrate their capacity to control their behavior. With careful and intensive work on the part of both the psychiatrist and the social worker it is possible to keep the therapeutic process in motion.

The principal difference between inpatient and outpatient treatment and the key to success of outpatient treatment is in the therapeutic management of the acting out in the initial phase of therapy. With inpatients the principal tool for controlling acting out is the use of the hospital environment that automatically places limits on patients' behavior. Clearly this is not available to the outpatient therapist whose only tool is the alliance established with the patient. But once the alliance is formed and the adolescent controls her acting out, treatment is identical to that for inpatients.

Jan, 16, was depressed, had difficulty concentrating, did poorly in school, lacked motivation, had difficulty socializing with her peers, and showed no interest in boys. She was occasionally truant. She described feelings of inadequacy about herself and had trouble sleeping. When she first came to therapy, overweight and sloppily dressed, she said that on her worst days she could not find a good reason for getting out of bed and going to school so she would roll over and daydream until her mother forced her to get up. In the first interview, she seemed eager to please as she reported her problems with her father's demandingness and her mother's indifference. She admitted to occasionally using marijuana and alcohol to feel better about herself.

Her mother complained that Jan was irresponsible and did not take care of herself, her clothes, or her room. She was distraught over Jan's sleeping all day and making inordinate demands on her time, claiming that Jan "wants me to wait on her hand and foot." Jan's father described her as selfish, lazy, demanding, spoiled, expecting to be waited on, and always attempting to get everything she could out of him.

Jan's father was narcissistic, often angry and demanding. Her mother was a borderline: compliant, idealizing of the father, emotionally empty, unable to be affectionate, and extremely resentful of the burdens of motherhood. She expected Jan to comply with her wishes in order to help her to feel better.

Jan's childhood seemed uneventful in terms of her later pathology. She had a sister four years older and a brother two years younger, who was viewed in the family as an "ideal boy." Jan was considered a contented and happy baby who gave her mother no problems. She seemed to look forward to school and did fairly well. She had no childhood symptoms except for attacks of asthma between ages six and eight. The family underwent many changes of residences during her first eight years because of her father's job with an oil company. Jan began menstruating without problems at fourteen, two years before entering therapy.

The arrangements we made were for Jan to see me three times a week and her parents to see a social worker once a week. Psychotherapy began by my confronting Jan with her maladaptive and regressive defenses. I asked her why she didn't take better care of herself, why she didn't do better in school, and why she let others abuse her. "Why can't you support yourself? Why are you so concerned with what others think of you rather than what you think about yourself?" I pointed out that her need to please others was so great that she would comply with their wishes to gain their approval, even at a great cost to herself.

Over the course of the first year, Jan gradually integrated the confrontations; she gave up her self-destructive behaviors and began to assert and activate herself. She took better care of her appearance and her clothes, did better in school, and took a more active role with her peers. As she activated her real self in these areas, her depression and conflict with her parents intensified.

"I feel cheated. They've given me nothing. I feel stuck, and I don't deserve it. All I do is suffer. My own feelings aren't important. I know I'm wasting my life being lonely and depressed all the time, but I just don't know where I belong. I feel deserted. I can't enjoy anything because I hate myself; I just want to curl up and die. In fact, I feel dead already so I might as well daydream. I know now that as a child I always felt that way and yet I always thought that mother was so wonderful."

As therapy progressed and got deeper, her perceptions of scapegoating by her parents became sharper and more continuous. "I feel rotten because they never notice or care about me. I'm a failure, but it's not my fault; it's theirs. They make me feel like a thing. But if I dare to fail or feel depressed, it's like stabbing them in the back. Mother is so sweet on the surface. She makes me feel so guilty that I want to cry. Daddy is so selfish that he'd sacrifice anything for his own interests. How come mother was never there for me? How come she treated me as nothing? Why does Daddy treat me like a slave?"

As Jan began to work through her rage and depression in sessions, her real self began to emerge even stronger. "I felt good after our last session. I realize I'm smart enough to do anything I want and I feel good about myself."

Near the end of the second year, her behavior took a dramatic change: she began doing excellently in school, she started dressing and wearing make-up to make herself look attractive, she made some good friends, and in general acted more assertively and self-assured. Throughout this time, the social worker met with Jan's parents to establish the goals necessary for her treatment to work. She tried to make them aware of their negative attitudes toward Jan and control them; to get the mother in touch with who it was in her background she was projecting onto Jan, making her unable to see Jan for who she really was; to teach them the basics of successful parenting and how to communicate emotions directly without acting out.

Near the end of the second year, I held joint sessions with Jan and her parents to reestablish a direct, verbal level of communications that would support Jan's emerging self. In the early sessions, both parents, despite treatment, still showed some negative attitudes toward Jan's assertiveness and autonomy, implicitly demanding that she comply with their wishes. However, with her newfound capacity to support herself, Jan confronted her father about his demands that she do only what he wanted and her mother over the ways she made Jan feel guilty. The conflict that erupted was verbalized and discharged. The family sessions lasted three to four months, and the three learned how to express themselves verbally. Jan learned she could hold her own in honest exchanges of feelings with her parents. Eventually they learned how to control their negativity.

In individual treatment, Jan focused on her anxiety about autonomy and in six months terminated therapy, having achieved fuller self-activation.

Fred, Scott, and many of our other adolescents were ill enough to be hospitalized after suicide attempts or other desperate pleas for help. Without treatment of the disorders that began in early childhood and were constantly reinforced up into adolescence, many of them would, no doubt, be dead, permanently hospitalized, or in prison. From this perspective, the results for many reflect a true triumph over tragedy. We found that 90 percent of the adolescent patients who received inpatient psychotherapy and were discharged as improved passed the test of time by maintaining that improvement four years later.[3] (This represents double the percentage reported as improved in other followup studies of the same disorders.)

For many, development almost reached full autonomy, with the elimination of their false-self defenses and the emergence of the real self. In all of them, individuality flowered; they became more creative, independent, and capable of demonstrating a capacity for intimacy. Another group showed dramatic improvement in functioning, self-assertion, and self-image, but still required pathologic defenses against separation anxiety and abandonment depression—including a clinging relationship—to maintain a high level of functioning. Even though they remained vulnerable to separation stress, they learned to assert themselves more successfully adapting to a range of life situations and challenges, thus lessening their reliance on their false self defenses.

The adolescents who improved were distinguished by an ability to live on their own, apart from their parents, and to stay in outpatient therapy for months or years if need be to support their real selves and to fight the pull of their parents' regressive wishes for them. Some patients had to cut off all contact with their parents for long periods of time to combat their negative influence. Those who did not improve often had more than usual overt symptomatology and more environmental separation trauma in childhood (like Jill) with clinical illness beginning before puberty. They also tended to have greater difficulty in the hospital setting, with both parents and patients resisting separation, and problems relating to the therapist. All these difficulties crystallized as plans were being made for the patient to leave the hospital, creating insuperable obstacles that were never overcome. Soon after discharge, the pattern of failure was set when the adolescent stopped outpatient therapy and returned home to live.

The improvement with hospital therapy was so closely related to the degree to which the patient's treatment followed the therapeutic model that we were able to predict at discharge with a high degree of accuracy how well the patient would be four years later at follow-up. These findings are compelling evidence for the accuracy of the theory and the effectiveness of the therapeutic approach. The inpatient or hospital segment of the long course of therapy these patients received was crucial in changing a regressive spiral of behavior into an adaptive spiral. The patients learned to replace defense with adaptation so that later they could participate in outpatient therapy where they found new capacities to direct their own lives, to perceive situations realistically, cope constructively with challenges at work and in relationships, and contain separation stress without sacrificing adaptation. These were the building blocks for a new life that could sustain and support them. This improvement was not based on a continuing transference relationship since the treatment had ended. They had internalized the work of the psychotherapy and changed their intrapsychic structure so that they could make it on their own.

10

PSYCHOTHERAPY WITH THE NARCISSIST

THE narcissistic personality disorder is more difficult to treat than the borderline patient because of the unique characteristics of the defensive tactics on which the grandiose self relies. It uses aggression to coerce others, including the therapist, to resonate with its grandiose view of itself. Furthermore, this stance is maintained nearly all the time. There are few lapses. Underlying this formidable stance, however, is an extreme vulnerability. The narcissist resembles a psychological turtle with a hard, impenetrable shell inside of which is an equally soft, fearful center: the impaired real self.

The therapist who has become comfortable utilizing a confrontive stance with the borderline patient has to change his approach in dealing with the narcissistic patient so drastically as to almost seem to assume another professional identity. It is almost as drastic as a runner changing from long-distance to sprinter or a musical comedy dancer attempting ballet. The therapist must be prepared for a wholly different kind of encounter and patient behavior. Instead of the avoidance of self-assertion, the clinging, and the acting out that the borderline engages in both inside and outside the sessions, the therapist must now focus on the fluctuations of narcissistic vulnerability and defense within the sessions. The basic therapeutic activity must change from confrontation to interpretation of narcissistic vulnerability. All the while the therapist needs to remain keenly aware, not of resonating with the rewarding element of the borderline's intrapsychic structure, but of possible failures in empathy with the exquisite vulnerability the narcissistic patient presents. The difference is due to the fact that the narcissist feels entitled to perfect responsiveness while the borderline will settle for much less.

The core of the therapeutic problem is that the patient presents three facades, two of which are full of defensive emotion and a third which displays no emotional involvement with the therapist at all and complete detachment of feeling. The patient either exhibits the grandiose self with the need for perfect mirroring or idealizes the therapist as the omnipotent parent figure and basks in his glow. But when the impaired real self with its anger and depression emerges, it brings with it the emotional detachment from the therapist in order to protect itself against painful feelings of vulnerability to loss. Thus, the patient may complain that the therapist "means nothing to him," he feels no involvement in the relationship, he has no reaction to the therapist as a real person, or that he does not think about therapy at all between sessions. I recall a patient who saw a psychiatrist three times a week for five years and then decided to stop, walked away, and claimed he never had another thought about the treatment or the psychiatrist. The therapist is either an idealized or mirroring object, an attacking object, or does not exist at all in the patient's psyche. How different this is from the borderline patients for whom the therapist becomes the center of their preoccupations and their psyches. Even when they are not in a session, they cannot get the therapist out of their minds. The transference acting out, the need for perfect mirroring, and the narcissistic wounds of the impaired self do not indicate a real emotional relationship with the therapist but are rather a defensive facade underneath which lies an extreme vulnerability.

And yet there is an illusion of stability in the narcissist because he or she has become a master at refueling the grandiose self by denying depression, devaluing social and environmental traumas, and using a variety of techniques to coerce the world to resonate with his grandiose self-image. Up to a point, the narcissist's denial of reality helps him to maintain his psychic equilibrium; but if the denial is too great, it will cause conflict. When the narcissist is forced by the demands of treatment to venture out of his safe, stable cocoon and activate his real self, it becomes clear how impaired that real self actually is. Then the patient will show immense difficulties in functioning and feeling.

For example, a narcissistic patient who was idealizing me as his therapist maintained that without my help he couldn't activate himself in the session. He was referring here to his impaired real self. He could not start the interviews, had no spontaneity, could not identify and express his thoughts or feelings. And on the occasions when he could activate himself, he was unable to acknowledge the fact that he had done so. The underlying lack of self-entitlement or sense of self-worth of his impaired real self was apparent. However, when his grandiose false self-image was reinforced by others' providing the admiration or attention he needed, he felt fine and was able to activate the false self easily and successfully. Small wonder that he confused his false self with his real self.

In dealing with narcissistic patients the therapist must avoid a number of traps. It is possible to overlook the patient's emerging grandiosity because it is disguised in conventional social terms, such as a normal need for approval, when in fact it is the narcissistic need to be perfectly admired and adored. For example, the patient may speak of occasionally feeling a need for the therapist to "like" him. What lies behind this statement is the need for the therapist to admire him, not occasionally, but all the time and perfectly. Another therapeutic trap is the temptation to attempt to overcome the patient's resistance by interpreting his grandiosity prematurely, before it has fully emerged in the relationship. A patient may talk about his need for approval without being aware that it is actually adulation he seeks. The therapist may be tempted to interpret this before the patient is ready to accept it.

Emotional involvement with the therapist stirs up such painful feelings of the impaired self that the patient defends against it by detachment of feelings and strict uninvolvement. There is either idealization of the therapist or no involvement at all. The only avenue to overcome this detachment and uncover the patient's vulnerability and pain is through the therapist's carefully formulated interpretations of the patient's narcissistic disappointment with the therapist's failure to mirror him. Exploration of the disappointment in the therapist leads to its source: the patient's need for perfect idealizing or perfect mirroring as defenses against his depression and impaired real self. In the course of this exploration, as the depression is worked through, the grandiosity of the false self and the underlying emotional detachment give way to a real emotional involvement with the therapist in a therapeutic alliance.

To illustrate the role psychotherapy can play in alleviating the narcissist's dependence on the inflated false self, consider the case of Walter, a 38-year old, married, successful lawyer with one child, who came to treatment because his wife of 20 years was leaving him because, she told him, she "didn't want to be abused anymore." He was depressed by this, as would be expected, but the overriding emotion was humiliation and rage at the outrageousness of her wish to leave him. "She is part of me," he fumed. "How could part of me separate from me?"

Walter had always treated his wife as a narcissistic object from whom he expected perfect mirroring and attendance, but when their son became an adolescent, she started her own business, which required her to be out of the home a lot. Walter became increasingly enraged at her, and he spent even more time at work, buried himself in his study at night reading, attacked her work and her relationships with friends and associates. Finally, she had enough and decided to leave him.

After his wife left him and he had to find a place of his own, he felt more angry, empty, impoverished, and depressed. He had difficulty arriving on time for sessions and trouble concentrating. He said, "I had this insane notion that everybody and everything should flow to me. I'm just waiting for some magical solution; I can't confront the reality that I am on my own. The idea of a task that doesn't feed my sense of self is impossible. You see I just don't want to do it alone. My wife was part of myself. I can't say goodbye. It's the price I pay for having lived in a fantasy. I can't believe this is happening to me. I'm thrown into the water and I imagine that if I close my eyes I won't get wet, and yet I'm soaked."

Walter could not accept my matter-of-factness as he related these feelings to me. Since I did not perfectly empathize with his situation, he raged at me. "I'm furious and fed up with your lack of concern about me. Here I am bleeding and nobody, not even you, will rescue me. It is humiliating. If I can't have the past back, I will do nothing."

Over the next sessions he continued talking about his narcissistic dependence on his wife. "I am whole only by union with another person. Separation makes me empty and collapsed. I feel like I'm walking through a movie set as an extra where I had once been the star. I didn't need intimacy with my wife. It was only when she began to frustrate my sense of importance that I grew angry and withdrew."

To create a therapeutic alliance and transference, I began to make comments—mirroring interpretations—about how his need for other people to admire him was a way of dealing with these painful feelings associated with being on his own. These led Walter to begin to recognize his grandiosity and open up and elaborate on it.

"The loss unmasks what I have tried to keep hidden all my life—my unwillingness to take responsibility for myself. I've always been terrified of being on my own, which means being alone feeling naked and vulnerable without my entitlements. I'm afraid without the dream of perfection I have no capacities. What tied me together, gave me discipline and grit, was the dream, the entitlement dream."

As he separated from his wife and began to build a new life, Walter started dating and became more aware of his narcissistic entitlement fantasies as they began to emerge in his new relationships. "I'm seeing this girl and realized that I want her to do what I want. When I talk, I want her to listen. I want to have sex when I want and not when she wants it. I find myself losing interest in her conversation and in her interests. Is this because we don't have anything in common or is it because I expect too much?" With time, Walter saw that he was only attracted sexually to women who saw him as a king or potentate, women who would belong to him and whom he could control. He admitted, "As soon as I'm interested in a woman, she is to amend her life completely to suit me."

Very slowly and painfully Walter began to activate his real self. He contacted his son who was living with his mother and began to see him. These encounters led to many sessions in which we discussed differentiating the son's needs from the father's and the need for the father to father the son. He also began to utilize his real self in sessions to reevaluate his relationship with his wife, not from the point of view of his loss of entitlements but rather from the realization that he had provided very little emotional satisfaction for her while they were married.

As his interest in work returned, he realized how his enjoyment of it had come primarily from its ability to boost his ego. He saw that his career satisfaction was a combination of mastery, achievement, and being the center of attention as the unique, idealized figure for his entire staff. He also began to understand how he created antagonisms among his peers because of his arrogant, harsh, and devaluing behavior.

In our sessions we discussed the principle of collegiality among peers and how it is necessary to acknowledge the real selves of others if one expects to have relationships with them. We also explored the roles that mastery and achievement play in deriving satisfaction. In time Walter began to see how he used work principally as a source of perfect mirroring rather than to satisfy and develop his real self.

Sometimes these discussions took place in the framework of communicative matching. For Walter, these sessions were his first encounters with the commonsense judgments that govern parenting, working, dating, being with others. For example, in work, Walter had been a workaholic, and his busyness reinforced his narcissistic armor and emotional detachment. We talked about how his schedule was "unrealistic" and that "the schedule is made for the man, not the man for the schedule." He also began to see the need for time to pursue recreational interests to balance the time spent at work.

The biggest arena for communicative matching was his relationship with women. He had had almost no dating relationships prior to marrying his wife. His whole perspective was dominated by his sense of narcissistic entitlement. He wanted to be the center of a woman's life and felt that she, like his mother, should subordinate herself to him in all ways. I explained to him how the real self forms relationships as opposed to the way the narcissistic self goes about it. But Walter found it extremely difficult to understand or implement this in his social life.

As a financially well-off, professional man, he soon became the center of attention for a number of women who pursued him. He would form instant relationships based on their providing social and sexual gratification, but when his partners would express their own needs for a more enduring relationship, he would explode with narcissistic rage and drop them. These experiences gave us opportunities to differentiate between the narcissistic and real self. We discussed his habit of impulsively initiating sex with women without first exploring their personalities, only to recoil in disappointment and rage when he discovered their shortcomings, inadequacies, or demands for a permanent relationship. This is a very common experience of people who have never learned the simple rules of how to go about discovering another individual's personality and evaluating how compatible it is with their own. He had trouble distinguishing whether he liked a woman for herself or because she mirrored him. More often, it was the latter. He would say, "I haven't learned how to be friends with a woman. I may only be attracted to women who see me as a king and who belong to me and let me control them."

He began to experience what he called "a profound change" in his lifestyle as his real self emerged. He was enjoying his mastery at work, relating more to his colleagues on a sharing basis rather than a need for mirroring and getting good feedback from them. He found more recreational time, curtailed his restless, impulsive manner of organizing his time, and was able to view himself and others, particularly women, more realistically as he experimented with his real self.

"I'm trying to contain myself and think rather than act," he explained. "I'm less afraid or uncomfortable with myself, more willing to try to understand what other people's needs are."

After extensive dating, he found a single woman about ten years younger than himself. Again he initiated "instant intimacy" and began to see her exclusively. They fell in love and talked about getting married, as Walter was in the final stages of clearing up his divorce. When the woman insisted that she wanted a child, Walter balked. As a result of both his narcissism and the fact that he already had two children, he told her he did not want another child. He at first denied to himself the potential conflict involved in marrying a woman who wanted a child when he did not. Could she be satisfied without a child? Eventually he realized she would not and broke off the relationship.

Because his company was going out of business, Walter had to find a new job. He ended up taking a position with a firm that he had not adequately examined and researched and discovered it was a bad "fit." He soon found that his coworkers were quite mediocre, and the combination of his outstanding ability and his narcissistic manner had them up in arms against him within a few months. He had to resign and move on. He learned from this experience, pursued his job search more thoroughly this time, and found a suitable position.

Finally, the day came when he said, "My real self is beginning to emerge. Although I'm not clear who I am, I am no longer a potentate or star, but there is more to me than that. There is something coming out that is authentic and real." He was no longer a workaholic and had a more flexible work schedule. He was far more aware and considerate of others' feelings. He was much better able to accept criticism and to involve himself in activities where he was not the center of attention. The old, rigid, detached need for entitlement was dissolving and a new, more flexible human concern for others as well as himself was beginning to emerge.

Frank's case demonstrates the difficulties in working with the closet narcissist who has built up barriers to avoid recognizing his grandiose self.

Frank, a 52-year-old single businessman, had two years of behavior therapy without any significant improvement before coming to see me six months later. His experiences with therapy had begun in his late 20s, and over the years he had been in and out of different types of treatment. Nothing worked. He said he still felt an inner grayness, anger, resentment, depression, and did not feel good about himself. He felt hopeless about treatment ever working because of his long history.

Frank was the second of four children in a middle-income family. His father was an arrogant, self-centered artist who was rarely home. He seemed more drawn to the outside world than to the family. His mother, whom Frank described as emotionally and intellectually dull, idealized and praised the father and supported his behavior. Frank felt he received no emotional or intellectual input from her or from his father.

He described himself as having been a quiet, obedient, "good boy," who did fairly well in school, rarely caused trouble there or at home, was average in sports, and was interested in outdoor activities. Nevertheless he felt, "I was boring, missing something. I had a fear of what it would be like to be out in the world on my own when I grew up." Frank finished high school, attended college, served in the Navy, and returned to establish himself in business, where he was both competent and successful.

Frank said he was absorbed in other people and things outside himself and that he needed a tight daily structure as well as a constant supply of friends, otherwise he would feel empty, angry, and depressed. He needed constant stroking from other people, yet he contributed very little of himself to his friendships and consequently felt isolated and alone most of the time. He tended to ignore his own wishes in order to please others and obtain their praise or approval. He was extraordinarily sensitive to and intolerant of criticism. He often felt frustrated. At work he would constantly criticize his employees.

When Frank came to me, he was not in a relationship with a woman. He had had a number of girlfriends over the years. The most recent exclusive relationship had been eight years ago with a woman he claimed to have loved but who turned him down because she said she felt he was unable to love. He had previously had an identical experience with another woman, and apart from these two relationships, most of Frank's involvement with women consisted of dating.

Outside of work, Frank spent his time playing on a local softball team, reading, and collecting antique guns.

Intrapsychically, Frank was typical of the narcissist in general and the closet narcissist in particular. From childhood he carried a grandiose self-image still fused to a combined maternal-paternal image that was omnipotent, capable of providing perfect wisdom, knowledge, direction, and care. Frank's mother idealized the exhibitionistic father so that this image of the father was superimposed on the image of his mother. His companion grandiose self-image felt good, unique, or special when he received perfect wisdom, direction, and knowledge from the omnipotent mother and father, which he equated with love. When he felt he was not receiving this emotional input from others, it evoked the underlying negative representation of the omnipotent figure which he then experienced as either withholding or harsh and attacking.

The companion self-image was of feeling empty, full of rage, depressed, confused, and helpless.

These omnipotent, grandiose images were allied with the pathologic ego's defense mechanism of avoidance, denial, splitting, mirroring, projection, and acting out. They operated as follows: Frank avoided asserting and expressing his exhibitionistic, grandiose self by posing as inhibited and passive, looking to others to acknowledge his greatness. This behavior was motivated by a fantasy that he must remain "hidden" and never express his grandiose self for to do so would frustrate and alienate his exhibitionistic, narcissistic father. By keeping the grandiose self hidden he was able to stimulate the omnipotent figure to provide the mirroring. When Frank's behavior was motivated by this need to hide, he was inhibited, compliant, eager to please, but suffered from much anxiety and tension. However, when this need was frustrated, it evoked the underlying depression and rage.

The psychotherapy began with this pattern: Frank's defensive strategy was continuously activated, so he avoided and inhibited self-activation, sitting passively without much awareness of his feelings. He intellectualized and rationalized his projection and acting out of the omnipotent figure onto me by saying that since he couldn't activate himself, it must come from me as his therapist. As the therapist I had the knowledge he required and he wanted me to provide it with direction, advice, and reassurance. My failure to do this and my quiet pursuit of therapy (listening silently, questioning when appropriate) triggered the underlying depression and rage. Frank then perceived me as withholding from him or attacking and demeaning him. Because he felt empty, fragmented, "missing a piece," helpless, and hopeless (as well as disappointed and enraged), he would be unable to act. Because he could not express his rage at me, he would handle it by acting it out on others for their "failure to meet his needs."

Whenever my comments or observations spoke directly to his problems, he seemed to respond to them with enthusiasm, but as they never reappeared in later interviews, it became evident that he did no further work on them nor did he apply them to his life between sessions. This apparent paradox can be understood in light of the narcissist's need for mirroring and the underlying impairment of the real self. While I spoke *to* him and *about* him, he was the center of attention and basked in the glow. Outside the session, however, he was unable to activate himself to integrate what I had said into his life. In fact, it was threatening for him to do so. Consequently, there was no continuity of theme from session to session.

The beginning of every session was agony for Frank because it confronted him with his basic dilemma: My silence left it to him to start the interview; he felt unable to do so on his own; when he failed at provoking me into initiating the session, he would feel angry, which he expressed by silence. On the few occasions when he would try to activate himself, he would quickly collapse with blocking, protestations of ignorance, and feelings of hopelessness and helplessness.

The first objective of treatment was to make Frank aware that beneath his need for continuous stroking and connection was the exquisite sensitivity to any and all failures to meet his need for perfect mirroring. It was also necessary to show him that his seeking of narcissistic mirroring, while it provided for psychic equilibrium, prevented him from leading a life of autonomy and real self-activation.

I began with narcissistic mirroring interpretations to remove the defense and establish a therapeutic alliance. I suggested to him that his silence was a reflection of how painful it was for him to talk about himself. When I further questioned why he had such difficulty overcoming his silence, he became mad at me, accused me of not doing my job, and pleaded that he was unable to talk about himself without questions from me. When I asked why simply doing my job as a therapist (listening) upset him so, he said it made him feel that I was withholding and that I was not truly interested in him. When I asked him where these attitudes came from, he was unable to elaborate. He repeated that my silence meant I was not interested in him.

The first two years of therapy consisted of the silence, arguments, and acting out of rage outside the office. No material from Frank's past emerged, for when the patient is engaged in transference acting out, there is no past. His attention and feelings are concentrated on his relationship with the therapist. Should the therapist bring up historical material by questioning the patient about his past, the patient would merely report facts but without feeling. When a patient discusses his past intellectually, there can be no real progress because the feeling component is missing. The patient may think he is dealing with the past by working it through, but in fact he is not.

Eventually my narcissistic mirroring interpretations that Frank's silence was due to his emotional pain began to establish a therapeutic alliance between us, and for the first time he gave up the silence and tried to activate himself to take responsibility for reporting his thoughts and feelings in the session and to make an effort to understand them. However, he became confused, would mumble, start and stop, and eventually say tearfully, "I don't know, I don't have the knowledge. I can't do it. The situation is hopeless."

My efforts were next directed at making him aware of his narcissistic vulnerability to me in the sessions—how extraordinarily sensitive he was to my every facial expression, the tone of my voice, and the nature of my comments. When I said something that Frank thought was way off target, his face clouded with disappointment. I had not mirrored him perfectly. This would occur even if I changed my facial expression or my eyelids flickered. These minute disappointments then became the focus of our discussion, and we discussed how his emotional antennae were six miles long. He was constantly plugged into a radar system that could pick up temperature changes of one degree or the slightest shift in the wind. He acknowledged the accuracy of these observations, elaborating that whenever he had to activate or assert himself at home or at work (give up his need for mirroring), he developed the same feelings of confusion, rage, and depression that he demonstrated in the sessions.

After about two and a half years of therapy a breakthrough finally occurred in the context of a new romantic affair Frank was having with a woman named Nina, whom he described as a "goddess of perfection." She was the ideal woman, physically, emotionally, intellectually, and her admiration for Frank was open and lavish. Their relationship included intense sexual activity. Frank was euphoric. However, after a period of several months, as the whirlwind romance settled down, Nina fell in love with him. At this point, Frank began to be bothered by her "flaws" and felt that she was no longer good enough for him. She had lost her perfection, and he focused on finding things wrong with her. His narcissistic glow had faded. He was not at all sure what had done it, but he no longer cared for her as he had before.

We were then able to link his need for perfect mirroring in sessions to his need for perfect mirroring from Nina. I suggested that it was normal in relationships for the initial romantic fervor to recede and the reality of the other person to come into focus along with the defects. Normal people do not have to see themselves or their loved ones as perfect. Lovers who are not narcissistic personalities continue to love each other "warts and all." But for Frank the disappointment was a fatal blow that led to depression and rage at Nina, which killed any feeling he had had for her. I pointed out that his disappointment was due to his need for her to be perfect and not to any fatal flaws in her. He was angry at Nina for the same reason he was angry at me. We frustrated his need for mirroring. I suggested that no one could possibly gratify this need and that if he really wanted to improve, he had better try to use therapy to understand why he felt the need for it.

As Frank's narcissistic defenses were broached, he reported for the first time the activation of his underlying angry self through a fantasy of smashing the desk in my office. "I wanted you to calm me down and be sympathetic, and you wouldn't and your outrage at my demand would be so great, you would throw me out." He went on to accuse me of being "hard and cold" and having "no feeling or concern" for him. He expressed his need for mirroring: "I demand and want you to care for me and stop pursuing your own objectives and withholding from me. I want you to give me something, not just leave me there hanging." This outburst of feeling triggered tears, but Frank could not identify their source, except to say they were a demand for me to "hold him and make him feel better."

In one session he recounted his anger at his lawyer, who made one mistake after ten faultless years of service. I pointed out the link between his need for perfect mirroring from both me and the lawyer and his rage when he did not get it. I added that even when I merely asked a question, it seemed to interrupt the mirroring and make him feel as if he were under attack.

As therapy progressed, sessions went reasonably well and Frank felt elated. "After the last session, I felt more like a peer with you. I felt great, but it stopped when I got back to work. I could feel the anger starting again. I get afraid that I might do something wrong or be caught messing up in some way. I only want to be seen doing something right" (that is, perfectly).

As Frank took a more active part in sessions, he began to introduce historical material, slowly, in bits and pieces. "In my family the style was to point out flaws and ignore achievement. As far as my father and brother were concerned, I didn't exist unless I did something wrong. Then they noticed me and criticized me for it." At one point he explained, "My father always asked, 'Why can't you be more outgoing?' But I was always afraid of screwing up or being laughed at if I was more outgoing with friends and family members."

Frank would relate his feelings stemming from his defensive self: "Part of me wants to be adored, receive all the attention in the world, and be loved." Then he would report criticism from the aggressive self: "Another part says, 'I'm no good.' I have to hide until somebody else makes me feel like a real person. On my own I'll show nothing until I know I'm the best."

As Frank activated his impaired real self in this way, the abandonment depression became more intense. "There's nothing going on in me, no motivation, direction, interest, or energy. I feel isolated, alone, on the periphery. I give to no one. I have to do it, live my own life, but I don't do it. I had a dream that I was with an old girlfriend, expecting sex. She seemed to go along with me and then said, 'No.'" He free associated: "No, you can't have that; you want it, but you can't have it. I feel disappointed, resentful, but recognize that she's playing it straight and that I'm the one who's playing a game. What do I want?" He projected the dream on to me. "I want you to be there, say something; but no, nothing you can say will make me better. Why don't I talk instead of just sit here thinking? To show off, get a response from you that will make me feel good? I want to take a trip, get away, escape, but I know it won't do any good. I hate it here, going around in circles. I feel helpless, like no one cares."

At this point his depression took over and he cried. "The crying annoys me. It gets nowhere. It interrupts my train of thought. I feel aging, dying, hopeless. I need you to say something, your voice, or I stay locked in the trap. Everything is in your voice, in women, in trips to escape, anything to get away from these feelings. In a later session, he said, "At work I'm being more realistic than perfectionistic. I don't have to eradicate all the problems. After all, I've been coming to you for four years now, and you're not upset that I'm no better."

At this first introduction of humor into our sessions, I responded in kind, "Well, if I can do so poorly in my job and get away with it, why can't you?" He laughed—the first small sign that the therapy was beginning to take effect and that he was beginning to change.

Frank continued to report further signs of improvement in the next months, feeling confident and taking pleasure in activating his real self. "I bought a wonderful antique gun. The salesman treated me as if I were ignorant about guns, and I was tempted to withdraw and let him put me down. But instead I decided to confront him and told him off." This direct self-assertive act contrasted with Frank's usual hiding and withdrawing. Then he teared as he thought about this, and he realized that he felt noble, solid, and free of what others thought about him.

His working through of these painful emotions led to fantasies. "I had a fantasy of you, father, and me on a huge stage feeling overwhelmed. I asked, 'What is going on?' I waited for father's approval, and it never came. Mother said father was intelligent. Well, where the hell was it? I rarely saw him at home."

As therapy progressed, Frank turned more and more to direct images of his family. "We never ate together. Mother and father's talk was trivial, boring, uninteresting. I feel scorn for father's self-centeredness. I'm helpless, know nothing, and father is supposed to help and teach me, but he doesn't."

In a dramatic session, Frank moved further into the working-through phase. He began by discussing his search for the perfect antique gun, comparing it to his search for perfection in women. He often couldn't make a choice because he felt that there was always someone or something else that would be better. He didn't want to be caught without the best. I pointed out that these two pursuits existed on different levels: one, the level of reality where he would like an antique gun and a girlfriend to enjoy; the other on the level of fantasy where he looked for perfection, which always seemed to lead inevitably to disappointment, whether it was with antiques, women, or me.

He responded that the fantasy of perfection gave his life excitement. Without it he felt disappointment and impending death. Only others—things or people—made him feel good.

Frank wondered out loud, "What's wrong with this therapy? Something is supposed to be happening here if I'm doing it right!" I replied, "Something is happening but it is unpleasant." "I have no inkling of improvement," countered Frank. "I want to feel good, and I'm not. If I'm handling this right, where are my rewards?" I explained, "The treatment leads you to recognize your imperfections, and then you get angry and begin to intellectualize." That is, there was a process involved and it was working. Frank was investigating how he protected himself from his bad feelings about himself. Therefore, the bad feelings emerged as a part of the process of getting to the bottom of the whole problem. Frank acknowledged that the therapeutic process of remembering and expressing feelings did seem to be working better than at any time before in his life—there did seem to be continuity and some kind of overall pattern emerging.

Frank arrived at the next interview with another positive breakthrough, reporting that he had a very exciting day after the last session. He felt good, spontaneous, involved, outgoing, "feeling his oats" as he had never felt before in his life.

Much remained to be done, and there were many further episodes of transference acting out; but the momentum of working-through had taken over, and Frank was solidly committed to the treatment process. Therapy with people like Frank with narcissistic personality disorders brings to mind the procedures necessary to allow an orbiting space capsule to reenter the earth's atmosphere. The capsule must be set at the right angle and the right speed at the appropriate time in order for it to leave the orbit and reenter. If any of these procedures are inappropriate, the capsule will not reenter but "skip off" into outer space. In an analogous fashion, the narcissistic personality disorder requires carefully timed interpretation of his or her narcissistic vulnerability in order to give up the self-defeating orbit of defenses and reenter the world of childhood to re-experience and work through early conflicts in order to be able to grow. Inappropriate timing or technique will cause the psychotherapy to fail, and the patient will not reenter the world of childhood but remain locked in the orbit of self-defeating defenses.

11

THE THERAPIST
AS THE GUARDIAN
OF THE REAL SELF

"WHY doesn't she talk more? Why doesn't she ask me more questions or give me more direction or advice? Why does she sometimes seem so cold and uninvolved? Yet she really does seem to know me, and what she says fits."

These perennial complaints at the outset of therapy from patients with an inflated or deflated self express their wish for the therapist to "take over" and reinforce their false defensive selves and enable them to "feel better." They become aware of the profound harm this response would do to their welfare only much later in treatment. The therapeutic relationship is not social but professional, and the therapist's challenge is to serve as guardian of the emerging real self by maintaining an emotionally neutral stance. This stance safeguards the patient and the therapy from the tidal wave of the patient's false-self projections and creates the conditions for the emergence of the real self.

The therapist's vital role in the psychotherapy of patients with a deflated or inflated false self is further complicated by the unique nature of the problems caused by the false self. The therapist must maintain strict emotional neutrality and objectivity in order to provide a neutral reality framework against which the patient can identify, contrast, compare, and work through her transference

191

projections. The neurotic patient, with a well-developed autonomous self and strong ego, has a good foundation for perceiving and accepting the neutrality of the therapist and the therapeutic alliance (the agreement between the therapist and patient that they will work together to help the patient get better through insight, understanding, and control of the thoughts, feelings, and behavior that constitute the problem). The therapeutic alliance becomes the framework against which to measure and understand the patient's projections. She and her therapist share a common perception and understanding of the reality of the relationship.

What are the motives of borderline patients? It is not strictly accurate to say that borderline patients come to therapy "to get better," although they will often word it that way. Perhaps 5 percent of their motivation is to get better. The other 95 percent of their motivation is to be taken care of by the therapist, although they do not articulate it in these terms. Nevertheless, they want "to feel good." To get better involves getting depressed, and most borderline patients do not want to get depressed. Their hidden agenda is to get the therapist to resonate with their need to be rewarded and supported and to serve as a new caretaker for them, so they will feel better and get the emotional supplies they wish they had gotten earlier in life. But if the patient succeeds in this and the therapist resonates with the rewarding pattern, he gives up his role as guardian of the real self; the patient will behave regressively, and treatment will no longer be effective.

The patients' other hidden agenda is to lure the therapist into resonating with the negative images they have of their parents. If the therapist will become the withdrawing parent, patients can discharge onto the therapist all the angry tension they could not discharge as children. Either way, the patients seemingly cannot lose. They get in fantasy all the supplies they wanted as children and still need, or they get the opportunity to relieve the anger and frustration over not getting them. In other words, the borderline patient can obtain in treatment the satisfaction he cannot get anywhere else in life. The narcissist's motives are similar to the borderline's but with the expected variations. Like the borderline, the narcissist uses therapy not to get better but to be admired and adored by the therapist. Failing that, he will use the therapist as a target for his rage and disappointment over not receiving the admiration and adulation he expects.

Patients with borderline or narcissistic disorders are rooted in defensive selves and poorly developed egos and live in a world bounded by their projections. Establishing a therapeutic alliance based on the therapist's emotional neutrality is difficult for these patients and, once it is established, it requires continual maintenance as treatment proceeds. Because these patients have a much poorer perception of reality, therapeutic neutrality is even more important with them than with neurotic patients. Their experience in treatment is probably the only place in their lives where they have the opportunity to be with someone who can remain objective in the face of their severe inability to cope with reality and treat them according to their best therapeutic interests. For these reasons, the therapist's neutrality and objectivity function for the patient as a life preserver that rescues him from his projections and safeguards his individuality.

In order to insure that he is indeed objective, the therapist must understand and screen out his own emotions, emotions that spring from his own personal past and have little to do with his treatment of the patient. He must also avoid responses that might jeopardize therapeutic neutrality—for example, reacting to the patient's angers, fears, or depression rather than reflecting them, or offering personal information about his own life or background. By monitoring what the patient can handle emotionally at any given point and limiting his interventions accordingly, the therapist can provide the most support. He becomes the guardian of the patient's real self. The therapist's emotional calm, together with his attitude of curiosity and investigation amid the patient's affective storm of hopelessness and helplessness, conveys a strong implicit message to the patient that she has the capacity to manage personal conflicts. This has a soothing effect and encourages the patient to persist with the struggle.

If the therapist loses his neutrality and objectivity and becomes personally involved with the patient, or steps into the patient's life inside or outside the sessions, he loses his most valuable tool in helping the patient recover: the objectivity of his perception and judgment. In addition, he confirms the patient's regressive projections and reinforces the patient's efforts at resisting therapy. By confronting the patient's projections, however, the therapist helps her to contain them, which is the first step in allowing the childhood source of these projections to emerge in memories, dreams, and fantasies. Only by controlling the transference acting out of her projections will the patient gain access to and work through the underlying rage and depression.

Because therapeutic neutrality is so vitally important for successful treatment, some therapists have adopted a distorted, rigidly overdeterministic view that they somehow must behave like inhuman blocks of wood for fear that expressing emotion or interest would threaten therapy. Nothing is farther from the truth. The therapist must be a real person, not in the sense of sharing his personal life with the patient but rather by showing an emotionally warm interest in the patient's problems, sympathizing with his real life defeats, congratulating him on his triumphs, and playing the part of an auxiliary ego in his confrontations. Throughout, the therapist must insist that the patient will survive emotionally only by learning how to cope and adapt. This does not mean that the therapist personally cares about the patient in the way that many borderline patients wish for and insist on. If therapists were to become personally involved with each patient, they would probably flee their professional calling due to emotional exhaustion.

A parallel misconception is that the *only* therapeutic force in treatment is the analysis and working through of the past. This view overlooks the fact that the structure of the treatment itself, based on the therapist's implicit assumption that the patient will always act in a mature, adaptive, and self-interested manner, provides enormous positive support. This attitude on the part of the therapist serves as a model with which the patient can identify. The therapist's confidence in the patient's ability to investigate and work through his past becomes a type of self-fulfilling prophecy if the therapist maintains the neutrality necessary to preserve it.

Additional support is created by the regularity of the sessions. The interview format itself is an opportunity to express and discharge painful emotions, to review and critique past efforts to solve problems, and to rehearse new adaptive solutions. If these components of the therapeutic process are properly managed, they constitute an emotionally soothing process and they aid the healing work without inducing regressions.

Though most therapists recognize that therapeutic neutrality is vital for successful treatment, they nevertheless are human beings with their own development, failings, and weaknesses. In the intense give and take of therapy, it is not uncommon for the therapist's own vulnerabilities to surface in what is called countertransference reactions. There are two definitions of countertransference. The strict definition is the transfer of infantile conflicts and feelings toward important persons in the therapist's early life onto the patient and treating the patient as if he were those projections. The broader definition, which I think is more suitable for work with disorders of the self, is *all* the therapist's emotions that interfere with the conduct of the psychotherapy. Using this broader definition alerts the therapist to possibly disruptive emotions whether or not he recognizes them as arising from childhood.

Our personalities develop through processes of identification, introjection, and projection as we take in the emotional messages that our parents send us. This is how we build personality structure while growing up, and those mechanisms remain alive and active even after we become adults. It is not possible to sustain a negative countertransference attitude to a patient's projection without somehow linking it up to our own developmental dynamics. It is somewhat akin to the Stanislavski method of acting in which the actor remembers and utilizes a past experience with the same emotional content as a scene that he is trying to portray in the present. As the therapist comes under the intense projections from the patient and begins to feel angry with him, the therapist will slowly, without being aware of it, search through his or her past to find some representation that will support the anger.

For example, consider a woman therapist whose patient, a teenage girl, peppered every session with rage and severe acting out. The patient hated the therapist, projected her rage onto the therapist, and assumed the therapist hated her. When the therapist came to see me, she talked about her patient in a snide, sarcastic way that was quite uncharacteristic of her. I pointed this out to her as a form of countertransference. Usually this would be enough to identify and control it, but repeated efforts to call this to her attention led nowhere. The sarcasm continued. I asked her if there was anyone in her background whom the patient reminded her of. Later she said that she was the second of two children, with an older sister who died at the age of three before she, the therapist, was born. The deceased sister had been the apple of the mother's eye. The therapist knew she could never compete with her dead sister to win her mother's approval. She realized that she was projecting her image of the dead sister onto the patient. Once she understood the source of her countertransference, she controlled it and continued with her work.

Sometimes countertransference can arise from the most mundane distractions or preoccupations. One day I was late and banged my car in the garage. A bit frazzled from the experience, I rushed into my office and admitted my first patient who asked me how another patient of mine was doing, calling her by her name. I was startled because they never had appointments around the same time. I wondered if they had met socially. Or was he dating her? Then I realized what had happened. Worried about my dented fender, I had inadvertently picked her file out of the drawer instead of his, and he had read her name on the folder. My distraction represented a countertransferential failure to pay proper attention to my patient. I apologized and told him about the accident in the garage.

Why is countertransference so important in the psychotherapy of disorders of the self? When patients with deflated and inflated false selves get into the working-through phase of treatment and begin to recall childhood memories, they describe their childhoods as if they were concentration camps and their parents were the guards. These patients survived by finding their parents' Achilles heels and using this knowledge to manipulate their parents to give them what they needed for survival. Consequently, they grow up to become masters of manipulation, keenly trained at evoking the desired response from others. They engage in provoking the therapist through their projections, never seeing him as a potential friend and ally who can be trusted. Unlike neurotic and psychotic patients, individuals with a false-self disorder make the therapist the center of the action by projecting upon him their manipulative strategies. It is difficult for a therapist caught up in this to maintain therapeutic neutrality.

In order to deal with the patient's projections and maintain therapeutic neutrality, the therapist must insist upon maintaining specific practical arrangements of the treatment, such as time, place, length of interview, fee, policy for lateness, cancelled appointments, vacations, and so forth. These arrangements help to manage the accidental and incidental events that can occur during the course of treatment. Strict adherence to these policies and arrangements will restrain the therapist from unwittingly playing into the patient's projections.

The vast majority of countertransference problems result from the therapist's unwittingly stepping into the patient's projection of the rewarding parent and functioning as a caretaker for her patient by altering the therapeutic framework thereby promoting the patient's resistance to therapy. The purpose of the therapeutic framework is to maintain the therapeutic objectivity. If the practical matters of treatment are not well established from the first and adhered to rigorously, they constitute "loopholes" or "leaks," which promote unnoticed transference acting out that can become institutionalized in the regular course of treatment. Each loophole gives the patient an edge in luring the therapist either into playing the rewarding parental figure by granting special concessions or into playing the disapproving figure, which becomes the target for the patient's rage. If these breakdowns in the therapeutic framework go unacknowledged, even the most skilled and dedicated therapist may not be able to avoid this subjective and defeating involvement in the patient-therapist relationship. Once the therapist has altered her therapeutic objective stance to resonate with the patient's resistance, she has lost her most powerful tool. The patient's persistent, artful, and insidious efforts are often pressed with such fervor and flavor of reality that the therapist is torn between humane considerations for her patient and therapeutic objectivity. Once a therapist even begins to think of herself as a caretaker for the patient, rather than the guardian of the patient's real self, she is already caught up in countertransference. She has already begun to respond to rather than reflect the patient's projections.

The field of psychotherapy is no more immune to life's vicissitudes than any other. It is not surprising, therefore, to discover that many psychotherapists also have deflated or inflated false selves, since therapists, too, emerge from the same background of family conflicts as their patients. In fact, certain characteristics of this work attract people with these personality disorders.

For example, the borderline therapist with a deflated false self can be attracted to the profession because of the protection it provides against fears of engulfment and abandonment which prevent him from enjoying feelings of intimacy in real relationships. The need for therapeutic neutrality can protect such a therapist from anxiety feelings, and he can use the professional relationship with the patient as a fantasy substitute for the genuine intimacy avoided in real life. The therapist with an inflated false self can enjoy treatment because he becomes the center of the patients' lives and this role feeds the sense of grandiosity and provides the narcissistic supplies he so desperately needs.

How well therapists perform professionally depends on to what extent they have become aware of their own problems of self-activation and self-emergence, and to what extent they have repaired them. Those who have repaired their real selves may be uniquely suited for this type of work, since they have been on both sides of the fence. If they are aware of their impairments, but have not rectified them, they can still do a good job as therapists if they know and can recognize the types of defenses they employ against their own abandonment depression. In this regard, it is most helpful if the therapist himself has had a course of psychotherapy or psychoanalysis. One of the reasons therapists choose therapy as a profession is to act out rescue fantasies that originated far back in their childhoods. The therapist projects remnants of his own deprived self onto the patient and then does for the patient what he always wanted done for him. In fantasy, then, he has the opportunity to remake his own childhood over and over with each new patient.

If the therapist has had healthy parenting, has matured successfully, and is capable of distinguishing clearly his own self and object representations, he can derive much pleasure and satisfaction as he helps patients to overcome and remake their childhoods. If the therapist is a borderline or narcissist himself, or does not make clear distinctions between his own self and object representations, he ends up projecting his deprived self onto the patient and treating himself through the patient. And of course the patient will not object since as long as the therapist continues to satisfy his own needs by treating the patient's problems, there is no pressing need for the patient to assume responsibility for getting better.

Consider the case of an otherwise excellent, well-trained analytic therapist being supervised by me whose patient, an hysterical, borderline woman, placed incessant demands on her, including late night phone calls. The therapist gradually controlled the patient's behavior. At one point the therapist called me to say that she had had a profitable session that day with her patient and thought everything was going well, only to receive a call from the emergency room of the local hospital that night informing her that the patient had signed herself in because of suicidal preoccupations. The therapist told me she suspected it was because the patient was mad at her for setting limits to her acting out. I suggested that the therapist tell the emergency physician to tell the patient to leave the hospital and come to the office to see her to work it out.

As treatment continued I scrutinized the therapist's reports to discover whether as she set limits to the acting out the patient would eventually become depressed. But abandonment feelings never emerged. I monitored the case for several weeks, wondering what was going wrong since the therapist's approach seemed to be proceeding normally. Still the expected depression did not seem to be emerging. Then in conversation with me one day, the therapist casually dropped the fact that the patient had not paid her bill in three months and she hadn't done anything about it. Here was the key: the therapist's not expecting the patient to take responsibility for herself and pay her bill had subtly reinforced her desire not to take responsibility for herself in therapy as well.

Another example is that of a teenage boy who dropped out of school, drank and took drugs, broke furniture at home, and developed severe obsessive-compulsive behavior. Both the patient and the therapist asked for a consultation with me. The boy came in, draped himself over the chair like a wet dishrag, and we stared at each other. I looked at him. He looked at me without speaking. Finally, he said, "Aren't you going to ask me any questions?" I replied that since he had requested the consultation, he must have a story to tell. He began slowly, haltingly. I didn't say much, and his body and facial cues clearly indicated that he wished I would take over. I told him that I thought another session would be necessary. He left, went home, and proceeded to break up the furniture. He then called his therapist and told him that I was a quack. His therapist suggested that he come back to see me again.

During our second encounter, after accusing me of quackery, he just sat there sulking. I explained that I wasn't sure why he was angry, since I had to get information before I could evaluate him. He saw the point of that but complained that I should be saying something to him. I asked if what I was doing was different from what his therapist did. His answer was exuberant: "Oh, he's very different from you. He's nice and makes it easy for me. If I don't have anything to talk about, he'll talk or suggest things for me to talk about. He asks questions and seems interested in me." I said, "There's the problem right there. Your therapist takes over for you and relieves you of the rage for having to take responsibility for yourself." Obviously, the therapist must ask questions, but they must be wisely chosen so that the act of questioning should not become a substitute for the patient's spontaneously reporting what he feels. Again the key to the problem was countertransference: the therapist was saving the patient from himself by acting as caretaker, relieving the patient of the need to activate himself.

Both of the above examples clearly show how progress can be impeded when the therapist steps into playing the rewarding role for the patient. Other types of common errors are changing the time of the appointments for reasons that are not legitimate, not charging for missed or cancelled appointments, allowing the patient to indulge in excessive phone calls to the therapist, not starting or ending sessions on time. Policies about these matters are important, not for the convenience of the therapist, but to protect both the therapist and patient from the therapist's countertransference and the patient's projections.

Countertransference does not have to sabotage treatment. The biggest aid in containing the effects of countertransference is the therapist's knowledge that something he is doing is going awry. The first step is for the therapist to identify the countertransference in terms of the feelings or attitudes that are emerging as he works with a particular patient. As long as the patient is not in a crisis state, the therapist can focus attention on his own countertransference as opposed to the patient's reports. In fact, the therapist must do this because at this point the obstacle to successful therapy is the therapist, and unless the problem is resolved, treatment will get nowhere.

The first step, then, is to identify the countertransference. The therapist must not share the problem with the patient, but keep it to herself until she has figured it out. At that point the therapist should look back over the past history of the treatment to see what the patient does to evoke the countertransference. Most often something in the patient's behavior provokes it, even though it is not the patient's problem but a problem rooted in the therapist's vulnerability. (Sometimes the patient is doing nothing to trigger countertransference. In this case, the countertransference is most likely a major, deep-seated problem of the therapist, and if it can't be resolved, the therapist should stop seeing this patient or get treatment for herself to help her overcome it.)

Once the countertransference is identified and controlled, and the therapist can see what the patient is doing to evoke it, the therapist can use these countertransference feelings as a signal to call the patient's attention to certain behavior. Or, if the countertransference has resulted in intrusive negative activity on the part of the therapist, she should acknowledge it to the patient so that the patient is aware of the fact that he is not totally responsible for the current problems in treatment.

For example, I once had a woman patient I was seeing three times a week to help her get in touch with her feelings of abandonment. As my scheduled vacation period approached, I became quite obsessive about all the necessary details that needed wrapping up before I could go away; a major one, of course, was to make a list of my patients and inform them that I would be gone for two weeks. On a Wednesday evening I was seeing this patient and listening to her efforts to deal with abandonment. Because I was distracted by my vacation details, I didn't realize that she was getting in touch with and expressing her feelings of abandonment for the first time. As the patient went out the door after this session, I announced that I would be leaving in a couple of weeks. As soon as she had left, I realized my mistake.

The woman had an appointment the following day, so I decided to wait to see how she had handled it before bringing up my behavior of the previous evening. I thought this would be a good barometer of how far she had come in treatment. If she denied and avoided the feelings created by this mistake, it would mean she was not as far along as I thought. If she took it up with me directly, it would confirm that she was making progress. She came in and laid it right on the line, telling me I had done a terrible thing by announcing my vacation at the end of last evening's session. She said I could have at least waited until the morning. She was right, and I apologized, explaining my preoccupations that had led me to be less sensitive than I should have been. (I have never found a patient who could not accept mistakes and apologies for them, as long as there are not too many. What patients cannot tolerate is lack of honesty.)

Often the patient's manner or behavior triggers the countertransference. For example, a lawyer I was once treating had a poker-faced style of presenting material in sessions. I was never quite sure if he was expressing real feelings or merely intellectualizing about them. After a long period of time, I found a countertransference response that answered this question. If I felt bored, I suspected that he was intellectualizing and not expressing genuine feelings. I could then ask, "Are you really feeling what you're telling me?"

Another patient was a successful, charming salesman and also served on the board of trustees of the hospital where I worked. In every session he engagingly told me how frequently my name came up at board meetings, always in conjunction with what a wonderful psychiatrist I was and how much good I was doing. He was obviously trying to seduce me. I got angry, lost therapeutic flexibility, and froze, at which point he accused me quite rightly of being "a cold fish." Later I examined my own feelings, and at the next session when he again tried to control me by flattery, I simply asked him why he felt the need to seduce me into his cause rather than assume that I was interested in working with him.

From the observing distance created by controlling the countertransference, the therapist can identify the principal clinical issue the patient is reporting and try to explain to himself the significance of that issue. With a borderline patient the issue could be any one of the parts of the borderline triad: self-activation, anxiety or depression, or defense. The next step is to devise an intervention strategy to deal with that issue and to hypothesize what the result of the intervention would be. For example, again with a borderline patient, the therapist might decide to confront defense and anticipate that depression will emerge if the intervention is successful. Lastly, the therapist must make the intervention and measure the response.

The dance of transference/countertransference between the patient and therapist is inevitable, whether the therapist has years of experience or is relatively new. It can be particularly troublesome, however, for new therapists who have yet to learn how to spot the clues of countertransference; do not know themselves very well yet, especially how they respond in treatment sessions to different types of patients; and do not know methods for handling and diffusing the countertransference. Case reports from 35 seminars I gave in which 12 new therapists presented individual cases clearly demonstrated the inevitable pattern of transference/countertransference. In each case the therapist stepped into the rewarding pattern with the patient.

At the beginning of treatment, the patient leads the dance through transference acting out because the therapist is caught up in countertransference. As the therapist gains better control of the countertransference, he slowly takes the lead as the patient shifts from transference acting out to real transference and establishes a therapeutic alliance. As therapy progresses, the therapist and patient trade lead positions as they slide back into transference acting out and countertransference. As each phase is resolved, the therapist assumes therapeutic control and the patient is led into further working through.

As a therapist becomes more knowledgeable about the dynamics of countertransference, its power to interfere with therapy is reduced. It is never completely eliminated since we are all human beings and cannot perform in relationships with patients as robots. Nor would we want to. What is important is for each therapist to know his own personal countertransference vulnerabilities and be guided by this awareness in the work. It also helps to have a supervisor or close colleague with whom one can share any problems that arise in this area. I had a close colleague for 25 years who, after a few minutes of consultation about a problem, could often tell me the countertransference binds that I had fallen into. I could do the same for him, simply because it is far easier to see countertransference activity in someone other than yourself.

Since countertransference is an inevitable factor in therapy, it is important for the patient to understand what it is and how it works. Borderline and narcissistic patients, however, are frequently not interested in identifying the therapist's countertransference as long as they can fit it into their rewarding or idealizing projections. Even when the therapist points it out to them, they might deny that it is interfering with their progress. It is helpful for the patient to keep in mind all the frame factors as a way of evaluating the degree of the therapist's countertransference, since most of the breakdown in the therapeutic framework involves the therapist stepping into a caretaking role for the patient. The framework is the practical arrangements within which the therapy is conducted: for example, does the therapist expect the patient to do the reporting, or does he take over with too many questions, or try to make decisions, or discuss his personal life, or get involved in the patient's life outside the office? Does he quietly insist that the patient face her conflicts or does he back off? Can he take hostility without becoming defensive? Is he responsive to the patient's moods? Does he charge an appropriate fee, and does he hold the patient responsible for missed appointments? Do his comments seem to fit what the patient is saying, or do they seem superimposed?

If a patient suspects that her therapist is handling the framework in a sloppy fashion, it should be a warning to the patient that a consultation on this matter is necessary in order to protect the patient's progress. It would be in order for the patient to bring it up with the therapist and suggest a consultation. Sometimes if the countertransference has not proceeded for too long a time or become too intense, a consultation can help the therapist identify it, and treatment can proceed from that point; but deep, prolonged countertransference becomes firmly ensconced in the relationship, making it highly unlikely that the therapist will be able to control it. If such is the case, it is a clear sign that the therapist has lost objectivity about this patient and should transfer the patient to another therapist.

A case of this sort involved a male therapist who called me for a consultation about a female patient he was treating as an hysterical neurotic. The patient had discovered that the therapist's wife was pregnant and had became overinvolved in preoccupations about the pregnancy. This tipped him off to the fact that something other than therapy was going on in their weekly sessions. I saw the patient in consultation and learned that she had "fallen in love" with the therapist at the very beginning and paid little or no attention to what he said in treatment sessions. The fact that he talked to her meant that he cared for her and that is all she was interested in. When I confronted her with the inappropriateness of this for therapeutic progress, she became angry at me. Later, I discussed this with the therapist; he realized that he was not familiar enough with working with personality disorders to rectify the situation, so the patient was transferred to another therapist.

Another incident in which the patient did not transfer to another therapist involved a patient who was an outstanding physician, twice divorced, who was taken by his current girlfriend to her therapist for a couple's session. The physician told the woman's therapist that he had been in analysis five times a week for the last eight years. Suspecting that something was going wrong with the physician's therapy, the woman's therapist suggested to him that he see me for consultation. I asked him how his analysis worked, and he replied that his therapist was insightful, charming, and always amazed him with brilliant interpretations of his dreams. The therapist was a wonderful person who always understood if the patient was late or had to cancel appointments because he was busy. I asked the patient if he ever felt angry at his therapist or had periods of depression with him. He said no, and went on to say that he could never find the perfect woman: there was always some flaw or disappointment. I asked if he had ever discovered flaws with his therapist or been disappointed in therapy, and he said no. In other words, the patient's perception of the therapist as perfect was an idealizing transference, and the therapist himself was probably using the sessions to fuel his own narcissistic needs and was probably bathing in a narcissistic glow along with the patient. Otherwise, he would have dealt with the idealizing transference, and there would have been a lot more progress. I suggested to the patient that the situation was not likely to change and that he should see another therapist. Much later, I found out that he had not switched therapists; he continued to bask in the narcissistic glow, there had been no progress, and he still continued to search for the perfect woman.

Patients with disorders of the self may benefit from other forms of treatment besides individual psychotherapy, such as group, marital, or family therapy, drugs, and hospitalization. In recommending or conducting any of these treatments, the therapist should keep in mind certain theoretical considerations as to how they should be approached with patients suffering with a deflated self. For the borderline patient, group, marital, and family therapy can be extremely effective if the therapist limits himself to confrontation dealing strictly with maladaptive behavior, such as drug abuse, sexual acting out, and avoidance of self-activation at work. It is not possible to work through the abandonment depression in the presence of others because the patient entertains a fantasy that he has exclusive possession of the therapist. The patient will invest emotionally in the therapist as a fantasy object only to the extent that this fantasy finds expression in the face-to-face relationship with the therapist. The presence of other people frustrates that fantasy, and the patient lowers his investment in the treatment to the point where it is impossible to work through the depression. Despite this, the very substantial goals of confrontive therapy, such as ego repair and improved ability to adapt to life, can be met in the group setting. If the patient wants to go further, however, and deal with the abandonment depression, individual therapy is necessary.

Drugs and hospitalization present a unique dilemma for the therapist. The borderline's philosophy of life is: life should be easy and I shouldn't have to take care of myself. The lesson the therapist is trying to teach is: life is not easy and if you don't take responsibility yourself, the price paid is always high. Drugs play into the patient's philosophy that life is easy and reinforce the rewarding fantasy, which acts as a resistance to therapy and must be dealt with in treatment. Drugs indicate to the patient that the therapist is willing to take care of her and will make life easy for her. If antidepressants are given to a patient working through the abandonment depression, the depression may disappear, along with the patient's motive for working through it. The patient would be under the illusion that the depression is gone, and yet she would still have the developmental arrest and be just as vulnerable to the depression when the drugs were withdrawn. Of course, drugs may have to be administered for clinical emergencies, but they should be used only for targeted symptoms, and eliminated when those symptoms clear up.

Hospitals are caretaking environments that promote regression, and their use, like the use of drugs, should be limited if possible. An exception to this rule is the borderline adolescents described in Chapter 9, who could not be treated except in a long stay in a hospital. Stays should be short and inpatient treatment focused on whatever stress (usually separation stress) brought the patient in. Contact with the outside therapist should be maintained, and the hospital therapist should devote herself to confrontation and avoid other aspects of the patient's problem. The patient should be discharged as soon as possible. Lower-level borderline patients who cannot function adequately may need more ego support than the therapist can provide in outpatient care. These patients may require hospitalization therapy over long periods of time, but this should be decided at the beginning of therapy.

Narcissistic patients do poorly in group settings (family, marital, group therapy). Most should not be placed in group treatment until they are aware of and prepared to work on their narcissistic defenses. They may require drugs and, less often, hospitalization.

Schizoid patients have a difficult time in group settings but, in contrast to the narcissist, probably should be placed in them where possible to begin to deal with their isolation. Drugs and hospitalization should be used sparingly.

The give and take between therapist and patient can, at times, be vexing and problematical for both parties. In the role of guardian of the real self, the therapist must recognize countertransference when it occurs and take the steps to diffuse it, or the treatment will cease to be effective. The therapist must be firm in resisting the borderline's and narcissist's attempts to manipulate the parameters of therapy for their own ends if the patient is eventually to take responsibility for his abandonment depression and work through it.

THE CREATIVE SOLUTION

Sartre, Munch, and Wolfe

PSYCHOTHERAPY is the best route to relief of the abandonment depression and discovery of the real self. But it is not the only one. Some people with impaired selves possess internal resources that they may draw upon to mitigate their pain and express at least part of their real selves.

The artist whose real self is impaired has a weapon for defending against the abandonment depression not available to the people we have looked at in the preceding chapters: the artistic talent which can lead to creative expression, which, in turn, can activate this function of the real self. The artist uses the creativity of his real self to find a way of dealing with the feelings of abandonment and engulfment and to temper the abandonment depression's power to ruin his life.

The birthright of the real self is creativity: the ability to invent, to perceive old patterns in new relationships, or to rearrange old patterns in new ways. Everyone with a healthy real self has the potential for leading a creative life and dealing with problems and challenges in innovative ways. Not all individuals have the same capacity for expressing their creativity, of course, since it, like all other capacities, is a product of both nature and nurture, of genetic inheritance and developmental encouragement.

Creativity often requires effort and struggle and the willingness to endure anxiety, since creative efforts usually have the potential of failing, of being critiqued unfavorably, and even of being rejected. Some people are unwilling to make the necessary effort to endure the unavoidable anxiety; as a result, they forego creative endeavors and, it is to be hoped, make their peace with living below their full potential. Still others may have been born with little creative endowment.

Stories of artists' struggles with their own personal muses are legendary. Creativity, it seems, does not come easy, even to those hailed as creative geniuses. Some of these difficulties may be related to disorders of the self or to scars left from the normal separation anxieties of childhood that impinge on everyone's creativity. One of the most common problems is avoidance, the inability to get down to doing work or follow through on it. This is typically seen in so-called writer's block, which may often be due to the writer's need to defend himself against the anxiety and depression which creative expression can cause. The other side of the coin is the artist who is able to complete a work, has a great creative success, and then, unable to endure the consequent anxiety of living up to this reputation, or the guilt of wondering whether it is really deserved, falls into depression and perhaps turns to drink.

The fully developed real self always has access to its creativity, but artistic creativity does not guarantee a fully developed real self. Many artists with severe disorders of the self are fortunate to have the talent that produces the urge to draw upon their creativity, thereby finding and establishing a segment of the real self that allows them to adapt to life more successfully than they probably would have without that talent. In effect, they ameliorate the depression and strengthen the real self—even though it remains impaired—through creative expression, which unlocks other impaired capacities, such as self-esteem and self-activation. Although these links are fragile, they can rescue the artist from the typical tragedies that result from a personality disorder. Creativity thus becomes the primary path in the artist's quest for the real self.

There is a host of writers, painters, artists, sculptors, and actors whose lives would ably demonstrate this. I have chosen Jeal-Paul Sartre, Edvard Munch, and Thomas Wolfe because they are well-known representatives of three different artistic media, and each used his medium to defend against the abandonment depression and express the real self. They are, respectively, the philosopher, painter, and novelist of the abandonment depression. Because they express the same theme and because that theme resonates with nearly everyone who encounters their works, their artistic achievements assume a universal quality, as is true of all great artists who deal with themes of developmental conflict, such as coming of age or loss of innocence, with which we can all identify.

Jean-Paul Sartre: Philosopher of the Abandonment Depression

Sartre's own insightful account of his childhood years vividly describes how his grandparents' and his mother's inability to acknowledge his emerging individuality and their need to idealize him inappropriately led to a severely impaired real self.

> I had no scene "of my own" . . . I was giving the grown-ups their cues . . . my own reason for being slipped away; I would suddenly discover that I did not really count, and I felt ashamed of my unwanted presence in that well-ordered world.[1] . . . My truth, my character, and my name were in the hands of adults. I had learned to see myself through their eyes . . . When they were not present, they left their gaze behind, and it mingled with the light. I would run and jump across that gaze, which preserved my nature as a model grandson . . . a transparent certainty spoiled everything: I was an imposter. . . . The clear sunny semblances that constituted my role were exposed by a lack of being which I could neither quite understand, nor cease to feel.[2]

Sartre's "lack of being" grew out of his recognition that he lacked a real self, that he had become "a model grandson" as a narcissistic defense against the emptiness of his own life. He defended against his fears of engulfment and emptiness by behaving in a manner that would satisfy the perfectionistic demands of the adults in his life. By identifying with the idealized projections of his mother and grandparents, he could ward off the feelings of fragmentation and nothingness. When these adults appeared to him as whole and perfect, he could bask in that wholeness and perfection as if it were his own. He performed as a mirroring object to meet their needs, rather than his own, to complete *their* selves at the cost of his own real self.

Overidentifying with the omnipotent images projected on him by the parent figures in his life precipitated the inevitable fears of engulfment and loss of self. He experienced his real self as empty, nebulous, without substance. Sartre dealt with this dilemma by beginning to write. At first he was motivated primarily to please the parent figures, as usual. His writing was ignored by the family, which worked to his advantage because without the need to mirror the adults in his creative efforts, he could enjoy the privacy and freedom to experiment with his emerging real self. Writing became a secret place where he could be himself. He had embarked on a quest that would begin to differentiate his real self from his false self; but to deal with the fears of engulfment that this quest precipitated, he maintained the split between his two selves and employed additional defenses, such as detachment, distancing, and intellectualization, against the painful feelings this splitting entailed. In Sartre's case, as in many others, this mode of being, combined with his high, probing intelligence, led him to become an intellectual and philosopher.

The major themes of the abandonment depression appear in Sartre's philosophy of consciousness, being, nothingness, and the human condition: the emptiness of the impaired real self, the lonely individual struggle to use creativity to establish a modicum of a real self, the fear of engulfment. He ultimately concluded that *being* in itself (i.e., consciousness) is nothingness, and nonbeing has no identity. Both positions reflected and reinforced his own experience of the emptiness he associated with his impaired real self. To him, the radical freedom of consciousness meant acknowledging that one is the absolute creator of oneself and one's destiny. *Being* for itself. The extraordinary responsibility implied by this role is felt as anguish, and a longing arises to escape from freedom into the secure solidity of self-identity possessed by things in the world. But we are not like the things in the world; we have consciousness and are condemned to be free. We escape this freedom only in death.

Because the adults in his family did not acknowledge and support Sartre's emerging self, he had to create it by himself. As a result, he assumed all human beings had to develop a real self without help, in a void, totally alone. The void and emptiness that encircled Sartre would fill up with the fears of engulfment he associated with efforts to activate the real self and to defend against it with the grandiose self. He could not see that a supportive, acknowledging environment could make the quest for a real self pleasurable and exciting, as it does for individuals who enjoy a normal development. He was equally unable to conceive of an autonomous self as being complete and whole without fears of engulfment, emptiness, loneliness, or anguish. "We are as alone as in our dreams," he surmised. His perception of social relationships was similarly distorted; he never found them to be based on emotional sharing and mutual enrichment. His concept of Being-for-others remained a threat to the autonomous state of Being-for-itself. His philosophy thus became a rationalization of his emotional dilemma—being and nothingness.

Edvard Munch: The Painter of the Abandonment Depression

Edvard Munch was born in Norway, the second of five children. His sister was one year older. His father, an army physician, was twice the age of his mother, who was already ill with tuberculosis when she gave birth to Edvard. She died when Munch was five. The mother's sister joined the household to care for the children. Edvard was often sick as a child. He became very close to his older sister, but she died of tuberculosis when he was fifteen. These early childhood events made an indelible impression on his character, his perceptions and feelings about women, and his need to create through his art the real self that was unable to emerge when he was a child. From his graphic portrayals of separation anxiety and abandonment depression and the difficulties he had in personal relationships in his life, I hypothesize that he was a borderline personality and therefore was unable to mourn the deaths of his mother and sister. It was not solely the deaths themselves but their occurring to an already borderline personality that had this effect on him. In the course of his long life of 81 years Munch produced over 50,000 drawings and paintings, a prodigious visual tribute to his search for a real self.

Munch led a nomadic life revolving almost totally around his painting. Depression, loneliness, and alcoholism plagued him, and he made frequent trips to health resorts but found no cure for his troubles. Throughout his life he was unable to commit himself to a long-term relationship with a woman; most of his liasions were tenuous, sporadic, and episodic, except for his two years or more of involvement with Tulla Larsen. But when Tulla proposed marriage, Munch literally bolted and ran. He rationalized that women might stand in the way of realizing his true potential for artistic self-expression, in other words they stood in the way of the development of his real self. His artistic quest for a real self was so fragile, he could not expose it to the threat of a relationship.

His paintings contain the most graphic visions of separation panic, abandonment depression, death, and grief. His famous painting *The Scream* is a dramatic evocation of the helplessness and panic of separation. He repeats over and over the feelings of loss and abandonment by death. The memories of his own pain-ridden childhood and the early deaths of his mother and sister recur in such paintings as *By the Deathbed* (1893), *Death in the Sickroom* (1893–94), *The Sick Child* (1885–86), *Melancholy* (1891), *Death at the Helm* (1893), *The Dead Mother* (1893), *Dead Mother and Child* (1897–99).

Munch's difficulties in understanding and perceiving women were portrayed in his paintings *Madonna* (1895), *Vampire* (1893–94), *The Woman (Sphinx)* (1893–94), *Jealousy* (1895), and his two paintings whose titles, *Separation* (1894, 1896) echo a key theme of the abandonment depression.

He said, "I have never loved. I have experienced the passion that can move mountains and transform people—the passion that tears at the heart and drinks one's blood—but there has never been anyone to whom I could say: 'Woman, it is you I love—you are my all'."[3] At age 45, his alcoholism worsened, he developed delusions of persecution and hallucinations, and he was hospitalized for 8 months, "My condition was verging on madness," he averred. He could have been experiencing a separation psychosis in a borderline or his condition might have been deteriorating into a psychosis. However, he recovered to do much productive work. As we will say of Thomas Wolfe, his ability to discharge painful feelings and to activate his real self through his art probably enabled him to have a far better adjustment than he could have had otherwise. His basic personality structure did not change, as it might have in psychotherapy.

Thomas Wolfe: The Novelist of the Abandonment Depression

The mountains that ringed his native town of Asheville, North Carolina, were a fitting metaphor for the defenses Thomas Wolfe erected around his imprisoned self. Only his writing and the acknowledgment of his unique talent by important people in his life freed the creative capacity of his real self from that prison, just as the train, one of his favorite images, was the only "way out or escape to freedom from the encircling mountains of Asheville." In describing his fictionalized alter ego, Eugene Gant, he wrote, " . . . the long retreating whistle wail had him dream and hunger for the proud unknown north with that wild ecstasy, that intolerable and wordless joy of longing and desire."[4]

Wolfe's real self was never able to escape totally from its psychic prison. Only the creative aspect broke loose; the rest of the capacities remained caught in the developmental arrest. He had little capacity for genuine intimacy and little autonomy; he was impulsive and disorganized with little ability to take charge of himself and his life. Only his writing gave him a more or less stable identity and a basis for relating to people. More importantly, from the intrapsychic point of view, his writing provided a more adaptive defense against his abandonment depression and allowed him to adapt to life in a far less self-destructive manner than he would have without it.

Wolfe's borderline dilemma was inexorably rooted in his unresolved dependency upon his mother. He was constantly motivated by a defensive need to comply with her wishes in order to relieve the severe abandonment depression associated with any attempt to separate from her and express his own individuality. His defensive false self was driven by a powerful wish for reunion (or fusion) with an idealized mother image. But the wish for reunion and the clinging it inspired carried with it a companion fear of being engulfed by the very person with whom he wished to merge and thereby lose himself. When Wolfe's clinging behavior became too intense, when he got too close to his mother, he would distance himself in order to preserve his fragmentary sense of self. His biographers often refer to this behavior as his compulsion to freedom. The issue, however, was not freedom but preservation of the self.

The need to distance himself from the maternal environment

brought additional problems. It interrupted his major defense against the abandonment depression—clinging—and the depression emerged, requiring other defenses, such as isolating himself geographically where he could relieve the depression by various forms of acting out such as drinking, sexual promiscuity, and the endless, aimless wandering that he captured so romantically in his writings. These themes of reunion and merger, fear of loss of self, distancing, depression, and self-destructive behavior dominated his life and literary works. The polar strategies of clinging and distancing were his principal defenses until he got in touch with the creativity of his real self through his writing.

Like most people, Thomas Wolfe was unable to face the infantile nature of his idealizing, clinging, and distancing behavior. But through his enormous creative talent he transformed his wish for a rewarding object, and expressed it as follows: "It was mostly of a search for a father. Young men sometimes believe in the existence of heroic figures, stronger and wiser than themselves, to whom they can turn for an answer to all their vexation and grief. Later they must discover that such answers have to come out of their own hearts but the powerful desire to believe in such figures persists."[5]

Wolfe's clinging fantasies were fueled by idealizing important people in his life: his mother, Mrs. Roberts, Max Perkins, Aline Bernstein. Time revealed their human inadequacies, however, and Wolfe grew disillusioned. None of them could measure up to his need for an omnipotent, rewarding figure who would support and nurture him. His desire to escape in order to relieve his fear of loss of self became so agonizing that it turned his feelings for them almost into hatred. "I see every wart and sore upon them, every meanness, pettiness, and triviality . . . and I hate these mutations."[6]

Wolfe's life story is the quest for a real self through exclusive dependent relationships with an idealized person, hoping he or she would provide the acknowledgment that would free his real self from its childhood prison. When the wish for union and merger became too intense, he would attack the idealized person because only by attack could he separate and preserve his sense of self. However, because he was unaware of and unable to take responsibility for the conflict, he would project, rationalize, and blame the idealized person for his or her deficiencies. In this way he freed himself from the person, but not from his eternal search for a rewarding object. His ploy left him alone, a wanderer, in need of other defenses against his abandonment depression.

This idealization of others has led students of Wolfe to suggest that he was actually searching for a Father-God whom he could not accept intellectually but for whom he still yearned. When he turned father substitutes into gods and then discovered they were only fallible and human after all, he felt betrayed. Was he searching for a father or a religion? My answer to both is no. He was seeking a rewarding object to help establish his real self, and he needed it.

Trapped in his search, Wolfe keenly perceived all the feelings and images of loss that borderline patients with an abandonment depression experience in psychotherapy as they activate themselves and individuate. His frequent use of the same images that borderline adolescent patients (see Chapter 9) use to describe their own abandonment depressions suggests a key to the popularity of Wolfe's books: he beautifully and eloquently described the vicissitudes of one of the most important phases of human development. He was the chronicler of human aspirations for individuation and a real self, as well as of the extraordinary power and depth of the feelings of loss when the real self's emergence is not acknowledged. Wolfe also deals impassionedly with the oedipal conflict (the conflict between the wish for the mother as a sexual object and the wish to emancipate from her) and the conflicts later in life between experiment and adventure versus safety and familiarity.

Tom was the last of eight children, six years younger than the next youngest, born to a couple who had formed a classic misalliance. They seemed to have come together mostly through a fantasy of escape from their individual fates. The mother was self-centered, domineering, possessive, stingy, ready to sacrifice any of her children's best interest to her own greed. The father, although sensitive, earthy, and lusty, was unable to take responsibility for himself or his family. He was plagued with severe depression, which led to catastrophic bouts of alcoholism. He vented his rage at life by relentless and bitter verbal assaults on his wife and children, blaming them for his dismal life and instilling guilt in his children to motivate them to rescue him.

Tom was treated as a baby by the entire family. His mother wrote: "I kept him a baby. He slept with me until he was a great big boy. He slept in the same room with his mother until he was twelve. He wasn't weaned until he was three and a half years old."[7]

It was this profound symbiotic dependent relationship with the mother that, on the one hand, probably laid the seeds for his rich creativity and, on the other hand, imprisoned his real self in the developmental arrest. His almost slavish dependence on the mother lasted until the age of 25 when he met Aline Bernstein. His relationship with his father was happier but much less intense. Although the father had many positive qualities, such as his interest in poetry, he seems to have been too depressed and immersed in his own problems to be much of a father to Tom, who was not his father's favorite, even though Wolfe claims to have worshipped him and enjoyed literature and poetry with him.

Wolfe's first experience of the abandonment depression occurred at age four when his mother left her husband for the first time and moved with Tom and his brother Grover to St. Louis, leaving Mabel, the oldest daughter, to care for the father. Grover caught typhoid and died, an event which Tom described as giving his mother "the most terrible wound of her life."[8] Thirty-four years later, when she was told that Tom himself was going to die, she reverted to the death of Grover and described it almost word for word as Tom had recorded it in his novel.

Tom's second experience of abandonment depression occurred at age six when his mother decided to move out from the father again and bought a boardinghouse to run. The other children "floated in limbo," living at one house or another, but Tom—the mother's possession—had to live with her: a clear example of her disregard for his best interests. He was taken from his father and siblings against his wishes to serve his mother. Repeatedly she betrayed him and exposed him to abandonment depression with all of its sense of loss and loneliness: first, by the basic nature of her relationship with him in which self-centeredness, possessiveness, and greed made her unable to acknowledge Tom's emerging self; and later by her depression at Grover's death, and her insistence that he live with her two years later. These events required an escalation in defenses to protect him from fears of engulfment, loss, and abandonment.

The groundwork was laid for retreat into fantasy and the development and use of distancing as a defense. After the painful, uprooting experience at age six, Wolfe's life took a decisive turn toward fantasy and reading to fill the emptiness. He would spend hours at the library reading every book, good and bad. The use of fantasy and words to defend himself against reality began to crystallize.

To deal with his feelings of disillusionment, betrayal, and loss, Wolfe submerged himself in self-dramatization, fantasy, and a lifelong search for an omnipotent mother figure who would acknowledge his emerging self and thereby permit him to free his real self from its prison. However, his disorder would compel him to experience the same disillusionment over and over in his personal life as well as portray it in his writings. In *Look Homeward Angel* he wrote, "All his life it seemed his blazing loyalties began with men and ended with images."[9]

It has been said that our parents give us our problems but also provide opportunities for solutions. The idealized mother who had betrayed and abandoned him developed severe attacks of rheumatism and went away for her health every winter, always taking only Tom with her, enrolling him in whatever school happened to be available. As disruptive as this was in certain respects, it also introduced Wolfe to the idea of using travel as a means of distancing himself from depression and fear of engulfment, and later travel did become an essential element in his lifestyle and literary works. In 1929 he wrote, "Thus did he see first the hillbound, the skygirt, . . . the mountains . . . the fabulous south, the picture of flashing field, of wood and hill which stayed in his heart forever."[10] But it was not a happy heart: their incessant travels (between the ages of 7 and 13 Wolfe spent winters in eight different places in the South) continually disrupted his development of peer contacts and the social skills needed to forge intimate relationships. Later in life he had severe difficulties in both areas.

It is possible that as the trips with his mother robbed him of his autonomy and individuality, the closeness with her became too great; it reactivated his fear of engulfment to an unbearable degree so that he could not indulge in his reunion fantasies with her in quite the same way. Instead, he projected his need for his mother onto the landscape, so that in his dreams of merging with the land he could feel the ecstasy and wonder that he previously imagined in a symbiotic fantasy with her. Thus, his lush, grandiose expressions of rapture with the landscape could be partially explained as a substitute for a gratifying symbiotic mother.

He also rhapsodized about trains, boats, cars, and all forms of travel, no doubt romanticizing his need to distance himself from his mother in order to deal with his fear of losing his identity. He wrote about leaving a place of commitment or entrapment for the open spaces which seemed to him like escape to freedom; and yet he was always able to deny that what lay at the end of the journey was not freedom or escape but the same abandonment depression, which always required additional defenses. He also could deny that the trap was internal, not external, and that travel only changed the scenery, not the problem.

My experience with borderline patients seems to prove Murphy's Law that life refuses to cooperate—whatever bad can happen will happen. Thomas Wolfe's life is an exception in that he was extraordinarily fortunate in meeting and allying himself with adults of upstanding character who were genuinely interested in and fostered his career. No manipulators or scoundrels used or abused him. He received loyal, steadfast support from people who were an almost perfect fit for the emergence of his creative self. The first was his teacher, Mrs. Roberts, who taught him composition, history, and English literature from age 12 to 16. She read a composition of his before meeting him and thought it was the work of "a genius." She was the first to acknowledge his creativity and encourage him to express his real self through writing. He wrote of her, "She was more than a mere teacher . . . [she was] mother of my spirit who filled me with light."[11]

In high school Wolfe won the bronze medal offered by a magazine for the best essay at his school. This event reinforced his desire to write and his inborn talent for words now found an outlet; but he still lacked a crucial psychological dimension for a sense of wholeness that would give him access to his creative source and activate his real self. He graduated from high school at 16 and wanted to go to Princeton, but his father would not support him, so he went to the University of North Carolina, his first trip away from home on his own. This first year living on his own was extremely painful: he was depressed; and his father developed the illness from which he would eventually die.

In his second year, Wolfe won a position on the college paper, and his life turned around. He joined everything, was initiated into fraternities, and began to get more external reinforcement for his writing. He was editor of the college magazine and associate editor of another magazine that published his poetry and stories. He found another mentor, Professor Greenlaw, with whom he studied Elizabethan literature and upon whom he projected his symbiotic needs. That summer, instead of returning home, he went to Norfolk to work; it was a difficult summer for him. On his own once again, he was exposed to the abandonment depression and took to roaming the streets and drinking—a harbinger of the distancing pattern that was to become one of the main themes of his life.

In his junior year, his favorite brother, Ben, who had always urged him to get away from home, died of pneumonia under a cloud of suspicion that his mother had not taken proper care of him. Ben had always championed Tom, who would always refer to Ben's death as the most tragic experience of his entire life. With Ben gone, Tom realized that he should leave home, but his mother clung to him and made him feel guilty about leaving her, since he was the only one left.

He returned to North Carolina and again was successful in all his literary activities, winning a prize for an essay on philosophy. Under the influence of Frederick H. Koch, who organized the Carolina Playmakers, he threw himself into writing a number of plays, which were well received. In spite of this he was still very confused about what he wanted to do. Since it seemed obvious that his talents and life pointed to writing, why was he unable to make the plunge into a literary career? I believe that he could not identify the wishes of the real self (i.e., to be a novelist) as long as writing was motivated by his defensive false self. In other words, he wrote in order to please the idealized authority figures like Professor Koch rather than to express his real self. Only after a long time when he discovered that playwriting was not the appropriate genre for him, could he tap into the great generator and reservoir of his creative talent and write the novels based on his childhood. Until then, his talent had to remain hidden and defended against because of his continued intrapsychic and external dependence on his mother.

Finishing college and having to be on his own brought Wolfe's underlying psychological dilemma to a head. Although unable to activate his real self, identify what he wanted, and implement it, he did realize that he could no longer cling to his mother. But where could he escape? This time the North became the fantasy, an as yet unexplored route of escape, a new environment to replace the omnipotent mother, a place that would acknowledge, activate, and fulfill his real self. He could no longer stay in Asheville, caught in the web of his relationship with his mother, so he went to Harvard to pursue graduate studies in playwriting under Professor George Baker, his latest symbiotic god. But Wolfe overwrote his plays with too many characters and scenes, and he was unable to cut them down. When he realized his plays were not "working," he decided to teach. He had still not, at age 24, discovered that his great desire to write would be satisfied most in writing novels and that his great talent lay there. He had not plumbed the reservoir. The disillusionment he suffered when his gods failed now characterized his relationship with Baker. He wrote to Mrs. Roberts: "I began to understand how bitter a draught it was that Professor Baker was an excellent friend, a true critic but a bad counselor. I knew from that time on that the disposition of my life was mainly in my own hands."[12]

Defeated, Wolfe entered the teaching profession with little enthusiasm. Although he had no great desire to teach, his new position placed him on his own in all ways, free from family and professors, so that he had to come to grips with his underlying problems. He wrote: "I had now committed myself utterly, there was no going back . . . I pulled up my roots bodily, broken almost utterly away from my old life, from my family, my native town, my earlier associations. There was nothing now for me except myself and my work."[13] He had temporarily given up his old defenses: drinking, sexual promiscuity, and clinging to his mother.

Desperate and determined to manage on his own, he worked himself to the bone day and night, containing his loneliness and desolation. He learned his job and enjoyed life again. This was a further, more decisive activation of his real self. The teaching duties were so demanding that he was unable to write. The major saving grace of his teaching job was that he was allowed to have the fall term off so that he could travel to Europe, which he believed was a necessary part of his education as a writer.

Who was this fully grown young man as he departed for Europe? He was tall, talkative, spoke with a lisp, and carried himself awkwardly; he was without conventional social skills. He had dramatic mood swings from states of euphoria to the blackest of depression. And yet despite all this, he was able to draw other people into providing for him what he was unable to do for himself. In the course of his travels, he amassed an extraordinary range of people throughout western Europe and the United States who were prepared to be his caretakers; and as long as a relationship was not prolonged or intimate, he was able to manage it. He had learned well his father's message that adult responsibility for oneself and others leads to depression and resentment, and he always managed to find someone else to take responsibility for him.

For example, Wolfe had a chronic inability to keep track of time and was late to meetings and to classes as well as with work assignments and publishing deadlines. He was unable to keep track of his belongings, losing various clothes, manuscripts, checks, and other important items. He always had problems managing his money. He was impulsive and basically undisciplined except when it came to his work, where he could lose himself for long hours at a stretch. He had difficulty organizing and coordinating his life's activities because of his faulty perception of reality and needed others to handle these affairs since his own real self could not. He was not even able to organize and shape his writing appropriately in order to have a realistic chance of being published.

And yet Wolfe was bright, had a good sense of humor, and was most likely an enjoyable fellow to have around. He had learned how to act out his helplessness in such a way as to provoke others to resonate with his need to be supported and taken care of. But he could grow suspicious of others; when in the depths of a depression, he feared a loss of self and the important people in his life appeared to him to be withholding their support and approval. At these times, he could accuse them of betraying him.

Wolfe's first trip to Europe was a notable turning point in his life, but it began badly. He was now alone, on his own, and his abandonment depression again surfaced as it had at Norfolk and Harvard. Again he resorted to acting-out defenses such as drinking and restless wandering, so that for months the trip was a disaster. He had enormous difficulty activating his talent and creativity on his own because of his depression: he would grimly sit down to write, but he would toss aside the few impatient fragmentary beginnings he managed to produce. Yet he did not give up. He kept at it, and suddenly, as he put it, "The words were wrung out of him in a kind of bloody sweat. . . . They were wrenched out of the last secret source and substance of his life and in them was packed the whole image of his bitter homelessness, his intolerable desire, his mad longing for return."[14]

Throughout this trip to Europe, Wolfe used distance to put himself in a place where he was alone both physically and psychologically, away from his usual supports. His depression and loneliness surfaced, as was to be expected, but he managed to control his acting-out defenses and in a titanic battle activated the creative part of his real self to overcome the regressive behavior. He wrote without purpose or direction. He described the process as "finding his own, i.e., America." What he meant was that he had found his childhood memories of Asheville and mother. Writing, for Wolfe, was a profoundly courageous and disciplined act by an otherwise undisciplined person. And yet he still could not further acknowledge and define his creative purpose without a substitute maternal figure. Again fate cooperated with his needs.

On the trip home from his dramatic discovery of Europe and, more profoundly, his rediscovery of America, home, and childhood, *and* the discovery that these could become the meat of his writing, he met Aline Bernstein on the boat, and they fell madly in love. Bernstein was a success in her own right as a stage designer and a person of grit, determination, and executive capacity. She was twenty years older than Wolfe. She assumed the caretaking functions he had such difficulty with, including supporting him financially as his mother had before. Having her to rely on fulfilled the remaining condition necessary to unleash the mighty engine of Wolfe's creativity.

Wolfe now transferred his symbiotic dependency from his mother to Aline Bernstein. Bernstein satisfied two other essential needs: she helped him once and for all to get over the notion that he was a playwright, convincing him that his style with its abundance of scenes and characters would never fit the stage; and as she encouraged his writing along other lines, she expressed a genuine sympathy for the deprivations of his childhood and youth. In effect, she acknowledged key aspects of his real self. Just prior to meeting Bernstein, Wolfe had controlled his acting-out defenses enough to get in touch with the emerging real self as it expressed itself through his writing, albeit falteringly and without direction or purpose. Bernstein's acknowledgment, encouragement, and support reinforced this emergence of his real self and gave it purpose and direction.

The dynamic that Aline Bernstein triggered in Wolfe's life is similar to what happens in psychotherapy to borderline patients with a similar type of symbiotic dependency upon the mother. In the beginning of treatment, the patient denies the negative feelings of anger, disappointment, and disillusionment at the mother's scapegoating, in order to preserve her as a rewarding figure, responding to his need (expressed through regressive defenses) to relieve separation anxiety and abandonment depression. The patient is afraid that expressing these negative feelings will bring on anxiety and depression. In addition, there is the fear that expressing them to the mother will cause her to withdraw. Therefore, these feelings and memories are defended against by splitting, avoidance, denial, and projection, and hence become unavailable to the patient.

Wolfe had been unable to get in touch with the great reservoir of his creativity—his childhood memories with their anger, disillusionment, and resentment—because to do so would have threatened his dependent relationship with his mother. When he transferred that dependency onto Aline Bernstein, he could then transfer the negative, withdrawing images of authority/caretaker figures back onto his mother without the threat of abandonment, since he was now dependent on Bernstein. This freed him to get in touch with "all the incidents he could remember from his youth." And as he tapped into that great wellspring of his creativity to fulfill his talent, he also fulfilled the expression of his real self. Wolfe's life now aligned itself with three vital conditions for unleashing the creativity of the real self: his attachment to the new maternal figure, Bernstein, did not require him to be her possession (on the contrary, she supported and encouraged the emergence of his real creative self while performing the caretaking functions for him that he was unable to do for himself); Wolfe himself controlled his acting-out defenses against the abandonment depression; the symbiotic union with Bernstein allowed him to be away from America, explore unknown foreign places, and deal with his fear of engulfment and loss of self.

These conditions are strikingly similar to the conditions that enable a borderline patient in psychoanalytic psychotherapy to work through the abandonment depression so that the real self can emerge: a real therapeutic alliance in which the therapist is supportive and acknowledging of the patient's real self; control of the patient's clinging and distancing defenses against the abandonment depression; emergence of the impaired real self and the abandonment depression with all its memories from the past. Whenever the defenses are interrupted or controlled, the force of the abandonment makes the feelings and their associations flow. The therapist's task then is to remove whatever additional obstacles of resistance appear to impede that flow.

The emotional force of the abandonment depression after the defenses are interrupted drives the treatment. The patient is not in charge of the process except to the degree that he controls his defenses. The force inevitably finds its way into sessions through memories and the discharging of rage and depression associated with these memories. Patients will speak of being "in the grip of a power" or of being the bystander at a process, often inundated and overwhelmed by the intensity and power of these feelings and memories. This is exactly how Thomas Wolfe described the emergence of his real self as it appeared in the creative writing process:

> It was a storm, a flood, a river, an elemental force which had to find release and if energy of this kind is not used it keeps boiling over and is given no way out. It will eventually destroy and smother the person who has it. I wrote about things that I had known, the immediate life and experience that had been familiar to me in my childhood. I had somehow recovered innocence, I have written it almost with a child's heart, it has come from me with a child's wonder and my pages are engraved not only with what is simple and plain but with monstrous evil as if the Devil were speaking with a child's tongue.[15]

When the creative self was in full sway, he had to

> . . . pour it out, boil it out, flood it out until he realized himself
> through a process of torrential production . . . but as he tried to set
> it down his memory opened up enormous vistas and associations
> going from depth to limitless depth until the simplest incident con-
> jured up a buried increment of experience and he was overwhelmed
> by this process of discovery and revelation.[16]

These same characteristics are seen in the working-through
process in psychotherapy: the innocence of childhood and the regaining of enormous floods of memories that have previously been
blocked by the need for defense. I think the psychological purpose
of Wolfe's writing is different from the purpose of the working-
through process in treatment. In the latter, the painful feelings of
loss associated with the abandonment depression are discharged
in order to free the real self to separate from the parental figure,
emerge, and become autonomous. Since Wolfe was not in treatment, this was not possible for him, but the psychological effect
of his writing was to recapture these painful feelings of loss and
memorialize them forever in writing so that they would never be
lost again. This process activated and consolidated the creative
aspect of his real self, but the remaining capacities of the self were
still impaired. He himself said that he wanted to "dig it up, get it
down, somehow record it . . . even upon thousands and thousands
of pages that would never be printed and no reader would ever
see."[17] It did not require public recognition; what was important
to him was the mere activity to "get it down, get it down."

Writing became his escape from the abandonment feelings, and
his daily life revolved around his need to write; but he could not
write continuously. When he stopped, he would get depressed,
brood and drink, and pace the streets all night, telephoning his
friends to accuse them of betraying him.

Throughout this phase of Wolfe's life, Aline Bernstein, who was
old enough to be his mother, functioned like a mother for him in
every way. Eventually the symbiotic relationship began to exacer-
bate and stimulate his fear of engulfment and loss of self. He began
to feel that if he continued this symbiotic fusion with her, he would
lose himself, meaning his creativity and capacity to write. It seems

to me that this was the ultimate reason why he had to leave her and return to Europe alone, although obviously there were additional reasons. Once abroad, his abandonment depression surfaced, and he resorted to wandering, drinking, and sexual acting out and found himself once again unable to write. He finally became disgusted with this self-destructive behavior and set to work.

The symbiotic fantasy includes a notion of exclusive possession of the object. Wolfe's projection of this fantasy onto Bernstein led to frequent paranoid outbursts of jealousy about her relationships with other men, for which there evidently was no basis at all in fact. He would accuse her of betraying him and then say that her betrayal was the reason he had to leave her. He recognized his self-destructiveness as "something that came from nature, from memory, from inheritance, from the blazing images of youth, from something outside of him and external to him, yet within him that drove him forever and that he could not help."[18]

As Wolfe was attempting to free himself from what he saw as the engulfing tentacles of Aline Bernstein, life again came to his aid with a substitute caretaker, his editor Maxwell Perkins, who came to perform the same psychological functions for Wolfe that Bernstein had. The same symbiotic dependency arose, as Perkins performed both the caretaking functions as well as organizing and synthesizing Wolfe's literary work. It appears to have been a mutually symbiotic relationship: Wolfe saw Perkins as an omnipotent, wiser, superior figure providing the support and nourishment that he required, whereas Perkins saw Wolfe, I suspect, as his alter ego, the author he had always wanted to be. Perkins acknowledged Wolfe's real self, and Wolfe's wish for the support of an omnipotent other was fulfilled.

When *Look Homeward Angel* (1929) was published and became successful, Wolfe exulted in this ultimate acknowledgment of his real creative self, but since the book was autobiographical, it caused an enormous critical furor in his hometown. Wolfe was forced to cut himself off from the town for the next seven years. He rationalized his use of old friends and family members as characters in his novel by saying, "No one in the end ever got hurt by a great book or if he did it was paltry and temporary compared to the amount of good that was conferred."[19] I imagine he meant both the good for humanity and for Thomas Wolfe.

Wolfe continued to write, spent a great deal of time with Perkins—who became his mentor, his savior, his advisor, his father-confessor—and continued to travel to Europe where he would repeat the same cycle: distancing to be alone, depression, acting-out defenses, control of the acting out, the return of the flood of memories, and return to writing. Finally, Perkins organized for Wolfe the vast amounts of material he had written, and it became *Of Time and the River* (1935). The subsequent barrage of accusations that Wolfe was not the author of the book in all probability heightened Wolfe's fear of loss of self in his closeness with Perkins and impelled him to leave Perkins as he had Bernstein. Again disillusioned and disappointed, he saw Perkins as the withdrawing parental figure, and accused him of betrayal. Another relationship had come full circle. Perkins was no longer the heroic figure, stronger and wiser than himself. He had become the enemy.

After much vacillation, Wolfe hired Edward Asner as his editor and went off on his ill-fated trip to the American West. His feeling of being caught in the web of a symbiotic bind with America—as well as with Asheville, Bernstein, and Perkins—was now diminishing. But on the trip, his impulsiveness and his not taking care of himself were as responsible as anything else for his eventual illness and death. When he caught pneumonia from sharing a bottle of whiskey with a friend, it precipitated a latent tuberculosis condition in his lungs, which resulted in the fatal tuberculosis of the brain.

This consideration of Thomas Wolfe's creativity is not meant to reduce him to a set of mechanical psychological principles but to offer another perspective on his enormous talent, the reservoir of which was his abandonment depression and his childhood memories. The driving force that opened up that reservoir was his quest to find a real self, expressed through his extraordinary writing ability. His control of his own acting-out defenses and endurance of his depression liberated the creativity of his real self and are a psychological accomplishment as remarkable as his literary triumphs.

We often think of creativity as limited to artistic expression, such as painting, writing, or performing; such examples of creativity are often quite dramatic and awe-inspiring so that they become one's standard. But there is a form of creativity that has nothing to do with artistic talent. It is the personal creativity of the real self that can make original, unique, and effective rearrangements of one's interior life, which are in turn expressed outwardly in new, more adaptive and harmonious ways of living. It involves the remaking of inner psychological patterns—images, feelings, values, thoughts—that can then be given outward expression to shape one's environment, activities, and relationships. For patients with an impaired self, creativity emerges in psychotherapy along with the other capacities of the real self, often announcing itself initially through a specific interest or plan, which the therapist reinforces by communicative matching. Over time, however, this single expression of creativity becomes a metaphor, a perspective, for both inner and outer life, characterized by spontaneity, flexibility, and originality.

Most people probably fulfill only a small percentage of their potential for creativity, unaware of the creative energies that are theirs either on the artistic or personal levels. There are many possible reasons for this failure. Since there are no perfect mothers and no perfect children, all individuals have scars remaining from the first three years of life when the real self begins to emerge and consolidate into its own unique autonomous self. This does not mean that most people have a disordered self, such as a borderline or narcissistic disorder. It does mean that many people have difficulties later in life that are a residue of the more minor conflicts of that early stage and that surface as more minor problems with creativity, autonomy, and intimacy.

Any creative endeavor, such as writing a book or a play, painting a picture, or beginning a new project at home or at work, can bring on anxiety, which may lead to symptoms, such as sleeplessness, irritability, or inability to concentrate. These symptoms are normal reactions to our fear of embarking upon the unknown, and can lead to defensive patterns, such as avoiding the activity or becoming obsessively involved in it. They usually do not go to the extremes that we have seen in people with a false self; our anxieties do not lead us to sabotage and defeat our creative goals. Rather, we persist through the anxieties and discover that they are relieved by the very act of completing the project.

It is in creative acts—from artistic masterpieces to everyday innovation and problem solving—that the real self is most alive. It is the real self that enables us to experiment in work, as in love, to find and achieve the sense of personal meaning essential for a fulfilling life. For many of those individuals with severely impaired real selves—the borderlines, narcissists, and schizoids among us— the psychotherapeutic techniques presented in earlier chapters offer real hope for overcoming the conflicts and inhibitions that have diminished their lives. For others among us, more minor fears of abandonment or engulfment are not crippling, but they may still pose threats to the autonomy and creativity of the real self. By recognizing the childhood roots of those fears we are empowered to loosen their grip on our adult lives—and the lives of our children.

Epilogue

RESURRECTION

I shied from what I considered real, building a world of my own . . .
impregnable; I was unaware of the slowly decaying castle,
a part of which would ebb away with every sudden storm.

Around the castle I had built a wall of sand,
within this, a wall of sturdy oak.
With grains of hate, I fortified the wall of sand,
yet I did not know that the blinding storm of tears
would dampen the sand, rotting the wood,

until suddenly, in a flash of lighting,
in a rumbling that shot and tore through the earth,
I, in my hate, attempted to destroy it,
ignorant of the consequences in my silent call for aid,

consciously rejecting all hands thrust in my direction.
I ran from my castle of dreams, attempted to escape from it—
the roaring of despair and the wind of self-pity
swept about me, and I rushed to the wall . . . tried to scale it,
and fell back, exhausted . . .

for my fingers could not grip
and I slipped in the sand, moaning, crying in the howling

wind, crawling to a corner to await my own destruction,
caring no longer for myself, my world, those within it.

Through the foul air, through the whirling mist
that surrounded me, a figure approached. It did not beckon,
but waited for me . . . it did not force me; it was I who
had the choice. And I, with tears of self-hate in my eyes
and venom in my lungs, confusion in my brain,

found, although I resisted, could not conquer it,
and defeated, surrendered my mind.
Surrender was not enough for him—apathy was not the answer.
I spoke through cracked lips, parched from lack

of communication, I finally asked the question aloud,
slowly, meaningfully . . . "what is this?",
for he took my hand and led me back to the world I had created
and I a fugitive feared to return.

But his grip was firm, yet gentle, and slowly,
I gave him my trust—a gift I thought I did
no longer possess. Following behind him, I came to the ruins,
closing my eyes for I could not bear to look,

and blindly, I stumbled to the wall, refusing to face
what I, in my own image, had created. He took my hand and placed
it on the sandy wall, instructing me to dig, and I obeyed
joyfully, for he allowed me to do it myself—yet soon I tired,
for I could not understand why, and the answer, "to help you"

was not familiar to my moulding ears.
I cried out in the darkness, "help me dig!"
and he replied that it was I who must help myself.
My fingernails were caked with sand, and I continued

to claw away at the cold wet sand, damp from a million tears,
and a decade of winter winds. Then through the blackness,
I screamed with pain, for oaken splinters had pierced my
fingers, and then with joy as I realized what I had reached.
I whispered in awe, "what now?" and the voice calmly answered,

"*climb over.*"
The wind began to howl, the wall began to rise,
and I faltered with indecisions. I moan with my inadequacy,
and with his aid, slowly pull apart the boards,

scraping my fingers on the nails I had once so proudly
driven. And beneath the boards, corroding with disease,
I found all human attributes thought so long ago
to be missing and presumed dead, and the realization surprised
yet frightened me. Time passed, and with the passage,

I accepted and no longer withdrew from
the world, pulling toward my soul
both the good and evil, so that I might
distinguish between them. I no longer wished to

return to the world I had once created, now it seemed
so long ago . . . I embraced the world totally and felt capable
to contribute to it while achieving what I wished from it.

Within it, I find all that was missing from the others—
mutual love, tolerance, understanding . . . caring.
I stir with the realization of the dawn.
Time's libation has accomplished its desired effect,
and I hear within myself satisfaction's sigh.
I rise, filled with the new-found freedom that was once
only tangible in dreams.

Beyond domestic panes of glass
I viewed the golden crescent
and feel its warmth caressing my cheek,
blinding my eye with the strength of its love.

In the silence of the early morn,
I walked the deserted streets, rushing to keep my rendezvous
with my newest love—the joy of living.
How many others share my love?
I am not selfish . . .
if only all might incorporate with my emotions!

Is it fair that I envision myself
as a free spirit, removed from the
human maladjustments that were once present within me?

It is fair to myself and fairer than I have ever been

. . . for I care.
My soul soars; I feel personally involved with others.

I stand alone now, yet am unafraid. No hand is held in mine;
I stand alone, independent . . . alive.
Viewing the dawn, I feel the blood surge through my body,
and laugh, grateful for the rebirth of my spirit.

But through the brightness of the dawn, memories still return.
There is a difference—they do not plague, but help to form
the future.

L.M.
(at the conclusion of her treatment)

Notes

Preface

1. Margaret Mahler, *The Psychological Birth of the Human Infant* (New York: Basic Books, 1975).

Chapter 2. The Development of the Real Self

1. Bruno Bettelheim, *Freud and Man's Soul* (New York: Alfred A. Knopf, 1982).

2. Over the years psychoanalytic researchers who see the self as the whole person have discovered some of the pieces to the puzzle of the real self. Otto Rank in *The Trauma of Birth* (New York: Harcourt, Brace 1929) suggested that the self's initial experiences center around the trauma caused by the emergence of the physical self at birth. Alfred Adler in *The Theory and Practice of Individual Psychology* (New York: Harcourt, Brace, 1940) emphasized the self's early feelings of inferiority and the defensive patterns to overcompensate for it that persist into adult lifestyles. In *Neurosis and Human Growth*, Karen Horney postulated an idealized self which produces a pseudo unity or wholeness that actually blocks the emergence of the real self. Harry Stack Sullivan in *Clinical Studies in Psychiatry* (New York: W.W. Norton, 1956) argued that the self is defined by its functions which fulfill our needs and maintain a sense of security.

3. The classical analyst H. Kohut in *The Restoration of the Self* (New York: International Universities Press, 1977) has adopted a wholly different theoretical approach based on his own theory of the psychology of the self. His clinical work, but not his theory, has been widely accepted.

4. Erik Erikson, *Identity, Youth, and Crisis* (New York: W.W. Norton, 1968).

5. Malcolm Cowley, "Looking for the Essential Me" (*New York Times Book Review*, June 17, 1984).

6. Margaret Mahler, *The Psychological Birth of the Human Infant* (New York: Basic Books, 1975).

7. T. B. Brazelton, "Joint Regulation of Neonate-Parent Behavior," in E. Tronick, ed., *Social Interchanges in Infancy* (Baltimore: University Park Press, 1982); R. N. Emde, "Toward a Psychoanalytic Theory of Affect," in S. I. Greenspan and G. H. Pollock, eds., *Infancy and Early Childhood. The Course of Life: Psychoanalytic Contributions Toward Understanding Personality Development*, vol. I (Washington, D. C.: National Institute of Mental Health, 1980); D. Stern, *The Interpersonal World of the Infant: A View from Psychoanalysis and Developmental Psychology* (New York: Basic Books, 1985).

8. Mahler, *The Psychological Birth of the Human Infant*.

Chapter 3. The Real Self in Action

1. D. W. Winnicott, *The Maturational Process and the Facilitating Environment* (New York: International Universities Press, 1965).

Chapter 4. Fear of Abandonment

1. J. F. Masterson and J. L. Costello, *Borderline Adolescent to Functioning Adult: The Test of Time* (New York: Brunner/Mazel, 1980).

2. Margaret Mahler, *On Human Symbiosis and the Vicissitudes of Individuation* (New York: International Universities Press, 1968).

3. J. F. Masterson, *Treatment of the Borderline Adolescent: A Developmental Approach* (New York: Wiley, 1972).

4. Ibid.

5. J. Bowlby, *Attachment and Loss*, vols. I and II (New York: Basic Books, 1969, 1973).

Chapter 5. Portrait of the Borderline

1. S. Freud, "Formulations on the Two Principles of Mental Functioning." In J. Strachey, ed. and trans., *The Standard Edition of the Complete Psychological Works of Sigmund Freud*, vol. 12 (1911), pp. 218–226. The child is initially motivated by the pleasure principle, the urge to seek pleasure and avoid pain. Disappointment in this pursuit leads to a new principle—the reality principle—that what is presented to the mind is what is real, even if it is not pleasurable.

Chapter 6. Portrait of the Narcissist

1. Eric Larrabee, *Commander-in-Chief* (New York: Harper and Row, 1987).

Chapter 9. The Borderline Syndrome in Adolescence

1. J. F. Masterson, *The Psychiatric Dilemma of Adolescence* (Boston: Little, Brown, 1967).

2. D. Offer and J. Offer, *Normal Adolescents: From Teenager to Young Manhood* (New York: Basic Books, 1975).

3. J. F. Masterson and J. L. Costello, *From Borderline Adolescent to Functioning Adult: The Test of Time* (New York: Brunner/Mazel, 1980).

Chapter 12. The Creative Solution

1. Jean-Paul Sartre, *The Words* (New York: Fawcett, 1964), p. 54.

2. *Ibid*, p. 52.

3. Ragna Stang, *Edvard Munch*, translated by Arnoldo Mondadori S. P. N. (Milan, 1979), p. 174.

4. Thomas Wolfe, *Of Time and the River* (New York: Charles Scribner's Sons, 1935), pp. 23–24.

5. Elizabeth Nowell, *Thomas Wolfe, A Biography* (New York: Doubleday, 1960), p. 157.

6. *Ibid.*, p. 28

7. John Skally Terry, ed., *Thomas Wolfe's Letters to His Mother, Julia Elizabeth Wolfe* (New York: Charles Scribner's Sons, 1943), p. XXII.

8. Thomas Wolfe, *Look Homeward Angel* (New York: Charles Scribner's Sons, 1929), p. 61.

9. *Ibid.*, p. 216.

10. *Ibid.*, p. 162.

11. *Thomas Wolfe, A Biography*, p. 30.

12. Elizabeth Nowell, ed., *The Letters of Thomas Wolfe*, collected and edited with an Introduction by E. Nowell (New York: Charles Scribner's Sons, 1956), p. 59.

13. *Thomas Wolfe, A Biography*, p. 74.

14. *Of Time and the River*, p. 859.

15. *Thomas Wolfe, A Biography*, pp. 105, 106.

16. *Ibid.*, p. 106, 107.

17. *Ibid.*, p. 194.

18. Thomas Wolfe, *The Web and the Rock* (New York: Harper and Row, 1937), p. 405.

19. *Thomas Wolfe, A Biography*, p. 361.

Selected Bibliography

Adler, G. *Borderline Psychopathology and Its Treatment*, New York: Jason Aronson, 1985.

Bowlby, J. *Attachment and Loss, vol. II, Separating.* New York: Basic Books 1973.

Erikson, E. *Identity, Youth, and Crisis.* New York: W. W. Norton, 1968.

Giovacchini, P., ed. *Psychoanalysis of Character Disorders.* New York: Jason Aronson, 1975.

Gunderson, J. *Borderline Personality Disorder.* Washington, D.C.: American Psychiatric Association Press, 1984.

Guntrip, H. *Schizoid Phenomena, Object Relations and the Self.* New York: International Universities Press, 1968.

Hartmann, H. *Ego Psychology and the Problem of Adaptation.* New York: International Universities Press, 1958.

Hortocollis, P. *Borderline Personality Disorders—The Concept, The Syndrome, The Patient.* New York: International Universities Press, 1977.

Jacobson, E. *The Self and the Object World.* New York: International Universities Press, 1964.

Kernberg, O. *Borderline Conditions and Pathological Narcissism.* New York: Science House, 1975, pp. 163–177.

Kohut, H. *The Restoration of the Self.* New York: International Universities Press, 1977.

Mahler, M. *On Human Symbiosis and the Vicissitudes of Individuation.* New York: International Universities Press, 1968.

Mahler, M. *The Psychological Birth of the Human Infant.* New York: Basic Books, 1975.

Masterson, J. F. *The Psychiatric Dilemma of Adolescence.* New York: Brunner/Mazel, 1967.

Masterson, J. F. *Treatment of the Borderline Adolescent: A Developmental Approach.* New York: Wiley, 1972, 2nd ed., New York: Brunner/Mazel, 1985.

Masterson, J. F. ed. *New Perspectives on Psychotherapy of the Borderline Adult.* New York: Brunner/Mazel, 1976.

Masterson, J. F. *Psychotherapy of the Borderline Adult: A Developmental Approach.* New York: Brunner/Mazel, 1978.

Masterson, J. F. *Borderline Adolescent to Functioning Adult: The Test of Time.* New York: Brunner/Mazel, 1980.

Masterson, J. F. *The Narcissistic and Borderline Disorders: An Integrated Developmental Approach.* New York: Brunner/Mazel, 1981.

Masterson, J. F. *Countertransference and Psychotherapeutic Technique—Teaching Seminars on Psychotherapy of the Borderline Adult.* New York: Brunner/Mazel, 1983.

Masterson, J. F. and Klein, R. eds. *Psychotherapy of the Disorders of the Self.* New York: Brunner/Mazel, 1988.

McDevitt, J. and Settlage, C. F. *Separation-Individuation.* New York: International Universities Press, 1971.

Modell, A. H. *Object Love and Reality.* New York: International Universities Press, 1968.

Olive Tree Productions. *Borderline Syndrome: A Personality Disorder of Our Time* [Videotape]. Albany, NY: Olive Tree Productions, 1988.

Olive Tree Productions. *Dr. James Masterson: Overview of the Borderline Syndrome* [Videotape]. Albany, NY: Olive Tree Productions, 1988.

Rinsley, D. *Treatment of the Severely Disturbed Adolescent.* New York: Jason Aronson, 1980.

Rinsley, D. *Borderline and Other Self Disorders.* New York: Jason Aronson, 1982.

Spitz, R. A. *The First Year of Life (A Psychoanalytic Study of Normal and Deviant Development of Object Relations).* New York: International Universities Press, 1965.

Stern, D. *The Interpersonal World of the Infant.* New York: Basic Books, 1985.

Stone, M. H. *The Borderline Syndrome: Constitution, Personality and Adaptation.* New York: McGraw Hill, 1980.

Winnicott, D. W. *The Maturational Processes and the Facilitating Environment.* New York: International Universities Press, 1965.

Index

The community that mother nature
made for us.

Talk about our experiences —
transformation then our experience
CsR— awareness

Want to share our intimate
relationship ō the healing powers
of CsR — while we teach
you how to rejuvenate your
relationship.